POSTHISTOIRE

POSTHISTOIRE

Has History Come to an End?

◆

LUTZ NIETHAMMER
in collaboration with
DIRK VAN LAAK

Translated by
Patrick Camiller

VERSO
London · New York

First published as *Posthistoire: Ist die Geschichte zu Ende?* by Rowohlt Verlag
This translation first published by Verso 1992
Rowohlt Taschenbuch Verlag GmbH 1989
English edition Verso 1992

Verso
UK: 6 Meard Street, London W1V 3HR
USA: 29 West 35th Street, New York, NY 10001-2291

Verso is the imprint of New Left Books

ISBN 0-86091-395-3

British Library Cataloguing in Publication Data
A catalogue record for this book is available from the British Library

Library of Congress Cataloging-in-Publication Data
A catalogue record for this book is available from the Library of Congress

Typeset by York House Typographic Ltd, London
Printed in Great Britain by Bookcraft (Bath) Ltd

For Regina Schulte

Contents

1

Invitation to a Tracking
of the Zeitgeist

> Don't start from the good old things but the bad new ones.
> *Walter Benjamin in 1938 on a Brechtian maxim.*[1]

There are many expressions which the Zeitgeist uses to avoid being specific about itself; it may refer, for example, to postmodern, post-industrial or postrevolutionary society. But of all such cutoff points, the most extensive only appears to be characteristic of the present conjuncture. Here and there, articles or research notes announce that history is over, that we are now living in a 'posthistorical world'. And usually that is the end of the matter, as if there were nothing more to be said. In general, the focus on posthistory or *Posthistoire*, with its arbitrary simulation of fragments of the past, belongs to an 'as if' aesthetic, a game with signs which, though quoted out of context and no longer 'in force', still seem to retain their power of attraction.

As historians read these scant reports that the object of their labour and curiosity no longer exists, they naturally feel a certain perplexity. For they are also living in one of those rare periods where history excites widespread attention in the media, and where the aesthetic imagination is frequently inspired by the cultural heritage. The heralds of posthistory therefore gnaw at the historian's self-confidence when they suggest that this reawakening of interest might come down to an exercise in simulation by the culture industry. Perhaps all he or she can do is try to gather together some little stones, without knowing whether they form part of a mosaic, or whether they will eventually appear as a mere scree devoid of form and plan. Is that strewn legacy what posthistory reflects from the past?

Before the historian's object turns into a mirage, it is worth taking a look at those heated discussions of the Zeitgeist which, in various ways, set forth a 'post' condition. In fact, this teeming output is not simply a question of fashion, nor is it confined to the literal sense of the term that something, one more thing, has come to an end. We are more likely to talk of 'our postmodern modernity' (Welsch), where the reflexivity signals not the termination of a dynamic structure but dispersal of the hope associated with it. Things go on, but the belief that they have a meaning fades away. If this shows both that the 'post' diagnoses are not just empty talk and that they mean something other than what they say, we have to consider the excess meaning contained within them. In other words, we have to investigate their origins – which is what we shall do here in the case of *Posthistoire*, or 'posthistory' as we shall call it for the convenience of English-speaking readers.

A journey through the history of this concept brings a number of surprises. First of all the unwieldy compound *Posthistoire*, which sounds like a French neologism, does not actually exist in French – and in German the addition of the article '*das*' makes it all the more conspicuous. In both languages, history as a collective singular is as feminine as its muse, Clio; apparently that is why *das Posthistoire* had to become a neuter noun in German. The word itself promises a descent into dark regions of conceptual history, and warns us that we shall not be able to grasp the concept if we move only at the level of the information supplied by its adepts. First, however, we must find the path of descent. After all, any statement merits a preliminary examination on its own terms and an investigation of the references that it uses to explain itself.

In our enquiry into the present-day use of the concept 'posthistory', we shall start from where it was taken up by the Left and promoted to a code of communication between various factions. This happened at the end of the 'German autumn' after 1977, when excerpts were posthumously published from the writings of Peter Brückner, a co-thinker and companion of the New Left and one of its last spokesmen. We then turn to the work of Arnold Gehlen, a co-thinker and companion of the conservative revolution in the Third Reich and one of its late spokesmen in the Federal Republic – a man who, in the early fifties, produced the preliminary formulations underlying the references to 'posthistory' among postfascist intellectuals. From Gehlen the trail may be followed back to an apparent progenitor of the concept, Antoine Augustin Cournot, a French philosopher from the time of the Second Empire who is little known in Germany. In Cournot, however, we find neither the word 'posthistory' nor that posthistorical melancholy typical of his new following, but on the contrary a technocratic programme for the overcoming of history, which is understood as a lengthy epoch of chaotic conflicts. This lineage might appear to suggest a kind of structural tradition of argument in which history is identified as a process of subjective, meaning-oriented disputes, and posthistory refers to a condition where world civilization functions as a huge, scientifically trained apparatus and culture becomes petrified into a natural phenomenon.

Considerable forcing is required, however, to construct such a tradition across highly varied historical contexts with contradictory political perspectives. I shall approach this problem in two separate ways. On the one hand, abstracting from the historical conjuncture of the posthistorical, I attempt to find in certain chains of association three diagnoses that have played a major role in the century separating us from Cournot. These three structural elements are: (1) the overcoming of historicism, and the growth of the notion that the universal historical legacy is accessible for 'dialogue' outside time between the leading minds or 'spirits'; (2) the self-regulation of the techno-economic structure of society as a 'megamachine' detached from subjects; and (3) the return of culture to natural premises with a long-term tendency to petrification, and its resulting inclusion in the nature–death nexus. My concern, therefore, is not to situate and evaluate the various authors within the history of ideas, but to use these three longitudinal sections to establish differences and common ground in their diagnoses of the age and in their topic of argument.

The chains of association will show that the key theses of 'posthistory' are by no means isolated within the past century of diagnostics; indeed, they can be incorporated into major traditions that have sought to arrive at an understanding of the age. On the other hand, their clustering in the idea that history is over, and that life will now continue in more or less animal form, appears to be specific to certain periods and groups of authors. Two aspects distinguish the posthistorical cluster of arguments from writings which may, in some respects, be quite similar: first, their reference back to, and self-location within, a tradition of the production of meaning for which they no longer see any social future; and, second, their avoidance of thinking about death, especially about the danger that modern civilization will annihilate itself and the world, which is the central preoccupation of other writers. Instead, the picture that looms for theorists of posthistory is of a mortal life lived without any seriousness or struggle, in the regulated boredom of a perpetual reproduction of modernity on a world scale. The problematic of posthistory is not the end of the world but the end of meaning.

This brings us on to my second approach to the specificity of the present interpretative conjuncture, in which we shall again find the integration of other diagnostic elements in a global account of the

transition to a posthistorical civilization. My main focus will be on the
formative stage of the posthistory thesis, amid the radical changes that
took place before and after the Second World War. For it is here that I
hope to forestall the literary game of quotations, and to encounter the
experiential premises which the authors of diagnostic fragments so
distinctively drew out of the contemporary arsenal in order to project
the negative utopia of a life continuing without meaning. This is all the
more difficult in that the forebears of the posthistory diagnosis almost
never offered an intelligible concretion of their own experience, but
preferred both to encode and to generalize it in the form of metaphors.
Their imagery points to a burning need for expression, an epitomiza-
tion of constellations which are under a reporting ban or are supposed
to be recognized in a flash, without any possibility of explaining them
through argument. In the metaphors of the interpretative conjuncture
we must therefore seek out the hidden history of the posthistorical. In
other words, we must discover the content of that unutterable life-
historical sensibility which, like a catalyser, takes otherwise disparate
elements from the spiritual household of the age and combines them in
a transcending global interpretation.

The metaphorical imagery – at once herald of potential knowledge
and encoder of the forbidden and forgotten – cannot be easily read,
because within it complex realities are compressed and associated with
one another. It rushes ahead of our understanding, and its content can
only ever be grasped by approximation, through the excess of its own
interpretations and the way in which they work themselves out in a
particular context. In attempting to understand the metaphorical
system of the posthistory diagnosis in its formation, I have mainly used
interpretations that refer to the history of its life and times. They are
not the only ones, of course; and others will be able to judge the results
of this historian's inclination to historicize posthistory.

None of the authors I have mentioned so far was a historian. That
induced me to test out the interpretation on the central imagery of
Walter Benjamin's reflections 'on the concept of history', a text which,
in recent decades, has been the most widely misinterpreted in the
German history of ideas of the 1940s. Benjamin's late work in literary
criticism and art theory was secretly accompanied by a kind of
attempted history of the everyday life of the metropolis in bourgeois
society – the so-called *Passagenwerk*, fragments which were first
published in 1982. Shortly before his death while fleeing from the
Nazis, in a state of extreme torment and disappointment, he set down a
piece rich in imagery as his first compressed attempt at an epistemology
of the historical practice in which he had himself been defeated.

Although some of Benjamin's analysis has points in common with the posthistory writers, it is diametrically opposed to their diagnoses. Benjamin was not interested in surviving to announce the end of meaning; he left a testament full of meaning to dig up repressed and buried hopes for the strengthening of those living around him – and then he died. Since the 1960s, however, his readers have divided over the dialectical tension of this new approach to history, and the actual text has been dehistoricized through a series of small, almost imperceptible reinterpretations of its imagery. In this way, Benjamin's fragmentary sketch of the development of his theory of history, with its register of precise metaphors, has been imported into that second leftist wave of posthistory from which we started out.

I have thus attempted to understand the posthistory diagnosis by means of three probes: the search for a tradition which, though perhaps a false lead, may yet provide valuable insights; the gathering of prefabricated parts of the argument from some intellectual workshops of the past century or so; and the attempt to deduce the hidden contribution to this diagnosis from the metaphorical system of its adepts. The material acquired from these probes is finally translated into a three-sided interrogation: (1) What exactly comes to an end in posthistory? (2) What is the historical site of this diagnosis? (3) Should it be of concern to historians? Since, for all my doubts and critical reservations, I would answer the last question in the affirmative, I would like to offer for discussion this report on my rather fragmentary investigations, together with further threads that have not been mentioned here and will be found in both the text and the supporting chapter notes. Up to now the question of whether history is finished seems to have haunted all the cultural sciences with the exception of history itself. Historians might with good reason adopt a wait-and-see attitude to all the other 'post' discussions about modernity, industrial society, revolution, the workers' movement, fascism, feminism, and so forth, with the aim of verifying whether such periodizations can yield positive concepts. But such patience seems less appropriate where it is a question of how and whether history in general, and not just the past, can be validly treated.

I would like to express my thanks to those who have assisted me with my investigations and discussed their own conclusions with me – above all, Dirk van Laak, who helped me find the relevant literature, took me on many new journeys, and gave me support in working up this text for publication after it had originally been written for a course at the Correspondence University in Hagen. In this respect I am also especially grateful to Ulrich Herbert and Nori Möding for particular advice and criticism, and in others to Michel Brélaz, Erich Kitzmüller, Karl-Siegbert Rehberg and Ingeborg Villinger. Early on, Dietmar Kamper made available to me the manuscript of a collection edited by himself and the late Jacob Taubes, *Nach der Moderne. Umrisse einer 'Ästhetik des Posthistoire'*, and this made it much easier for me to work myself into the project. The first discussion of my thoughts was with Jörn Rüsen's graduate students at the Ruhr University in Bochum, during a conference on 'Posthistory or Neohistoricism?' in October 1987, and with Thomas Lindberger from the Berlin History Workshop. In the following year, at the Berlin Wissenschaftskolleg, I received advice, criticism and encouragement from, among others, Cesare Cases, Lazlo Gloser, Wilhelm Hennis, Reinhart Koselleck, Wolf Lepenies and, above all, Victor Gourevitch, to whom I am especially grateful for our day-long conversations. I completed the chapter on Benjamin's angel early this year, working at night in the still empty spaces of the old Town Hall of Heisingen, a suburb of Essen – the days were given over to founding a cultural studies institute here in the Ruhr. Dan Diner and Saul Friedländer, after reading the manuscript, invited me to publish a version of the concluding remarks as 'Afterthoughts on Posthistoire' in their new journal *History & Memory* (Tel Aviv). Regina Schulte's anthropological vision accompanied my detective's obsessions in gaining forcible entry into the posthistorical set of quotations, often raising questions that indicated productive lines of enquiry or, at times, simply brought me to a necessary halt. That is why this book is dedicated to her.

L.N.
Institute of Cultural Studies
Essen, May 1989

Note

1. Walter Benjamin, *Understanding Brecht*, London 1973, p. 121.

2

Retrogression:
Loss or Overcoming of History?

I THE END OF THE HISTORY OF BOURGEOIS SOCIETY?

In the 1970s Peter Brückner personified the attempt of post-'68 radical intellectuals to extend the openings made by the New Left in the Federal Republic. More than once he was presented as an associate of the Red Army Faction and suspended from his post as professor of psychology at Hanover University – the last time being from the 'German autumn' of 1977 until 1981. When he died at the age of sixty, a year after the ban had again been lifted, a file marked '*Posthistoire*' was found among the papers he left behind. It contained a collection of material for a planned course of lectures – mainly extracts from other authors[1] and the fragment of a manuscript on changes in the concept of revolution.[2] Here we can read:

> Bourgeois society[3] was thus the truly historical society, in the sense that within it different epochs overlapped in a state of high tension and that its radical changes bound together, both in national states and on a world market, a multiplicity of regions, populations, social processes and economies that had hitherto been only loosely touching one another. There can be no doubt, however, that it was precisely within this interlinking process that the mode of production of industrial society began, for the first time in history, to create a relative universality of living conditions for many castes, classes, layers and provinces – in their labour and commerce, free time and communication, in the social organization of the family, in sexuality and the clinicity of dying. . . . All the equalizing elements of the industrial milieu thus bring in their wake the shadow of 'posthistory', a humanity whose members are alike in their 'attitudes and behaviour', their 'interests and value-judgements'.[4] . . . The outcome of such normalization and integration is a new form of 'reality' – that is, normality which registers

particularity or qualitative difference only as a deviation, usually a matter for the doctor or the police. Specificity vanishes off the track [*im Abseits*].[5] The differentiation of overlapping epochs is flattened out: city centres and transport systems, education and speech colours, forms of sociability and modes of perception are 'modernized'. This one-dimensional reality, unlike in the slowly dying historical period, is no longer space and time for competing parties; it is itself a party. . . . Even in countries with a developed class structure, classes and their destinies come from the fringes into the shadow of the new version of the 'fundamental contradiction' – on one side, the forces preserving (technological) rationality and the administration or production of normality; on the other side, 'non-simultaneous' revolts which encompass elements from pre-bourgeois and post-industrial critiques. Here is a potent source for that second paradigm of transformation: the resistance to the structures of posthistory. And this emerging population no longer allows us, who are in the 'breach', to construct a synthesis around a 'collective subject', at least not as a class subject.[6]

These notes are just one text among many in which the radical Left has had to admit to itself that the concepts of the Marxist tradition no longer describe the experienced reality of its surrounding society in a way that offers any guide to action.[7] This realization came later in West Germany than elsewhere, because here the Marxist tradition was for long interrupted by fascism and the Cold War and had first to be rediscovered before it could be worked through.[8] Divorced from a corresponding tradition within the labour movement, the younger intelligentsia underwent a change of orientation all the more hectic in that the generational turn to radical action in the second half of the sixties recharged the Marxist tradition with the absoluteness of the revulsion against fascism. It thus fed the longing to identify with a collective revolutionary subject of victims, sought first among the working class and then in solidarity with Third World liberation movements. But the tensions which stemmed from such identification – tensions between the theoretical revolutionary tasks of the 'subjects' and their actual reality – destroyed the hope in a transformation of capitalism, and therefore in history itself as a dialectical structure of social movement.

In the course of the seventies, the perspective of overcoming the system was increasingly replaced by definitions of a system which, no longer capable of being influenced, already cast forward the shadows of 'posthistory'. A standardized humanity would now treat otherness as a pure deviation and place it in the hands of doctors or the police – a one-dimensional normality in the face of which specificity would disappear off the track. A delusive integration[9] of the once-central contradiction between labour and capital would convert it into a driving-force of the system's destructive dynamic and bring about a change in the lines of confrontation. Organized struggles on the front of the main contradiction would give way to a multiplicity of particular rebellions, the cultivation of alternative forms of life in the margins and cavities of the system, and the mobilization of coalition movements against existential dangers (nuclear power, environmental pollution, the arms build-up). From one fundamental social contradiction to a plurality of alternatives, from the revolutionary subject to vital subjectivity, from history to 'posthistory'?

Brückner's notes, written down in the midst of this regroupment and reorientation of the Left, treat 'bourgeois society' and 'history' together in a kind of retrospect, as an overlaying of epochs in Europe. What is emerging in their place is the perspective of a posthistorical world civilization, which those two categories are no longer able to grasp. Any hope of movement is invested in the multiple, existential contradictions between standardized normality and the appropriate Other, which is beyond any great designs or grand organizations. The role of prophet also ceases to apply, and the intellectual is either shifted to the interpreter's balustrade or reduced to earning a living.

This characteristic mixture of ideas – which equates bourgeois society with history, defines the contemporary world in terms of systemic dangers, and maintains hope in the future mainly at the level of individuality – was by no means confined to Brückner or to left-wing theoreticians. It is only one variant of a diagnosis of the age, whose contours can also be discerned elsewhere with surprising correspondences. Let us just take the example of the most productive and controversial conservative interpreter of modern Germany, Ernst Nolte, whose trilogy on the ideological content of German and world history in the last two centuries starts out from a similar problematic, even if it involves different concepts and cognitive interests.[10]

Using the term 'liberal system' to denote civil or bourgeois society, Nolte derives its historical impetus from the tension inherent within its contradictory, non-synchronous character (Brückner's 'overlaying of epochs'). The attempt to dissolve this tension is responsible for the utopian frustration of anarchism, but also for the extermination potential of bolshevism and fascism. For Nolte and for Brückner, however, the future has not yet crystallized out, and he hopes that 'under the threat of catastrophe' the inner mobility of the liberal system will finally allow it to be adapted to man. But he realizes that progress, which has become a structural feature within civil society, 'can lead, even as it safeguards peace, to the self-destruction of humanity'. Only a concentration of individuals with the power to think and educate – a kind of decentralized force of subjective elites – might become 'the main factor in a gradual change of the whole system'. The problem of posthistory is then posed within the overall framework of the post-national condition. After Hitler's attempt to usurp history and bring it to a halt, the East–West accords divided Germany and removed it from the 'centre of the world'. Then the Federal Republic, as the vessel of a non-political, economistic society of private happiness, roused itself at most for a short period – that is, during the 'German autumn' – to act as a historical unit and to draw some of the contours of a bourgeois state.[11] We could hardly find two analyses that were more opposed politically and yet more similar historically!

The inflation of the various 'post' concepts might suggest that we are no longer able or willing to define the content of where we are and where we want to go;[12] that we seek only to know where we come from. What used to appear self-evident or desirable has lost its inno-cence, and now words more or less fail us. 'Posthistory' is the most far-reaching of these concepts, for it denies a future not only to one characteristic element of a phase of history (modernity, revolution, industry, etc.) but to the idea of history itself. Brückner's last writings show that this notion of a dawning posthistorical culture – which was first formulated on the right of the postwar German intelligentsia,[13] and whose approval by the older 'Frankfurt School' generation was criticized by the student movement and its mentors[14] – later spread quickly among the Left, at least as regards its exotic keyword.[15] Why was this seemingly French word so much quoted in German, and why did it acquire its neuter gender?[16] Its conspicuous air of pedantry should actually make our task easier in tracking down the historical origins and significance of this whole conception.

Brückner himself makes a number of casual yet significant references to the work of Arnold Gehlen, who made his name in the Third Reich as a philosopher specializing in social psychology, and whose conserva-tive anthropology and cultural criticism had a considerable influence in the Adenauer period.[17] Disgust with the masses first appears already in 1952, when the need for security is indicated as an unconscious drive of contemporary humanity (the 'id'): 'They no longer bother about the old magical word freedom; they think in terms of plans. Perhaps a still higher degree of mistrust is thereby reached – the wish to make the world futureless and at that price to buy security. Are we already outside history and in posthistory?'[18]

A decade later Gehlen was noting 'the concept of "posthistory", taken from Cournot (1801–1877), with which the author has recently tended to work'.[19] Now it is no longer the mass 'they' which thinks but an ego which reasserts itself and projects global sterility, where the 'Coloureds' are not even able to think again that which has been overtaken:

> If we now turn to the two great halves of the world and their ideological foundations, my conclusion will perhaps be less surprising when I say that there is nothing more to be expected in terms of the history of ideas, that humanity has to settle down into the present broad surroundings, with of course all the many different variations of which one can think. Just as humanity securely depends in religion upon the great doctrines of salvation that were formulated long ago, so it is firmly committed in its sense of civilization – which leads me to make one plausible assumption that the so-called developing nations will not find a positive third ideology. For global ideologies of that kind – including historically surpassed ones like fascism, or undeveloped ones like Rousseau's or Nietzsche's doctrine of salvation – are without exception a European product that does not exist outside this area. I will therefore stick my neck out and say that the history of ideas has been suspended, and that we have now arrived at posthistory. Thus Gottfried Benn's advice to the individual – 'Count on your own resources' – should now be issued to humanity as a whole. In the very epoch when it is becoming possible to see and report on the earth as a whole, when nothing of any import can pass unnoticed, the earth is in this respect devoid of surprises. The alternatives are known, as in the field of religion, and are in every case final.[20]

In the 1960s, at the Congress of Sociologists for example, Gehlen stood at the opposite pole from Adorno. And yet, in private correspondence they assured each other – like 'people lost in the forest. . .despite the wolves' – that their cultural critiques were in agreement about the abdication of the subject, the predominance of evil and the petrification of the conditions of life. In the face of Nietzsche's 'age of darkness', which coincided with the most widespread general education, the philosopher would again simply 'thrash around like Hercules'. Gehlen put this down to the 'secular disappointment which socialism had brought in its cultural wake'. Consequently the culture of feudalism and of the *haute bourgeoisie* could not be replaced, even after their epochs had passed away into industrial society. The fourth estate, always led by 'class aliens', had produced a 'zero balance-sheet'; and what industrial society contained was actually a 'post-bourgeois culture', which could no longer be described as positive.[21] The *embourgeoisement* of the masses was of no avail, since one could not expect this formation to generate a distinctive new culture. On the contrary, the decrepit culture into which the structures of society congealed was also losing its characteristic possibilities – which, in the case of bourgeois culture, meant the subjectivity of great individuals. The kind of subjectivity now piling up in a heap was no longer of any historical relevance, its room for manoeuvre reduced to that of an amoeba within a 'second nature'. 'There has never been so much differentiated and articulate subjectivity as there is in the world today, nor have there ever been so many people equipped with the most sensitive antennae.'[22] If such statements somehow took on a positive inflection in the phase of modernizing restoration, when the great individual at least still felt sustained and recognized in the role of herald, they turned a somersault in the face of the student movement and the moral discourse that paved the way for it. The typical gesture then became one of dismissive irritation:

> Self-reflecting, overwrought individualism means subjectivism, in which the destructive series of supports and meanings races to an end; they are pumped out from their unconscious compulsiveness and then chewed over and used up in the processing of experience, reflection and 'testimony'.[23]

Already during the Adenauer period, this aggressive resignation fed on the popular appeal of its brusque gestures and so on a kind of 'empirical a priori', as Gehlen called it. In private he also borrowed from his teacher Hans Driesch the term 'prior knowledge of disorder', and traced it back to feelings from his childhood in Imperial Germany.[24] However, the perception of postwar culture as absurd had deep roots:

> Now there is no longer any internal development within art! It is all up with art history based upon the logic of meaning, and even with any consistency of absurdities. The process of development has been completed, and what comes now is already in existence: the confused syncretism of all styles and possibilities – posthistory.[25]

Arrogance, if only as an armour of solitude, often has a fascinating side to it. And among the defeated Germans, the dismissive gesture of the post-fascist intellectual rapidly won a following. There used to be a spirit of Europe – but now that was all over. After us would come the flood of arbitrariness, perhaps including some coloured variations. Did not Goebbels's gutter press warn that Americanization would spell 'niggerization'? The masses, the other races, were just the impersonal 'they' or 'id'. Without a heroic subject, no history. All one could count on now were the existing contents of one's bookcase – it was not worth opening one's eyes to anything beyond. And yet, the Cassandra-type prophecies became even shriller in tone as his eyes opened wide in terror.

Our investigation into the origins of New Left 'posthistory' has thus led us – apart from some references to the Frankfurt School – to Arnold Gehlen's core writings of the fifties and sixties and to the first quotable use of the term in 1952. Before we turn to the source mentioned by Gehlen himself, A.A. Cournot, we must ask what paved the way for the introduction of this idea into his own work. Is posthistory post-fascism? Carol Hagemann-White points out that in an essay from 1943 Gehlen had already evoked the idea of social-historical 'crystallization' – or 'consolidating systematization', as he called it then – which was to be the substantive filling of posthistory.[26] In the middle of January 1943, two months after the Allied landing in North Africa and not long before the Sixth Army surrendered at Stalingrad, Gehlen gave a lecture on 'Problems of a Philosophy of History'. According to the critical notes taken by agents from Rosenberg's bureau, he there formulated in cautiously groping German the idea of posthistory *avant la lettre*:

> How little Gehlen considers history to be action or at least development was made plain by a revealing turn of phrase: 'By that I do not mean that there can be nothing really new in history.' But in fact, for this existentialist and so ultimately timeless interpretation of history, nothing decisively new, surprising and radical can happen any longer. Gehlen also maintained that European painting has now passed through its complete range of 'possibilities', and that the Indian myths had already developed all the basic possibilities of religious belief. For Gehlen, history is in the end a self-enclosed arsenal of experience which, though perhaps capable of elucidation by a careful interpreter, basically lies behind us – or in which everything is at once contemporary and timeless as a 'possibility'.

And a superior added to this:

> In the course of his remarks, Gehlen produced no more than purely abstract historical parallels: he did not reach the question of the real historical basis of such parallels, nor therefore the question of history as such. Whereas Max Weber, to whom he referred, started out from highly concrete social matters, Gehlen got no further than an intelligent but essentially sterile juxtaposition and abstract ordering of historical types.[27]

The distance which is here expressed between Gehlen and the keepers of National Socialist ideology previously went unnoticed, as it had been effectively bridged in practice. Before fortunes turned in the war, Gehlen had not come to the fore as a philosopher of history. In pursuing his academic career after 1933, he had joined the Third Reich as an official of the University Teachers' Association in Leipzig, paid fulsome tribute to the regime in various lectures and publications,[28] and then, at the beginning of the war, made his name with a philosophical

anthropology according to which humanity was by nature dependent upon 'supreme leadership bodies' (or 'institutions', in the denazified postwar edition).[29] Its unhistorical character never became an issue
so long as the supreme leadership bodies had a clear historical significance within the theory. But when their failure became apparent,
Gehlen's 'anthropo(bio)logy'[30] required a framework in which their
historical connection was first provided for and then abstracted into
institutions.

This outcome points back to the origins of Gehlen's biological
reduction of anthropology, which can be located in his postdoctoral
thesis *Real and Unreal Spirit* in the final crisis of the Weimar Republic.[31] The problematic of this work turns away from the traditional
horizon of idealist systems and rejects their epistemological assumptions. Instead it sails into aporias in which the 'impotence of spirit'
compels resignation, unless they can be reconciled through leaps of
thought and decision. 'The. . .systems, knowledge and statements that
are not met with in experience, the objective contents of earlier ways of
thinking [should be] brought to life only insofar as we can apply them
to the one thing adequately accessible to us, namely, the individual
person.'[32]

Considering Gehlen's scepticism about the knowableness of the
Absolute, the hope of a philosophical–anthropological link-up with
that tradition must appear forlorn. The individual microcosm, faced
with the infinity of the historical macrocosm, can be made knowable
only through biological reduction. Yet Hegel's dialectic reproduces
itself in relation to the person – that is to say, in the negation of
youthful naturalness through subjectivist reflection, and the overcoming of the 'unhappy consciousness' through self-sacrifice in action. It is
in action that the 'genuine reality' is experienced beyond the subject–
object division, as 'unconscious certitude of being'. In other words,
individuals recover themselves when they have 'risked a leap into
being'.[33]

But why does reflection appear as a paralysed disunity, so unbearable that it triggers the longing for a leap into being through unconscious action? Gehlen himself refers in this connection to Alfred Seidel's
Consciousness as Misfortune – a truly symptomatic cry of despair from
the interwar intelligentsia, brilliantly expressing its political tensions
and the nightmare of its bewildering ideological heritage.[34] In fact,
Seidel hanged himself in 1924, on the very day that he finished the
book. Born into a business family, he had been brought up an orphan
and suffered from depression and physical illness. He threw himself
into the November Revolution of 1918 as an idealistic communist and,

after an unsettled, hyperactive period of study in Heidelberg, worked as a private scholar utterly impoverished by inflation. All he lived for was to complete the book. The intellectual forces that had him in their grip are described in the Introduction:

> This work came into being out of the spiritual and political struggles of the time. It began with an attempt to combine problems from Marx and Freud, and an application of psychoanalytic theories to their own effects. Above all, it was influenced by the thinking of Goethe, Hegel, Dostoevsky, Nietzsche, George, Klages, Alfred Adler, James, Simmel, Max Weber, Jaspers and Spengler.[35]

At the end Seidel plunges with the cry '*Destructio destructionis*' from reflection into religion – but effectively into death. In between, he develops a psychological theory and a diagnosis of ideologies and analytic consciousness within the framework of the philosophy of history. Culture is interpreted as the sublimation of a hypertrophied sex drive,[36] and the phase of self-analysing consciousness – as opposed to the certainty of instinctive values – is regarded as both the blossoming and the end of a culture. In conclusion, Seidel confronts Spengler and Hegel with each other. Dismissing Spengler as a political reactionary and illusionist, he nevertheless admires his analysis of history in *The Decline of the West*. It is in this light that he reads Hegel: 'The dawning of consciousness is the result and culmination of the unfolding of the *Volksgeist*. It fulfils the meaning of this people or culture within world history, signifying its completion and hence its decline.' But Seidel then goes on to castigate that process of growing consciousness as a breakthrough by 'the demonic instincts of the Western spirit' and – 'for the sake of spiritual purity and true culture' – to 'nihilize that nihilism' which, with its 'talk of positivity', seeks a further growth of consciousness as a means to construct something which 'by its very nature [cannot] be consciously willed'. In this view, there is nothing more negative than talk of positivity, which the truly positive never engages in. The destruction of nihilism, however, can only arise out of the spirit of nihilism itself, insofar as 'analysis is propelled against analysis'.[37]

Gehlen saw another exit from the 'unreal spirit' of modernity in the crisis that was reorganizing bourgeois society as a mass society: human behaviour *secundum naturam*. But the idea that action could overcome the disunity of thought was later perceived to be a subjective illusion.[38] On the one hand, the person who engages in action is embroiled in social relations of power where the 'certitude of being' is by no means necessarily experienced. On the other hand – and in the late thirties

Gehlen developed this as the cornerstone of his philosophical anthropology – man is distinguished from other forms of life by his deficiency
in instinct. In order to compensate for this, man's conceptual orientation in the appropriation of nature must hold its numerous attrac-
tions at bay[39] and constitute through authority the contexts of his
self-preservation in action. Thus, the overcoming of the disunity of
consciousness leads the individual into social space, but since this is
structured only in categories of power and technique, it makes the
individual dependent on the power that exists at any given time. There
is no support for resistance against it, only memory of the 'objective
contents of earlier modes of thought'.

II Posthistorical Modernization

Since Gehlen the literature has been haunted by talk of Antoine
Augustin Cournot, the French mathematician and philosopher from
the time of the Second Empire. Instead of page references, however,
which are never given, we often find a presentation of biographical
details, as if encyclopedias had been consulted more than the work of
the apocryphal Church father of 'posthistory'.[40] In fact, when we
examine Cournot's writings, we do not actually meet the central
concept of 'posthistory',[41] but a related idea. History 'in the narrower
sense' or 'as it is normally understood' (Cournot's usual way of
referring to what is essentially the whole of previous history since the
emergence of the advanced European and Asiatic civilizations) is
reserved for a heroic and turbulent period of transition between two
non-historical, stable conditions: that is, between the tribal cultures of
early times and ethnology, and the socio-economic human civilization
of the future. The relationship between history and humanity's final
condition is seen as a drawing together that can never be fully completed – a process which, in the metaphor of a river, is drawn off into an
irrigation system.

> History, as it is normally understood, has its starting-point in those primal
> facts whose description and, if possible, explanation are the task of ethno-
> logy: it progressively leads humanity towards a final state where, in terms of
> social organization, the elements of civilization properly so called have
> assumed a preponderant influence over all the other elements of human
> nature, thanks to the continual intervention of experience and general
> reason. All the original distinctions are tending to fade away, even the
> influence of historical precedents is losing its strength, and societies are

tending like a beehive to arrange themselves in an almost geometrical
fashion, whose essential conditions are ascertained by experience and
demonstrated by theory. The truly historical phases of human societies are
situated between these extremes – that is, the phases in which political and
religious institutions play the main role, the periods of wars and conquests,
of the foundation and destruction of empires, of the rise and fall of
dynasties, castes and aristocratic or popular governments. That, above all,
is what has attracted the attention of historians right up to the present day,
whether they have approached history as artists or as philosophers. For the
group of such grand scenes is much more fascinating than the ethnological
origins of history, or the often hidden movement of the civilizing current
which has awaited our own times to begin displaying to all its irresistible
force. . . .

It is between the two extremes in the development of societies that superior
men of all kinds – conquerors, legislators, missionaries, artists, scholars,
philosophers – exercise the greatest influence over their century, and that
the strokes of fortune have the greatest force and resonance. For its
capricious power is not then held in check to the same extent, either by the
primitive instincts of Nature and a necessity that might be called vital or
organic, or by another necessity, physical or economic, whose principle is
more abstract but no less powerful, because (at least in the main) it
determines the economies of societies in the last instance through reciprocal
repression of all individual instincts. Thus, just as human societies went on
existing before they lived the life of history, so we can imagine that they can,
not exactly attain, but stretch out towards a condition where history is
reduced to an official gazette recording regulations, statistical data, the
accession of heads of state and the appointment of officials, which therefore
ceases to be history in the customary sense of the word. . . .

We are leaving the historical phase in which caprices of fate and acts of
personal or moral vigour have had so much influence, to enter a new phase
in which people weigh up the masses pen in hand, and are able to calculate
the exact results of a clockwork mechanism.[42]

The new condition is presented in this text as an overcoming of
chaotic historicity,[43] and as a hope of world peace and prosperity.
Cournot was certainly not alone in looking with expectation towards
social-technological self-regulation of a world society existing at one
and the same level; indeed he stood here within the French tradition of
early socialism and positivism.[44] This idea that history would be
overcome through the unfolding of bourgeois society was ultimately
part of the Enlightenment programme, which in Germany was most
clearly expressed in Immanuel Kant's 'Idea for a Universal History with
a Cosmopolitan Intent' (1784).[45] According to this conception, after a

long period of military conflicts in which the historically established states had fragmented and thus neutralized one another on a manageable scale, developed bourgeois society would 'maintain itself automatically' [*als wie ein Automat*]. In the nineteenth century, therefore, the concept of 'posthistory' (if it existed at all) did not contain the frustration of cultural pessimism, but rather the hope that the chaos of history and the ubiquitousness of historicism might finally be overcome.

We might thus reformulate the question of whether history is over, and ask instead whether, in the judgement of contemporary mentors of the Right and the Left, the Enlightenment prophecies are beginning to be fulfilled. We might then further consider how and why nineteenth-century programmatic visions have become images of terror in the second half of the twentieth century. But before we attempt to trace the route from the future of the past to the nostalgia of the present, we need to establish the principal coordinates: that is to say, what Cournot understood by history and civilization, and how his distinctions should be translated into the language of contemporary historical thought.

On the one hand, Cournot saw all previous history mainly in terms of great personalities and events and the category of freedom (although elsewhere in his discourses he thought that regularities could also be detected in the succession of religions, cultures and empires[46]). On the other hand, he saw the tide of civilization irresistibly gaining the upper hand: its movements and exigencies might often lie hidden, but they pushed forward through the accumulation of experience and rational planning, forced the renunciation of instincts within the socialization process, and determined in the final instance the economic life of society. The last formulation, in particular, now sounds almost like Marxism put back on its feet. But the remarkable metaphor of the geometrical beehive suggests a concept of social structures neither clearly determined nor unequivocally rational, which – as Norbert Elias put it in his analysis 'On the Process of Civilization' – come down to 'configurations' where hierarchies based on power, division of labour and levelling do not exclude one another. What Cournot formulated was not a democratic programme but a technocratic prognosis.

In a series of non-specific remarks on the development of human relations, Cournot anticipated the twentieth-century overshadowing of the history of events by structural history. It is thus not without a certain irony that the French pioneers of this shift – the so-called Annales School[47] – did not primarily concern themselves with the modernization processes of world civilization, but sought to relate the narrative history of feudalism and the ancien régime to the social-structural levels of the economy, material civilization and *mentalités*. In other words, what Cournot saw as characteristic of the future, they tried to establish as the element already determining the past. It was only in a second wave, coming from the USA in the mid twentieth century, that the social modernization processes associated with industrialization became the dominant theme of a discipline that redefined itself as 'historical social science',[48] and global, 'geometric' models were derived from dynamic societies and set as yardsticks for the assessment of all other countries.[49] This notion of a unilinear objective, which shot ahead of experience and reason, fixed what Cournot had had in mind with his image of the beehive. But in the course of its realization, this promise was increasingly felt to be a danger – of a history without alternatives, and without the possibility of establishing in historical research those degrees of freedom which threaten to disappear in the contemporary experience of all-powerful systemic connections.

A direct application of Cournot's concept of history, however, seems rather problematic in the contemporary world, at least as a route-marker along the winding paths of the history of ideas. For we have lost sight of our goal: instead of remaining with Gehlen's outdated posthistory, we have landed amidst historical social science and a modernity of anonymous process-structures which promises the freedom that Hegel defined as the knowledge of necessity. Indeed it may be concluded that, in terms of cognitive content, modernization and posthistory lie less far apart than one might suppose from the affirmative or disappointed tone of their champions. But we cannot yet understand why the one is hailed as a tendency of bourgeois society while the other is registered with a sense of resignation. We must therefore look more closely at the accompanying tones. If we do not wish to overburden ourselves with the intellectual history of the past hundred years, it might be useful to draw out Cournot's basic intentions and to identify their sequels and associated approaches in the period since then. Three areas need to be stressed for our present purposes: (1) Cournot's hope of overcoming the rampant historicism of his age; (2) his aim of a social science based upon laws and predictability, which would be capable of 'weighing up the masses'; and (3) his use of social metaphors – beehive discipline, a river diverted into irrigation canals, approximation to a final condition – as an indication that nature and technology stimulated him with ideas for the development of social models and instruments.

Notes

1. These included Daniel Bell, Jürgen Habermas, Herbert Marcuse, Henri Lefebvre and Claus Offe.
2. 'Geschichte und Posthistoire', appendix to Peter Brückner, *Psychologie und Geschichte*, ed. Axel-R. Oestmann, West Berlin 1982 – presumably written in 1980.
3. It is one of the specificities of the German notion of history that the concepts of 'civil society' and 'bourgeois society' are denoted by the same term: *bürgerliche Gesellschaft*.
4. The quotations are from Arnold Gehlen.
5. An allusion to Brückner's autobiographical account of his youth in the Third Reich: *Das Abseits als sicherer Ort*, West Berlin 1980.
6. Brückner, *Psychologie*, pp. 264–66.
7. The two best-known texts – both characteristically written by émigrés – have a similar perspective and span nearly the whole period of this literature, which should be distinguished from an earlier wave of renunciations of Stalinized Marxism. See Herbert Marcuse, *One Dimensional Man*, New York 1964; and André Gorz, *Farewell to the Working Class*, London 1982.
8. Provisional appraisals may be found in collections such as: Frank Deppe et al., eds, *Abendroth-Forum*, Marburg 1977; Jürgen Habermas, ed., *Observations on the 'Spiritual Condition of the Age'*, Cambridge, Mass. 1985; and Rolf Ebbighausen and Friedrich Tiemann, eds, *Das Ende der Arbeiterbewegung in Deutschland? Ein Diskussionband für Theo Pirker*, Opladen 1984.
9. Cf. Bernward Vesper, *Die Reise* (first edition published in 1977), Jossa 1981, p. 433.
10. See Ernst Nolte, *Marxismus und Industrielle Revolution*, Stuttgart 1983. Cf. *Der Faschismus in seiner Epoche*, Munich 1963, and *Deutschland und der Kalte Krieg*, Munich 1974.
11. See Nolte, *Was ist bürgerlich?*, Stuttgart 1979, pp. 11ff., and 'Pluralität der Hitlerzeit?', in ibid., pp. 88ff., as well as the overview in *Marxismus*, pp. 533f. For a more cautious assessment, see Karl Dietrich Bracher, 'Ende des bürgerlichen Zeitalters', in idem, ed., *Geschichte und Gewalt. Zur Politik im 20. Jahrhundert*, West Berlin 1981.
12. See the magnificent survey of the many different aspects of the 'post' phenomenon in the introduction to Hans Robert Jauss, 'Der literarische Prozeß des Modernismus von Rousseau bis Adorno', in Ludwig von Friedeburg and Jürgen Habermas, eds, *Adorno-Konferenz 1983*, Frankfurt/Main 1983, pp. 95ff. See also the informative overview by Hans Egon Holthusen, 'Heimweh nach Geschichte. Postmoderne und Posthistoire in der Literatur der Gegenwart', *Merkur* 430 (1984), pp. 902ff.
13. This is most apparent in the case of Gehlen's old colleague from the thirties in Leipzig, Hans Freyer. See his late work *Theorie des gegenwärtigen Zeitalters*, Stuttgart 1955, esp. the section 'Die Vollendbarkeit der Geschichte', pp. 62ff. This whole tradition will be discussed further in chapters 3 and 5 below.
14. See chapter 6 below.
15. Ten years after 1968, it became quite common on the Left to picture the coming of a protracted apocalypse and to reject 'ticket inspection by the World Spirit' – a sensibility to which Hans Magnus Enzensberger, as so often, gave early expression. See his 'Two Notes on the End of the World' (1978), in *Political Crumbs*, London 1990. In the eighties, the greatest interest in *Posthistoire* was to be found among young Berlin philosophers and sociologists in the circle of Jacob Taubes – Böhringer, Bolz, Kamper or Kittsteiner – and among other writers with a background on the Left, such as Gumbrecht or Sloterdijk, who diagnosed a sense that time and history were over, not mainly from the crystallization of socio-cultural structures but from the broken connection between experiential space and horizon of expectations (Koselleck), given that nothing was to be expected any longer. International parallels might be seen in the writings of Vattimo, Baudrillard or Cooper, for example.
16. A few authors deviated by using the feminine article – for example, Rolf Schwendter (*Zur Zeitgeschichte der Zukunft*, Frankfurt/Main 1984, pp. 320f.) envisages '*eine*

Posthistoire' which, following Comte, is 'the posthistorical future as an endlessly prolonged past'.

17. On the biography of Gehlen, see Karl-Siegbert Rehberg's obituary 'Metaphern des Standhaltens', *Kölner Zeitschrift für Soziologie und Sozialpsychologie* 28 (1976). On the problem of continuity between the 1940 and 1950 editions of Gehlen's main work *Der Mensch. Seine Natur und Stellung in der Welt*, see Carol Hagemann-White, *Legitimation als Anthropologie. Eine Kritik der Philosophie Arnold Gehlens*, Stuttgart 1973 (which lists the divergences on pp. 274ff.) and Gabriele Althaus, 'Zucht-Bilder', in Urs Jaeggi et al., *Geist und Katastrophe*, West Berlin 1983, pp. 60ff.

18. Gehlen, *Studien zur Anthropologie und Soziologie*, Neuwied/Berlin 1963, p. 246: 'Über die Geburt der Freiheit aus der Entfremdung'. [The German impersonal '*es*' construction, here rendered by the use of 'they', alludes to the Freudian id in a way that cannot be conveyed in English. *Trs note*]

19. Ibid., p. 344. The editors of Gehlen's collected works also came to realize that the unusual concept was not to be found in Cournot. *Gesamtausgabe*, ed. Karl-Siegbert Rehberg, vol. 7, Frankfurt/Main 1978, pp. 468ff.

20. Gehlen, *Studien*, pp. 322ff: 'Über kulturelle Kristallisation'.

21. Gehlen, 'Über kulturelle Evolutionen', in H. Kuhn and F. Wiedmann, eds, *Die Philosophie und die Frage nach dem Fortschritt*, Munich 1964, p. 219.

22. Gehlen, 'Das Ende der Persönlichkeit', in *Studien*, p. 331.

23. Gehlen, *Moral und Hypermoral*, 2nd edn, Frankfurt/Main 1970, p. 157. In this repudiation of the extra-parliamentary opposition, he joined with an ideological hardliner from the GDR, Wolfgang Harich, who in his old age sought out Gehlen's authoritarian anthropology as a way of completing Marxism, so that the Eastern bloc countries might be further developed into egalitarian eco-dictatorships. I do not have sufficient knowledge to say whether, as a result of this exchange on the plasticity of needs, Gehlen became an authoritarian Green shortly before his death. Cf. Harich, *Kommunismus ohne Wachstum? Babeuf und der 'Club of Rome'*, Interview with Freimut Duve, Reinbek 1975, pp. 177ff.

24. On Driesch's 'vitalist solipsism', see Lothar Samson, *Naturteleologie und Freiheit bei Arnold Gehlen. Systematisch-historische Untersuchungen*, Freiburg 1976.

25. Gehlen, *Zeit-Bilder* (first published 1961), 3rd edn, Frankfurt/Main 1986, p. 206. Gehlen's concept of posthistory is often cited in the literature but has rarely been looked at in any depth. But see the interpretations in Wolf Lepenies, *Melancholie und Gesellschaft*, Frankfurt/Main 1969, pp. 232f.; Martin Greiffenhagen, *Das Dilemma des Konservatismus in Deutschland*, Frankfurt/Main 1986, pp. 329ff. – with further discussion of the impossibility of conservatism in modernity, pp. 374ff. I was kindly given a copy of Werner Röhr's *Arnold Gehlens negative Utopie vom 'Post-histoire'* before it was to be printed in Poland, in 1987 or thereabouts. This is generally a judicious reappraisal and critique, written in the GDR, but it gets out of hand in its sweeping social-functional conjectures.

26. Hagemann-White, p. 172, referring to Gehlen, 'Formen und Schicksale der Ratio', *Blätter für deutsche Philosophie* 17 (1943).

27. The sociologist who edited Gehlen's collected works, Karl-Siegbert Rehberg, kindly drew these notes to my attention (*Bundesarchiv* NS 15/204).

28. See, for example, Gehlen, *Deutschtum und Christentum bei Fichte*, Leipzig 1935.

29. See the references in n. 17.

30. This characterization is used by the philosophical editor of his writings, Lothar Samson: *Naturtelologie*, p. 139.

31. *Wirklicher und unwirklicher Geist*, Leipzig 1931. This 'philosophical investigation into the method of absolute phenomenology' (1931) is treated by Samson (pp. 68ff.) mainly as an existential-Hegelian setting of the course of his thought; while Hagemann-White (pp. 52ff.) chiefly considers its consequences (e.g. the completed break with Kierkegaard, more or less at the same time as Adorno's) and its account of Freud.

32. Gehlen, *Wirklicher und unwirklicher Geist*, p. 8.

33. See Samson, pp. 91f.

34. Alfred Seidel, *Bewußtsein als Verhängnis. Aus dem Nachlaß* , ed. Hans Prinzhorn, Bonn 1927, which carries the subtitle *Fragmente über die Beziehungen von Weltanschauung und Charakter oder über Wesen und Wandel der Ideologien* [Fragments on the Relations between World-View and Character, or on the Nature and Change of Ideologies]. The editor's introduction draws a delicate picture of the author's personality. On the surrounding climate of cultural pessimism (Ludwig Klages, Oswald Spengler, Theodor Lessing), see Samson, pp. 75ff.

35. Seidel, p. 72.

36. In one fragment (p. 212) he writes: 'The scientist is a sublimated pervert. Scientists are so good – not just generous but weak, good-natured people – because they do not have to live out their anti-social, evil characteristics. . ., but sublimate them precisely in their intellectual activities; for that reason, however, such products have a correspondingly destructive effect.' Hagemann-White (p. 163) suspects that in Seidel as in Gehlen there is a confusion between sublimation and reaction formation: 'Seidel despaired of his own thoughts, because he. . .could only understand culture as neurosis and civilization as a curse. Gehlen turns things round and legitimates every neurosis with culture (instead of charging the latter with the former), so long as it makes possible behaviour in accordance with norms.'

37. Seidel, pp. 201ff.

38. Around 1933 Gehlen undertook a number of idealist detours so that, 'in accordance with his nature', he might invoke repression and discipline and call for affirmation of whatever happened then as an expression of the highest freedom. See Hagemann-White, pp. 52ff.

39. In Gehlen's philosophical anthropology this is valued as a 'productive achievement of release': see Axel Honneth, *Kritik der Macht. Reflexionsstufen einer kritischen Gesellschaftstheorie*, Frankfurt/Main 1989. Honneth further argues that if the signs are reversed, one can see here a structural parallel with the critique of reification and domination in a slightly later émigré work, Horkheimer's and Adorno's *Dialectic of Enlightenment*, whose moulding by the life-philosophy and cultural criticism of a Ludwig Klages or Alfred Seidel took the edge off 'critical theory' and turned it into a doctrine of the convergence of totalitarian domination.

40. Concise biographical information about Cournot is provided by J. Feller in *Dictionnaire de biographie française*, Paris 1961, pp. 983f.; and more details about his work are in the editor's introduction to Cournot, *An Essay on the Foundations of our Knowledge*, ed. Merritt H. Moore, New York 1956. A special issue of the *Revue de Métaphysique et de Morale* (13/1905) contains an assessment of his work – see, in particular, the contributions by C. Bouglé and G. Tarde on his conception of history.

41. Nevertheless, the literature on Cournot baldly uses the term 'phase posthistorique'. See, for example, Henri Berr, *La synthèse en Histoire*, 2nd edn, Paris 1952, p. 206, as well as the older studies. Informative contributions by two of Gehen's collaborators, apparently sent to Paris to discover *Posthistoire* in Cournot's writings, also contain no quotations: see Roman Schnur, 'Ein Prophet der verwalteten Welt. A.A. Cournots Prognose des posthistorischen Zeitalters', *Wort und Wahrheit* 16 (1961), pp. 743ff.; and Friedrich Jonas, *Geschichte der Soziologie*, vol. 1, Reinbek 1976, pp. 323ff. For the present state of research, see Stephan Meier, ' "Posthistoire". Versuch einer historischen Annäherung', in Dietmar Kamper and Jacob Taubes, eds, *Nach der Moderne. Umrisse einer 'Ästhetik des Posthistoire'*, unpublished manuscript, 1986; and Meier's summary presentation in 'Geschichte und kein Ende', *Bauwelt* 74 (1983), nos 1/2, pp. 22ff.

42. Antoine A. Cournot, *Traité de l'enchaînement des idées fondamentales dans les sciences et dans l'histoire*, vol. 3 of *Oeuvres Complètes*, Paris 1982, pp. 484–5. On the prognostic dimension in Cournot's work that remained virtually unknown in his time, see Raymond Ruyer, *L'Humanité de l'avenir d'après Cournot*, Paris 1930, pp. 47ff.

43. For Cournot this clearly includes revolutions. He also predicts that the socially and economically managed society of the future will no longer face revolutions, only riots and rebellions which will not alter its basic character and will thus give it an affinity to earlier societies. Ibid., p. 552.

44. One thinks above all of Saint-Simon and Comte; and of the more far-reaching perspectives of Marx and Engels for a transition from the domination of people over people to the administration of things — which would, of course, require radical changes and by no means dispense with further revolutions as in the positivist tradition.

45. In Immanuel Kant, *Perpetual Peace and Other Essays on Politics, History and Morals*, trs. Ted Humphrey, Indianapolis 1983, pp. 29ff.

46. Cournot, *Considérations sur la marche des idées et des événements dans les temps modernes*, vol. 4 of *Oeuvres Complètes*, pp. 9ff. Cf. idem, *Matérialisme, Vitalisme, Rationalisme*, vol. 5 of *Oeuvres Complètes*, pp. 220–1.

47. See Claudia Honegger, ed., *Schrift und Materie der Geschichte*, Frankfurt/Main 1977.

48. See Hans-Ulrich Wehler, *Geschichte als Historische Sozialwissenschaft*, Frankfurt/Main 1973, and the subsequent editorial work of *Geschichte und Gesellschaft*.

49. See Wehler's critical research report in *Modernisierungstheorie und Geschichte*, Göttingen 1975.

3

From 'End State' to 'Exterminism': On Some Sceptical Tropes Used in Diagnosing the Twentieth Century

I DIALOGUE OF SPIRITS

While Cournot was still alive Nietzsche – a cult figure in recent postmodernist writing[1] – wrote his diagnosis of the 'historical malady' of his age.[2] Antiquarian ballast in the form of pointless knowledge, relativism, illusory constructions of meaning, artificial barriers to the contemporary presence of genius from the past – these all lay like an incubus on individual vitality and threatened to prove 'harmful and ultimately fatal to living being'. For Nietzsche, 'historical men' were bound to a process which led them to believe in a future happiness denied to them in the present. 'Powerful instinct' broke down when it was necessary to forget or to remember: 'the unhistorical and the historical are necessary in equal measure for the health of an individual, of a people and of a culture'.

> But the world must get on, that ideal condition will not be created by dreaming, it must be fought and struggled for, and the path to redemption from that owlish earnestness lies only through cheerfulness.[3] The time will come when one will prudently refrain from all constructions of the world-process or even of the history of man; a time when one will regard not the masses but individuals, who form a kind of bridge across the turbulent stream of becoming. These individuals do not carry forward any kind of process but live contemporaneously with one another; thanks to history, which permits such a collection, they live as that republic of genius of which Schopenhauer once spoke; one giant calls to another across the desert intervals of time and, undiscovered by the excited chattering dwarfs who creep about beneath them, the exalted spirit-dialogue goes on. It is the task of history to be the mediator between them and thus again and again to

inspire and lend the strength for the production of the great man. No, the *goal of humanity* cannot be in its end but only *in its highest exemplars*.[4]

Such lines, with their longing for life and their cult of genius inviting identification, have been a powerful stimulant for the fantasies of grandeur entertained by younger members of the educated middle classes. They found the meaning of history in present experience and made deferred hopes in the future as laughable as the critical-historical barrier to contact with things handed down from the past. Regardless of the political utilization or ostracization of Nietzsche in the twentieth century, his offer of subjectivity, greatness and immediacy ensured that he would continue to fascinate when the identification with great historical-philosophical frameworks crumbled in the face of reality.

In the nineteenth-century variant of historicism, the pathos of progress already counterposed a concept of sequentially unfolding historical epochs to one of cumulative development,[5] but it was Oswald Spengler, just before the First World War, who conceptualized what would be the most resounding break in the upward continuity of the Enlightenment philosophy of history. The publication of the first volume of his *Decline of the West* at the end of the war ensured that, through a promising misunderstanding, it would become a bestseller.[6] Breaking with the Eurocentric perspective of historical ascent, he embarked upon a comparative study of the course of advanced cultures and ended with a prognosis of the end of Western civilization. Even for contemporary readers who had little taste for the conservative-ideological charge of Spengler's critique,[7] his theory of cultural cycles functioned as a liberation from the hold of historicism and the evolutionary philosophy of history, whose 'tapeworm' he had severed 'with particular resolution' so as to grasp 'individual parts as closed totalities'.[8] The general overview of history, not so much for professionals as for the short-term public interest in the subject, thus came to focus on natural forms of blossoming and passing away. History thereby opened itself to selective access which, given the subjective observational interests, could cancel its sequential order and split off the developmental forms of cultures. In this way Nietzsche's dialogue of trans-historical geniuses was supplemented by dissociated observation of their respective cultural constraints, whose complexity naturally required the introduction of particular viewpoints to be authenticated by history.

Nietzsche's plea for a dialogue of spirits across or outside time and Spengler's vegetative world-history have become less and less rarefied as a result of mass communications and the reproducibility of all cultural traditions. The perspective of history thus shifted from what happened at a particular time, and from the reconstruction of an overall evolutionary coherence, to a randomly accessible storeroom of what once existed. The individual was thereby estranged from roots in tradition and from the interconnections established by the philosophy of history, which both shrivelled into 'mega (or grand) narratives' without any binding force.[9] Not without reason does the 'time machine', which abolishes both temporal and spatial distance, stand at the beginning of twentieth-century science fiction.[10] The twentieth century is distinguished by the fact that the abstract, linear understanding of time which marked the human sciences in the eighteenth century, as well as the historical conception of nature in the nineteenth, have entered into the everyday life of society and increasingly provoked individual escapes from its unilinear regime.[11] In a kind of reversion to the idea of unhistorical cultures, this may take place in drug-induced fantasy or through the power of electronic media to store and call up the cultural heritage outside the constraints of time and space.

For half a century, Ernst Jünger devoted himself to such escapes from time and reported on them in journals, essays and first-person novels.[12] The last work in this series on time dissociation and cultural decline is still the most developed 'posthistorical' novel that can be read today. In *Eumeswil* – a hi-tech staging of Nietzsche full of quotations – the author adopts a posthistorical optic for his tale of a master-race 'anarch' within a 'fellah society'. On cooler examination, of course, all that happens is that a collaborator of a dictatorship declares himself a baron (*Freiherr*) by an act of subjective will, and a miracle machine provides him with the greatest spirits of all ages for a dialogue outside time. The narrator calls himself a historian and is carrying out research, removed from any cognitive interest, with his *Luminar*, a mixture of a time machine and a comprehensive video data-base of everything handed down by history, which can be instantaneously called up at any time according to the subject and situation.[13]

One would make too light of this novel if one simply demonstrated that Jünger had derived the idea of his hero and the cognitive structure of his *Luminar* from Spengler's *Decline of the West*.[14] The postmodern appeal of his conception consists rather in its schizophrenic range. For the paradigmatic occupation in 'posthistory' is that of the historian, who on the one hand plays with total knowledge of everything that has previously happened, and on the other hand practises participant observation as a night-waiter eavesdropping on some small-town potentate. And out of the threatening sameness, everydayness and fear of 'fellah society',[15] the compromised individual rises to the nihilistic awareness that he could kill if necessary and to his fantasy existence as 'anarch'. This is a king without a country, who divests himself of morality without taking on any responsibility – a self-image of greatness, won through autosuggestion, which empowers him for the dialogue of spirits. After socially meaningful movement has come to a standstill, or at least can no longer be discerned, posthistorical culture plays with history as a technical arsenal of ever-available analogies. If the reference to society holds out no prospect of meaning, the individual is free to dispense with it and is thrown back on his own continued existence. And here Jünger recommends his own biographical endowment as a military man and member of the educated classes, because of the self-sufficiency that it provides.

Jünger thus epitomizes, in a distinctively bourgeois-elitist manner, certain basic problems of the postmodern culture to which neo-conservatism also in part refers,[16] but which cannot be reduced to it. That culture really begins in the America of the 1950s with a revolt against the elitist *l'art pour l'art* of the literary avant-garde, seen as the very embodiment of modernism to be opposed, for example, with the great variety of Pop culture. Since the 1960s this turn against the rigidity and unilinearity of the recent European heritage has spread to other areas of culture in the USA. Particularly noticeable has been the general opposition to what is known there as the International Style, derived from the tradition of Bauhaus émigrés, and thus to functionalism and the ontological ethic of 'doing justice to the material' in architecture. It has defetishized advances in form – which, in alliance with the capitalist culture and construction industries, threatened to lead to the skimming off and freezing of culture – and instead advocates popular use of technical possibilities and quotation from earlier historical forms as a way of breathing in new life.[17]

This impulse was subsequently picked up by a current of French philosophy in the 1970s, which developed a critique of the self-grounding notion of social progress and underlined the historical character of its epistemological presuppositions. In the wake of de-Stalinization and the events of May 1968 – when French intellectuals distanced themselves from the Communist Party with which they had largely sympathized in the postwar period – the philosophy of history stemming from Marx and Hegel finally lost its hegemony, and it was denounced for its pretensions as an authoritarian language-game invented by master-thinkers.[18] Politically these disputes mainly involved a regroupment within the Left; only a few writers completely turned the page with the energy of the renegade. It was at a fairly late stage that postmodern tendencies began to influence the culture in the

Federal Republic, where they coincided with the imitative 'turn' towards Anglo-American neo-conservatism and with the political organization of the alternative scenes. This caused intellectual authorities of
the established Left to misinterpret such trends as the cultural planking
on a new political and axiological conservatism and thus to wage a
bitter struggle against them. In fact, their response might be understood
as the disappointment of those who, in the postwar decades, had
argued for a rediscovery and reimportation of the progressive part of
German culture repressed and expelled by the Nazis, with which the
international modernist culture had been largely impregnated.[19]

The real problems of postmodern culture, however, cannot be forced
into a Right–Left schema and can only be partly explained by the kind
of national shifts that have been mentioned here. Nor can they be
averted by a simple reaffirmation of the inherited ideals of modernist
literature and architecture or the basic assumptions of the Hegelian
tradition of the philosophy of history – especially since these appear
mostly to degenerate into a kind of aesthetic or philosophical immuni-
zation against systemically deformed interest structures within industrial society. Rather, the problems consist in the arbitrary nature of the
alternatives which, arising from the consumption-oriented techniciza-
tion of the elitist dialogue of spirits, become a self-service store in the
cultural market of mass society. The modern media eliminate the
spatial and temporal distances between cultures and tend to make it
impossible to distinguish between passed-down quotations, lived reality and fantasy. Intensifying the pressure on individuals to find their
bearings, they trigger defence of their self-esteem against the flood of
unmediated arbitrariness, so that the levels of fantasy and reality
become more and more blurred. Jünger's posthistorical parallelism of
collaborator-existence and *Freiherr*-fantasy is thus only one example
among many – one which, in its combination of contempt for the
masses and obsession with greatness, also demonstrates the legacy of
bourgeois culture to the postmodern phase of bourgeois society itself.

In this connection, there are one or two things to be found in the
work of the French Germanist and sociologist Jean Baudrillard, an ex-
Communist intellectual and translator of Marx, Brecht and Weiss who
after 1968 became a semiologist in the train of the PCF structuralist
Althusser, and who since the mid seventies has been active as an
essayist on the alternative literary scene.[20] Baudrillard writes in an
associative language of outpouring images or – as he puts it – analogies,
in which society and history are described with physical metaphors that
thrive on mere plausibility. We shall consider in more detail below the
significance of analogies from the natural sciences and technology. But

we should point out here that for Baudrillard realities can apparently be grasped only in physical intuitions, to which findings about society from everyday experience are then assigned in the manner of quotations. In a radical sequel to American media criticism,[21] he argues that social reality and its 'simulation' in the media can no longer be distinguished in terms of their reality: the 'hyperreality' conveyed by the media fades all primary experience and removes its capacity to function as a control.

In 'L'An 2000 ne passera pas'[22] – a text satirizing the technological modernization programme of the Socialist government in France – Baudrillard does not predict the physical collapse of the world in the near future, but rather the social volatilization of 'history' and thus of the possibility of recognizing or differentiating a future period of time. The 'exit from history' is not an end but an eternal sameness, and what he presents is 'not at all an occasion for despair', but rather for that cheerfulness which Nietzsche already praised as the road to redemption. Despair would presuppose some historical coherence of meaning or a goal that might not be attained. But the poststructuralists seek precisely to dissolve such determinations of meaning that appear in the meta-narratives of the master-thinkers of the philosophy of history.[23]

This 'posthistorical' arbitrariness is evoked in Baudrillard's essay by the reciprocal mutation of social–philosophical and technical–scientific codewords – a kind of 'war of words in outer time'. The volatilization of history is derived from three 'analogies':

1. The exchange processes underlying economic, political and sexual liberation have expanded and accelerated to such a degree that they resemble an artificial satellite which has attained 'free flight', broken away from its orbit and taken leave of reality, meaning and history, scattering into discrete atoms.

2. The opposite tendency of deceleration is true of 'the mass'. On the surface of dense bodies time stands still. An 'inert mass' has arisen from the excessive thickening of the social processes of circulation – a mass without meaning which, as the 'residue of history' or as 'inverse energy', absorbs any strategy pointing beyond it. The 'massification' is thus irreversible, and signifies 'a slowing down of history when it touches the astral body of "the silent majority"'.[24]

3. Finally, in a process analogous to the acoustic disappearance of music in the ultra-perfection of a quadrophonic system, history reaches a 'vanishing point' in the surfeit of information about events that are both too many and too close, and through the dissolution of social interrelations in microanalytic research. Each

event sinks 'with musical accompaniment' into the timeless store of too many events, into a proliferation of memory without experience.

Before the referent himself collapses into the delirium tremens of such metaphorical rhapsodies, he might do better to snap out of it. But instead he feels compelled to report a little piece of nostalgia standing out from further developments in this direction:

> May '68 was an event of this kind: funny, mysterious and not very historical; with its power of non-meaning, however, it was a pure effect of sudden crystallization[25] with hardly any noteworthy consequences (apart from the slowing-down that it entailed for socialism). But all in all it was an intense turn of events, which took place at the right time, with a special tone colour.[26]

II THE MEGAMACHINE

At the beginning of the bourgeois epoch, the dangers of its distinctive ideal of greatness were already conjured up in *Faust* and *Frankenstein*. In Germany the industrial revolution still lay far ahead around the year 1800, so that the gold- and man-producing genius in *Faust* could eventually be redeemed. But in England the material preconditions were already laid for the future dynamic of bourgeois society. Here we do not find the homunculus in a test-tube; rather, in *Frankenstein* the hubris of human inventiveness brings forth a monster who breaks free of his creator and threatens to develop a pernicious, superhuman power.[27]

A hundred years later Germany was catching up and had become the most dynamic industrial state in Europe. It was around this time that Max Weber – now a classic to whom the most diverse authors refer – spoke in the languages of social science and liberal politics of the contradictions between personality and trends in modern society. He drew from Nietzsche the cult of great individuals, whose values, productivity and power were the only truly creative phenomena in history, and he felt himself similarly bound to produce an *oeuvre* so gigantic that it brought him to the point of mental derangement. Unlike Nietzsche, however, he became capable of work again, and by submitting to the rules of the academic world he even worked his way up to become one of its most restrictive guardians. Despite his many-sided and thoroughly political personality, Weber reduced his science to an instrumental rationality which, obliged to practise academic ascesis with regard to value judgements, theorized the discipline of consistency. It drew its references from, and conceptually structured, the whole course of world history, and laid major emphasis on the 'disenchantment of the modern world' through calculating domination:

> The increasing intellectualization and rationalization does not, therefore, indicate an increased and general knowledge of the conditions under which one lives. It means something else, namely, the knowledge or belief that if one but wished one could learn it at any time. Hence, it means that principally there are no mysterious incalculable forces that come into play, but rather that one can, in principle, master all things by calculation. This means that the world is disenchanted. One need no longer have recourse to magical means in order to master or implore the spirits, as did the savage, for whom such mysterious powers existed. Technical means and calculations perform the service. This above all is what intellectualization means.[28]

Weber propagated this limitation of science to instrumental rationality as a course of intellectual honesty, which in principle offered the reward of omnipotence over nature through technology and calculation. At the same time, however, this self-limitation was intended to keep the political space for decisions and for individual value premises free from the structural tendencies of rationalization and bureaucratization. In great personalities he saw the forces that really drove and structured history; science should merely help them to remain true to themselves and to evaluate the consequences of their action.[29] For his attempts to grasp history in a conceptual framework had taught him to understand the world as essentially a conflict between existential impulses and social trends.[30] On one side were the irreducible powers and values of religion and personality, whose intervention in society constituted the fundamental creative element. On the other side were trends involving rationalization of culture and bureaucratization of social domination, which he considered to be the decisive ones of the modern world. Weber thus developed a thoroughly old-Prussian view of the military and civil-service 'apparatuses' as intrinsically rationalizing instruments:

> When fully developed, bureaucracy also stands, in a specific sense, under the principle of *sine ira et studio*. Its specific nature, which is welcomed by capitalism, develops the more perfectly the more the bureaucracy is 'dehumanized', the more completely it succeeds in eliminating from official business love, hatred, and all purely personal, irrational and emotional elements which escape calculation. This is the specific nature of bureaucracy and is appraised as its special virtue. The more complicated and specialized modern culture becomes, the more its external supporting apparatus

demands the personally detached and strictly 'objective' expert, in lieu of
the master of older social structures, who was moved by personal sympathy
and favour, by grace and gratitude.[31]

Apart from the dehumanized nature of this concept of rationality, its
identification with an apparatus built out of men proved to be of little
use since it was incapable of confronting the huge expansion of
bureaucratic apparatuses in the twentieth century, with all their arbitrariness, inefficiency, unmanageability and corruption.[32] That may be
a matter of debate. But at any event, the trends of modernity[33] seemed
to Weber to involve an irresistible dynamic and filled him more with
fear than with admiration, because their tendency to shape ever more
rigid structures locked the individual into a 'steel-hard casing':

> No one yet knows who will live in that casing in the future, and whether new
> prophets or a powerful rebirth of old thoughts and ideals will stand at the
> end of this awesome development, or – if neither of the two – a mechanized
> petrification, veiled in a kind of frantic self-importance. But in that case, the
> word could become truth for the 'last men' of this cultural evolution:
> 'experts' without spirit, hedonists without a heart. This nothingness
> imagines itself to have climbed a hitherto unattained level of humanity.[34]

In order to ward off this threat of posthistorical petrification, Weber
appealed during the First World War for a constitution based on
representative democracy – as the most likely vessel in which the
charisma of historical personalities could assert itself and be protected
from sterile banalization of their domination in successive bureaucra-
cies. Faced with the professional politicians of Weimar, however, who
lacked any real 'vocation', Weber looked in the long term to a plebisci-
tary leader-democracy as the only way of channelling revolutionary
violence to force open the cramping structures of market and
bureaucracy.[35]

What Weber split apart conceptually, the history of the twentieth
century would join together. Precisely because science imposed political ascesis, its misuse could involve the legitimation of politics through
constructions of reason; it thereby became all the more effective as an
instrument of rationalization and all the more exploitable for charismatic domination, functioning in the end as a kind of binding agent.
Conversely, bureaucratization proved to offer no protection against
irrationality, either of the system as a whole or of individual
bureaucrats.

A number of writers critically analysed this massing together of
political and military power, market economics, bureaucracy and
scientific technique – what Lewis Mumford referred to as a 'mega-

machine' reversing the instrumental relation between man and machine.[36] In this view, the period of the Second World War was a major turning-point, when the upward spirals of power and rationalization fused into dynamic systems on which individuals were now so utterly dependent that their very nature was adapted to the system.

Two dystopian novels from this period have come to epitomize the threat posed by technocracy and totalitarianism to civil society: Aldous Huxley's *Brave New World* (1931) and George Orwell's *Nineteen Eighty-Four* (1949). In retrospect, the imagination of such critics of the age seems to have lagged behind the real dynamic of society. Indeed, in 1959 Huxley returned to his vision of a technocratic future in the coming centuries, and concluded that in his own lifetime reality had already started to catch up with it.[37] And when the year 1984 actually arrived, the main concern of the media was to impress upon the public that Orwell's novel did not look ahead thirty-five years to a future state of Western society but was simply a critique of contemporary totalitarianism (especially in its Stalinist form) – so great was the fear that readers would misjudge the literary genre.

In the reconstruction and modernization boom that Western Europe experienced during the first two postwar decades, the problematic of the 'megamachine' was rarely taken up again, although there was no lack of voices warning that the drive for social rationalization found no equivalent in the substance of individuality.[38] The émigré legacy of the Frankfurt School, whose discussion of fascism, Stalinism and the American culture industry negativized the Enlightenment concept of progress as part of a universal process of domination over external and inner human nature, was initially not given very much attention.[39] Walter Benjamin's final testimony remained unknown for the time being – a text which, though akin to Adorno in its renunciation of progress, is of greater interest to us here because its indelible imagery maintains a fundamental tension between the 'piled-up wreckage' of progress and an active hope in the redemption of the repressed here on earth.[40] His reflections first came to notice in West Germany when the repressed Marxist legacy, and then its limitations, were discovered anew.

In the Adenauer era, however, a greater impact was made by the 'posthistory' diagnoses of sociologists who had either exercised or received a formative influence in the Third Reich – men such as Hans Freyer and Helmut Schelsky, respectively.[41] In writings less marked by despair that those of the émigré Left-Hegelians, the denazified Right-Hegelians maintained their distance and searched for elements of civilizational continuity that would be powerful enough to explain the

historical failure of national (or, more precisely, *völkisch*) subjectivism, and to provide a warning against overestimation of the room for manoeuvre at the disposal of welfare-state democracy.[42] They conceptualized scientific-technological civilization as a 'second system', whereby man detached himself from the compulsion of nature and created a world of his own with self-generating structural and practical constraints. The theme of 'man as such' was thus not an anthropological archetype: it arose out of man's encounter with, and responsibility for, himself in those objectivized structures, precisely insofar as they placed in question the meaning and room for manoeuvre of the individual.[43] In this analysis, the space for politics was whittled down and the substance of democracy exhausted, because the practical constraints of the system's technical regulation made citizens dependent upon political managers and these in turn upon scientific 'advice'. At this level of power structures the diagnosis became more entrenched, while in relation to meaning the proffered therapy involved continual historical or metaphysical reflection. Instrumental rationality remained undisturbed as the working capital of the 'megamachine'.

Where the chains of the past did not fix minds so tightly to the ground but allowed the scientific and anthropological dimensions to be thought together, consideration of the autonomous objectivization of the human spirit yielded much more far-reaching perspectives of a fundamental and thoroughly positive change in human existence. Thus, in the postwar years the much-read Jesuit paleontologist Pierre Teilhard de Chardin saw the earth as wrapped in a kind of spiritual atmosphere. This consisted entirely of networks – as we would say today – of social and technical inventiveness ('noosphere'), which would bring forth a new man.[44] Pierre Bertaux, a Resistance-fighter who after the Liberation became head of the Sûreté and subsequently a professor of German, foresaw the end of all previous history because demographic growth and the exhaustion of raw materials necessitated a 'mutation of man'.[45] The American futurologist Roderick Seidenberg expressed similar expectations,[46] though more in the spirit of Cournot and without the contempt for the masses common among European intellectuals at that time. Already in the early postwar years, when demands for an intelligent organization of society were making themselves felt, Seidenberg saw the maturing of a fundamental differentiation between the two conflicting human endowments of instinct and intellect, which he thought would favour the latter in its objectivized form of 'universal organization'. He derived this perspective from a past in which man evolved from the harmony of animal instincts through the conflict of instinct and intellect – 'along a precarious path of unstable syntheses[,] and that path is history'.[47] However, the objectivizations of human intelligence (in industry, for example) were cumulative – the key point missing from Spengler's theory of cycles[48] – and achieved freedom vis-à-vis nature. On the other hand, they exerted a growing force for order which tended towards satisfaction through universal organization. Seidenberg was aware that this must mean an extensive and irreversible change in what had previously been understood by human nature. Moreover, he would seem to have coined the actual phrase 'post-historic man' – contrasted, as in Cournot, to both prehistoric and historical–transitional forms – which was then popularized and criticized by Mumford as a 'climactic dream . . . at the mercy of an infantile scheme of life'.[49]

Meanwhile in German-speaking culture, in a development mainly influenced by the émigré experience and the persecution of the Jews, an occasional but journalistically effective series of pieces analysed the relationship between machine and man not simply by establishing or taking for granted an immanent apparatus rationality, but by trying to work out its catastrophic dynamic in the wake of Auschwitz and Hiroshima. This critique was, of course, still more sombre than the contributions of the Frankfurt School or of futurological writings in other countries, but it was worked out through personal resistance in the anti-nuclear movement which involved, as in the case of Benjamin, a courage born of the loss of hope.

Günther Anders referred to the fact that technocracy was bound up with social changes which made it largely immune from revolts against the real possibility of man's self-destruction.[50] He saw this possibility in the deeply rooted expectation of infinite progress, in the evacuation of death from the experiential context of modern civilization, in the discrepancy between the customary horizon of responsibility and the field of action of technology, and above all in the moulding of man by the media. By the latter he understood the indirect, fragmented and manipulated perception of reality by the media, as well as the disintegration of the individual into spheres of activity without any clear responsibility.[51] As a result of – and in partial contradiction with – his practical commitment to the peace movement and the opposition to the war in Vietnam, Anders's diagnosis became so radical that he saw technology as the new subject of history. At most, men were now 'also historical' – that is, resistant or reactive – as the proletariat had been in a history made by male members of the ruling class. With the emergence of technocracy man's 'nature' was fundamentally changed, and the relationship between the two became 'final and irrevocable'. It did not depend on when the destructive powers of technocracy would bring about the 'end of time', because 'end-time' was already with us and one could speak in the traditional sense of the 'antiquation of history'.[52]

The 1970s were strongly marked by discussions about the limits to growth, pollution of the environment, human capacity to endure stress, governability of the system, the coming of postindustrial society and the spectre of nuclear catastrophe. As the impression became more widespread that the great machine itself was spluttering out of control, views such as those of Anders began to have a broader resonance. Scientific investigation of science was placed on the agenda, and Schelsky's continuous metaphysical reflection at least came to the attention of scientists – both in their specialist work and in their public opposition to the unrestricted use of their products. At the same time, however, 'research and development' was revealed as the essential factor in production and growth and, to a hitherto unknown degree, the object of political, military and economic encouragement and demands. (Robert Oppenheimer had already justified his role as physical coordinator of the first atom bomb programme, working alongside the army man in overall charge, with the words: 'It's technically sweet.')

With the shift towards a 'postindustrial society', mainly characterized by the development of encircling technologies and media and hence the perfecting of 'secondary systems',[53] a whole series of inherited social facts and perspectives that had once seemed self-evident finally broke into pieces. The so-called collapse of trade-union solidarity is perhaps the most conspicuous example. Dissolution of the basic structures of industrial society points not towards a breakdown of the system but to new, more fluid forms of opposition which feed off existential and cultural experiences and can scarcely be brought under the control of representative democracy. Today, of course, these are no longer particular domains such as class cultures, of which bourgeois society was once composed and which seemed to point beyond its structure; they are now simply the 'system' itself.

The question that Weber or Benjamin turned around in their minds is now constantly posed – namely, whether the iron casing of rationalization or the catastrophic 'advance' of history can still be interrupted, and what alternatives can be ranged against it. Who today still presumes to manage the systemically intertwined interest-structures in accordance with a higher viewpoint? But nor is it possible to stop them operating. If the megamachine is no longer an instrument, can its modes of functioning still be influenced and, if necessary, disrupted? And if trust in the historically determined alternatives for the future has run out of steam, which forces will have the will and the capacity to measure up to them? Since the answers to these questions are unclear and point to various possible differentiations rather than alternatives,[54] the notion of a self-generating catastrophe has suggested itself – including in the form of indefinite advance.

III NATURE AND DEATH

Our third chain of associations is triggered by Cournot's natural and technological metaphors for the structure and motion of society: for example, the beehive, the river petering out into an irrigation system, or the 'end state'. They gain significance against the background of his work as a theoretician of mathematical–economic probability and his attempt to produce a philosophical–encyclopedic conceptualization at once of history, nature and social science. In the human sciences, particularly history, there was hardly any basis within Wilhelmine culture for such a synthesis; historicism was in its late bloom, and attempts were being made to distinguish precisely the methodologies of the natural and human sciences. In other cultures, too, such a linkage was left to figures on the margin of the academic world.

Among historians the most prominent outsider was Henry Adams, a successful publicist and productive private scholar who felt himself to be a failure because he measured himself by his own ancestors. His great-grandfather had been a leader of the American Revolution and second president of the United States – an office in which Adams's grandfather had later followed – and his father had become one of the most outstanding diplomats in the USA.[55] This may explain why Adams's most important theoretical works, though written during the turn-of-the-century boom, concern themselves with the fall of civilization, and why his first novel already criticized the decline of American democracy.[56] Apart from his activity as a publicist, his annual trips to Europe or around the world, and his medieval studies including a Harvard professorship, he filled nearly a whole bookshelf with writings on early American democracy and assumed the presidency of the American Historical Association. Finally, when he was sixty-five, he began to address the problem of a theory of history which would draw programmatically on the natural sciences and catch up with them by working out social regularities and scientifically based prognoses.[57]

Adams took up two themes that were topical then and still are today – the growing social use of energy and the historicity of nature – and combined them in a prognosis about the acceleration of history and, in moral–ironical vein, the threat of the end of civilization in 1921.[58] His

aim, then, was to free himself from the external appearance of the
industrial revolution and to draw up calculations about the social use
of energy. He concluded that the bend in this energy curve lay not in the
early nineteenth century but around the year 1600, and that since then
the speed-up in growth had become ever more marked. Industrialization was just one stage within a long-term acceleration process, whose
phases[59] were becoming ever shorter and which was not carrying the
world to a new plateau of civil society but exhausting it in a dynamic of
increasing fury. This 'law of social acceleration', worked out from
empirical data (though with anything but rigorous measurements), was
then combined with a transposition of the second law of thermodynamics into a social metaphor. The general formulation of this law had
been achieved shortly before through statistical advances in probability
theory. The propositions concerning entropy in the theory of heat
would have a fundamental significance for atomic physics, modern
astronomy and the development of a new social understanding of
nature that supplanted static-mechanical ideas about the regularity of
nature.

In the theory of heat, which starts from the premiss that in a closed
system energy does not change over time, entropy measures the energy
lost in the conversion of heat into other forms of energy. This yielded
the basic insight that our world is finite and its processes are irreversible, so that differences in heat, which are the precondition of all life,
ultimately balance out and result in 'heat death'. In the theory of
elementary particles, on the other hand, entropy is formulated in such a
way that 'orderly movement can be fully transferred to disorderly
movement, but disorderly movement cannot be fully transferred to
orderly movement'.[60] For a metaphorical mind, which sought an
underpinning in laws of nature for its sense of *décadence*, this must
have reinforced the idea that in society too all order, which rests upon
inequality, tends towards dissolution and that levelling is a fatal
disease.

The objections are obvious enough: the temporal dimension of the
earth's history is not the same as that of the class formation of
bourgeois society; man cannot be compared to elementary particles, or
heat differences to class distinctions, and so on. Thus, Adams's social
entropy might be dismissed as the early science-fiction of bourgeois
decay, were it not for a series of irritating elements that make such
judgements seem overhasty. First, Adams combined a very productive
'natural scientific' approach (the observation of acceleration on the
basis of energy transfers) with a questionable but still highly topical
metaphorical procedure (transposition of the law of entropy to the

history of society).[61] Second, in spite of this combination, Adams arrived at diagnostic insights far in advance of expert judgements concerning, for example, the technologization of atomic physics:

> The assumption of unity, which was the mark of human thought in the Middle Ages, has yielded very slowly to the proofs of complexity. The stupor of science before radium is a proof of it. Yet it is quite sure, according to my score of ratios and curves that, at the accelerated rate of progression since 1600, it will not need another century or half century to turn thought upside down. Law in that case would disappear as theory or *a priori* principle and give place to force. Morality would become police. Explosives would reach cosmic violence. Disintegration would overcome integration.[62]

Adams called for the moral challenge of the newly released forces to be recognized in time. In place of the old regulative systems of social morality based upon prohibitions and taboos, it was necessary to develop institutional safeguards to control the exponential growth of energy.

Third, our picture of the world has been fundamentally transformed in the twentieth century by the theory of evolution and the law of entropy, as well as by theories of historical cycles, systems theory and sociobiology which have shown that it is possible to merge basic categories of the natural and social sciences.[63] Finally Adams and others (among whom he stands out only in his posing of the problems) took up from the optimism of progress the theme of the irreversibility of nature and the exhaustion or self-destruction of expanding civilization.

Not long after these attempts to grasp the macroworld with the aid of rather crude instruments, Sigmund Freud was making similarly tentative and speculative efforts to decipher the microlevel. In a radical departure from psychiatric conceptions of mental illness as a physical defect of the brain or nerves, his theory of psychoanalysis had placed the major causal emphasis on the long-term cultural effect of curbing the libidinal drives (above all in children's experience within the family).[64] But after the First World War he gave death and aggression a new role, especially in a text which even today is largely disputed or ignored by his followers.[65] In this interim balance-sheet of psychoanalysis, written with his characteristic clarity and curiosity, Freud attempted to develop a biological conception of memory on the basis of his work on the remembered and the repressed. This model, which in its essentials still structures physiological research into memory, led him to a cautiously expressed but far-ranging hypothesis about one of the two basic human drives: the death instinct (the other being the libido).

The writings of Freud's later years, from the interwar period, mainly extend into the realm of cultural diagnosis the insights that he originally obtained through analysis of individuals, and they are marked by a profound scepsis about one-sided hopes in progress and the capacity of societies as a whole to live in peace.[66]

These elements of Freud's later theory of the instincts, which so embarrassed many of his followers, give it a particular interest for our investigation: namely, the abandonment of human perfectibility and the correlation of the cultural and mental findings of psychoanalysis with a biochemical model of its natural presuppositions. The course of the discussion, which was triggered by the problems of the repetition compulsion as the decisive medium of psychoanalytic therapy and by the challenge of the war traumas, cannot be properly examined here. I shall refer to only two of the observations to which it gave rise. First, whereas Freud begins the essay by declaring irrelevant any crediting of his libido theory to the philosophical tradition of the Enlightenment, he ends with the almost frightened realization that 'we have unwittingly steered our course into the harbour of Schopenhauer's philosophy. For him death is the "true result and to that extent the purpose of life", while the sexual instinct is the embodiment of the will to live.'[67] It sounds as if the author has found himself transposed, by a kind of practical constraint of his own research, from the tradition of the Enlightenment to that of bourgeois cultural criticism.

The second observation concerns an idea related to the entropy metaphor, which Freud enlists to interpret the 'conservative character' of the instincts as a micro-physical discharge of energy, so that the sexual or life instinct leads to short-term stimulation of vital energy tensions and thereby arrests the tendency to adjustment of this tension involved in the ego or death instinct. The following quotation, which joins together two separate passages, brings out Freud's view of life as a detour towards death, a return of the organic to the inorganic which becomes ever more 'complicated' in the course of evolution. This was the aspect of his theory taken over by such champions of the posthistory concept as Arnold Gehlen or Ernst Jünger, in the metaphor of 'levelling' as a first step towards 'crystallization' (postvital petrification of culture) at the level of society.[68]

> If we are to take it as a truth that knows no exception that everything living dies for *internal* reasons – becomes inorganic once again – then we shall be compelled to say that 'the aim of all life is death' and, looking backwards, that 'inanimate things existed before living ones'. The attributes of life were at some time invoked in inanimate matter by the action of a force of whose nature we can form no conception. . . . The tension which then arose in

what had hitherto been an inanimate substance endeavoured to cancel itself out.... For a long time, perhaps, living substance was thus being constantly created afresh and easily dying, till decisive external influences altered in such a way as to oblige the still surviving substance to diverge ever more widely from its original course of life and to make ever more complicated *détours* before reaching its aim of death. ... Seen in this light, the theoretical importance of the instincts of self-preservation, of self-assertion and of mastery greatly diminishes. They are component instincts whose function it is to assure that the organism shall follow its own path to death, and to ward off any possible ways of returning to inorganic existence other than those which are immanent in the organism itself. We have no longer to reckon with the organism's puzzling determination (so hard to fit into any context) to maintain its existence in the face of every obstacle. What we are left with is the fact that the organism wishes to die only in its own fashion. Thus these guardians of life, too, were originally the myrmidons of death.[69]

He opposes to this the effect of sexual coalescence:

But how is it that the coalescence of two only slightly different cells can bring about this renewal of life? The experiment which replaces the conjugation of protozoa by the application of chemical or even of mechanical stimuli enables us to give what is no doubt a conclusive reply to this question. The result is brought about by the influx of fresh amounts of stimulus. This tallies well with the hypothesis that the life process of the individual leads for internal reasons to an abolition of chemical tensions, that is to say, to death, whereas union with the living substance of a different individual increases those tensions, introducing what may be described as fresh 'vital differences' which must then be lived off. ... The dominating tendency of mental life, and perhaps of nervous life in general, is the effort to reduce, to keep constant or to remove internal tension due to stimuli (the 'Nirvana principle',. . .) – a tendency which finds expression in the pleasure principle; and our recognition of that fact is one of our strongest reasons for believing in the existence of death instincts.[70]

Freud saw in growing personal and cultural awareness a hope of mastering the destructive potential of the death and aggression instinct, with its catastrophic social effects. But although he considered himself a pacifist, he thought it unlikely that in the foreseeable future there would be 'a community of men who had subordinated their instinctual life to the dictatorship of reason', and who would therefore be truly capable of peace. Freud's ideal consisted in Kant's old programme of a world-wide, law-governed civil society; for he too regarded man – in Kant's words – as a beast that needed a master, but he did not consider any individual as suitable for that role. However, the Enlightenment faith had grown old, and although Freud saw the need to fight for it, the tail wind of history already seemed to him to be making itself felt. 'An unpleasant picture comes to one's mind of mills that grind so slowly that people may starve before they get their flour.'[71] And he added with an almost desperate irony:

> The death instinct turns into the destructive instinct when, with the help of special organs, it is directed outwards, on to objects. The organism preserves its own life, so to say, by destroying an extraneous one. Some portion of the death instinct, however, remains operative *within* the organism, and we have sought to trace quite a number of normal and pathological phenomena to this internalization of the destructive instinct. We have even been guilty of the heresy of attributing the origin of conscience to this diversion inwards of aggressiveness. You will notice that it is by no means a trivial matter if this process is carried too far: it is positively unhealthy. On the other hand if these forces are turned to destruction in the external world, the organism will be relieved and the effect must be beneficial. This would serve as a biological justification for all the ugly and dangerous impulses against which we are struggling. It must be admitted that they stand nearer to Nature than does our resistance to them for which an explanation must be found. It may perhaps seem to you as though our theories are a kind of mythology and, in the present case, not even an agreeable one. But does not every science come in the end to a kind of mythology like this? Cannot the same be said today of your own Physics?[72]

The question was directed in an open letter to Albert Einstein, whose scientific theories and anti-fascist commitment were major prerequisites of the construction of the atom bomb during the Second World War. This war unleashed a hitherto unimagined force of technological and bureaucratic destruction, with such a systematization of the potential for violence that it was difficult to see individual human aggression in its instruments. Rather, the experience conjured up the image of a 'megamachine', in which social structures and dynamics were reified and which threw individuals back upon themselves. From now on, after Auschwitz and Hiroshima, man would appear to be an 'antiquated' being.

In the face of the deep crisis that had carried Europe into two world wars, the United States became the strongest power and the most functional model of modernization, forming a world empire that made history. Its power, often compared to Rome's, appeared to lack the inner disunity of European bourgeois society in the epoch of imperialism, especially since the socialist alternative – which had first become organized on a large scale during the economic crisis of the thirties – was witchhunted as 'unamerican activities' in a xenophobic atmosphere of rivalry with the Soviet Union and struggle against the heterodoxy of many of the intellectuals driven from Hitler's Europe. On the road to becoming a superpower, most of the American ruling layer was able to keep the clear conscience it had developed in overcoming its policy of neutrality vis-à-vis the Axis – which now asserted itself against the new totalitarianism in the formation of a world in the image of the 'first new nation'.

Whereas the first two postwar decades in Europe laid the basis for growth and modernization within this framework, the same years had the significance of an interwar period for the USA. At the same time, a fundamental intellectual opposition took shape through a critique of power and of its manifold risks, and then achieved a widespread impact in the movement against the Vietnam War and the formation of an alternative youth culture. Only a minor role was played in this by the legacy of socialist alternatives in Europe. For the new power and its anti-totalitarian conscience called for a critique based on a distinctive set of themes. Alongside the questions of race, poverty and civil rights, this democratic–ecological critique mainly focused on the nexus of power and technology (the 'megamachine'), drawing on the explosive force of psychoanalytic insights into culture and history to expose the WASP potential for repression and its elevation to a seamless ethos of work and domination. Such new paths, which sometimes veered off into mystical life-practices, coalesced around the late-fifties cult book *Life against Death*, by the classical philologist Norman O. Brown. Its translation into German at the end of the Adenauer period, with the innocent title *Zukunft im Zeichen des Eros* [The Future under the Sign of Eros], went almost unnoticed.[73] But in America it had a powerful effect which, in the early fiction of Thomas Pynchon, linked up with the entropy tradition stemming from Henry Adams.[74]

Brown had begun to concern himself with psychoanalysis in 1953, at the age of forty, when the replacement of the liberal New Deal ideals by 'the politics of sin, cynicism and despair' became unbearable to him.[75] Contrasting Freud's later work on the death instinct and cultural analysis to the mundane adaptationism of the American therapeutic machine, he reread psychoanalysis in the light of Nietzsche and Jacob Böhme and saw in its historical and anthropological extension

> a way out of the nightmare of endless 'progress' and endless Faustian discontent, a way out of the human neurosis, a way out of history. . . . If historical consciousness is finally transformed into psychoanalytical consciousness, the grip of the dead hand of the past on life in the present would be loosened, and man would be ready to live instead of making history, to enjoy instead of paying back old scores and debts, and to enter that state of Being which was the goal of his Becoming.[76]

Brown's view of history and culture as an ever higher degree of neurosis was opposed both to Enlightenment optimism and to Marxism, which made up for its lack of a utopia of love and peace with a biological spiral of needs, and remained trapped within the nexus of repression and sublimation associated with the compulsion to work.[77] Brown's own theorization involved an emphasis on the death instinct, understood as a striving for separation, alongside the love or life instinct with its striving for unity. In this respect, and in his attempt to hold together the symbolic dimension and the biological presuppositions of psychoanalysis, he remained faithful to Freud. But he believed that the conflict between libido and death instinct had come to structure the late Freud's deep pessimism about the perspectives for human culture, and he sought to go beyond this conflict as well as culture itself, with its compulsive disorder of progress and discontent.

Brown arrived at this solution through a seemingly minor shift. With the help of Kojève, Nietzsche and Hegel, he reinterpreted the instinctual polarity – which Freud had cautiously seen in terms of a heuristic dualism – as a dialectical relationship. By then setting Freud's history of life together with Hegel's philosophy of history, he opened up a broad programmatic perspective for the halting of progress and the overcoming of history.[78] This parallel between an instinctual dialectic of psycho-physical individual history and a dialectical development of human culture and domination seemed to provide a key for the future, whereby a change in individual life – above all the elimination of repression, the freeing of sexuality and a return to nature – might also stop the further propulsion of the historical dialectic. For Brown, all the Faustian energy of domination hindered man from achieving peace, being, pleasure and therefore a graceful death, and prevented the dissolution of historical time in an eternal satisfaction which would also make it possible to accept death. Only a 'reanimalization' of the individual could nullify that energy, which was the result of the suppression of death. At the end of this dialectical argument suggesting that history itself could be overcome – an argument which he tried to make clearer with an ingenious critique of anal fixation in the culture of protestantism and capitalism[79] – Brown saw a mystical 'resurrection of the body' beyond repression, history and time.

The powerful impact of this book on the protest movement in the USA was intensified by Pynchon's adoption of its dialectical theory of repression, in connection with an entropy-based macroperspective which he, like Adams, extended from nature to an interpretation of the historicity of society.[80] While the forms of the protest movement were directly emulated throughout the world and utilized as the expressive medium of local programmes, it was at best with astonishment that Europe learned of their roots in a cultural critique which sought to overcome the suppression of death – and hence the repetition compulsion of deadly violence – through a return to the animality of nature. Here too, as Pynchon's novels were published and read over the next two decades, the imaginative world of an escape from history, filled with nature and death metaphors, became increasingly conspicuous, long after it had freed itself from the existential movement of intellectual protest against the protestant–capitalist Cold War culture of the new superpower. In Europe the clocks were set differently.

When the Soviet Union began to build its own hydrogen bomb in the 1950s and a struggle was launched in West Germany against atomic rearmament of the new Bundeswehr, scant attention was paid to the diagnoses of Günther Anders and others about the machinery of death that was sucking humanity into a dynamic of catastrophe.[81] At that time it was a voice like that of Karl Jaspers which won a greater hearing, with its emphasis on human responsibility and its denunciations of the impermissible 'Gnostic' speculations of the prophets of posthistory.[82] From the late seventies on, however, as the arms drive accelerated and the energy and ecology crises became more widely known, a prophetic tone also appeared among scientists and others in Europe which stamped intellectual perceptions of the future with metaphors and arguments derived from the natural sciences.[83]

Such prophecies conjured up a systematically organized tendency to death within world society – whether in the form of straightforward annihilation ('exterminism'), or through the plundering of irreplaceable resources from future generations. We thus find again the keyword 'entropy' expressed in programmatic visions where the room for manoeuvre is extremely limited. Such visions still cling to the responsibility of individuals, by appealing to their capacity to think again, to change their behaviour, to join with others in the practice of resistance. But the characteristic element is that such responsibility is hardly to be expected from those who are actually 'responsible'. At most politics, bureaucracy, industry and army are regarded as cogs in the 'megamachine', which they cannot steer differently even if they wanted to. The race of petrified apparatuses towards catastrophe must be stopped through outside resistance and the withdrawal of allegiance, so that any space won in this way can be used for a radically new praxis.

At the end of these chains of association we may single out three prophecies, coming from quite different backgrounds, which appeared a decade or so ago in the USA, Britain and France and have since been translated into German.[84] This will allow us to grasp the central role of systemically inflected metaphors from nature and technology in the contemplation or avoidance of the death tendencies within contemporary society.

First, in a bestseller originally written for an American economic trends institute, Jeremy Rifkin developed a 'new image' for the dissolution of world civilization: 'entropy'.[85] Like Adams, though initially with less use of metaphor, he made the second law of thermodynamics the basis for a dynamic theory of society. He predicted neither physical heat death nor the cultural death of social levelling, but set out to construct a kind of historical–ecological materialism that assumed the exhaustibility of the energy or matter base of a social formation. The scarcer the resources became, the greater would be the compulsion on society to switch to a different form of energy use, and thus to a new economic structure with corresponding social forms and values. Rifkin used the term 'entropy watershed' to denote these negatively determined transitions. One such point was immediately in store for world society, since fossil fuels and other key raw materials were becoming exhausted, and the growth economy (including population increases) typical of the past formation could not be saved through nuclear energy because this was neither safe nor practicable on a world scale. For the coming solar age there was a clear alternative: either society could adapt to the rhythm of natural renewal, which would entail a drastic reduction in world population, a return to agriculture and organization in small, semi-autarkic communities;[86] or an attempt could be made to maintain the socio-economic growth structures through an acceleration of biological renewal based upon genetic engineering.[87] In deciding between ecotopia and the nightmare of a genetically manipulated solar age, Rifkin was helped by a kind of 'meditative' use of the second law of thermodynamics.[88] If our earth is 'ultimately' finite and will return to dust after the cooling of the sun, then this entropic *memento mori* helps us to understand that we must accept the finiteness of life and therefore a return to agrarian modes, since a civilization centred on objects and growth is doomed to fail.

Edward Thompson's lengthy and similarly plausible analysis of 'exterminism', in which the arms build-up appears as the driving-force of both the USA and the USSR, also reaches a crux in a short-circuit between nature and society.[89] Thompson, who left the Communist Party in 1956 and became a leading figure in the New Left, subsequently committed himself to European Nuclear Disarmament and attempted to convince the Left that it should not slide into anti-Americanism through the use of traditional anti-imperialist concepts – for the danger came equally from the Soviet Union. Even if it rested there upon political–institutional and ideological factors rather than upon the military–industrial complex of the Western world, the growth in arms production characterized both systems and had to be analytically traced back to its roots. The protracted Cold War had blurred the difference between the systems, so that a fundamental change from within could not be expected on either side.

> No doubt we will have one day a comprehensive analysis of the origins of the Cold War, in which the motives of the agents appear as rational. But that Cold War passed, long ago, into a self-generating condition of Cold Warism (exterminism), in which the originating drives, reactions and intentions are still at play, but within a general inertial condition: which condition (but I am now asking a question which will, I hope, be refuted) is becoming irreversible as a direction. . . . (T)he inertial thrust towards war (or collision) arises from bases deeply enstructured within the opposed powers. We tend to evade this conclusion by employing concepts which delimit the problem: we speak (as I have done) of the 'military–industrial complex', or of the military 'sector' or 'interest' or the arms 'lobby'. This suggests that the evil is confined in a known and limited place: it may threaten to push forward, but it can be restrained: contamination does not extend through the whole societal body. But the more apposite concept, which is employed by some peace researchers, is that of isomorphism: 'the property of crystallizing in the same or closely related forms'. . . . Viewed in this way, the USA and the USSR do not *have* military–industrial complexes: they *are* such complexes. . . . Isomorphic replication is evident at every level: in cultural, political, but, above all, in ideological life. . . . Gregory Bateson, the social scientist, employed an analogy from biological systems: 'The short-time deterrent effect is achieved at the expense of long-time cumulative change. . . . It is this fact of cumulative change from one act of threat to the next that gives the system the quality of *addiction*.' Frustrated aggression 'backs up' until it permeates whole cultures. It is within ideology that *addiction* to exterminism is distilled.[90]

This brief extract contains a whole panoply of social metaphors from nature: the image of irreversibility with which we are already familiar from the theory of heat, and simpler ones such as contamination, societal body, crystallization, addiction or distillation. Even the Marxist 'drives' seem here to be a slave to the death instinct – or to evil. The central concept of isomorphism, derived from chemistry, denotes a form of crystallization: 'the appearance of crystalline forms with very similar plane angles, in crystals with a different chemical composition' (*Brockhaus* Dictionary). 'Isomorphism', the dictionary adds, 'is a very widespread phenomenon' – as common as the arms production of great powers. Its inscrutable danger conjures up awesome images of disease and inorganic lifelessness. But if social space is thus emptied in the prophecy, are its appeals to social change and intervention not likely to go unheeded?

Michel Serres, a mathematician by training who teaches the history of science at the Sorbonne in Paris, has offered a whole series of multidisciplinary contributions as the basis for a constructive role of philosophy in the society of the future. In his view, however, such a role can be established only if science withdraws from the space of politics – otherwise it will inevitably be pulled into the system of 'thanatocracy'. Serres's interpretation of this 'rule by death' – all political leaders have followed Hitler in dealing with the means of mass destruction – is evoked in a lengthy and rhapsodic text. At its centre stands the fusion of domination and science in the dynamic 'military–industrial complex', which no less a figure than President Eisenhower warned against in the 1950s.

> In almost every case today the programmer is the one who holds sway in the ministry of death. Therefore the history of science has a direction, an orientation, a single destination. This can be proved. There is no longer any real history of the sciences, because their course is now overdetermined. Science has left history behind. It has entered a posthistorical era. It is utterly in the grip of the death instinct. . .the abduction of knowledge by the powers of death. Conjunctural, economic, strategic or political reasons are rehearsed; the most recent past, the study of conflict, the game matrix, the behaviour of rats are called up for consideration. . . . No variation across countries and systems: the association of industry, science and strategy, wherever and however it takes shape, rapidly metastasizes and conquers space – economic space, political space, in short: space. It is the association of the best-protected theory and the most effective procedure for the most exacting, domineering and imperial goals. Or more accurately: the fully thought-out alliance of theoretical reason, practical reason and calculative, predictive, purposive reason. All reason is reduced to Reason. The most potent and productive triangle that history has ever installed. . . . The abominable engine of the new history – which produces itself by sucking everything into its exponential growth. . .: theoretical innovation, industrial product-lines, strategic rivalry. One feeds off the other. This triangle never varies, because it is the tissue called for by certain products. Those who own the product – ballistic missile, thermonuclear bomb, orbital weapon – must necessarily instal the triangle in the infrastructure.[91]

We again find the daring interdisciplinary imagery, deriving its authority from the prophetic gestures of a Frankenstein who has looked the monster in the face.[92] The system here frees itself from all human needs, values and influences; it is the very engine whose ever faster conversion of energy must lead to all-destroying collapse or to final exhaustion.

The death instinct, which Freud developed as a genetic hypothesis concerning the ego-instincts, has taken the form of an epidemic disease that 'infests' the dual power–knowledge superego.

In a further metaphorical speculation – namely, that engines can be everywhere but not everything – Serres opens some tiny room for manoeuvre. The eros of the simple life, together with a primal curiosity scientifically controlled in dialogue, might make it possible to jump clear of the raging machine, to starve out its scientific need for energy, and to stretch out again the span of life as a detour on the road towards death. It is the resistance of a vital energy which Luther, at the beginning of the bourgeois epoch, already opposed to the chiliasm of his time: 'And even if I knew that the world would come to an end tomorrow, I would still plant my little apple tree today!'[93]

Notes

1. Clear evidence of this was provided by Jürgen Habermas's first response after he had been attacked by the French champions of postmodernity (above all in Lyotard's *The Postmodern Condition*, Minneapolis 1984) as a master-thinker from the Hegelian tradition. It was a damning survey of Nietzsche's work first printed under the title 'Der Eintritt in die Postmoderne' (*Merkur* 421/1983), in which he refrained for the time being from directly confronting his adversaries. In a critical analysis of this text, Rolf Günter Renner then developed his heuristic model of an aesthetically, rather than historically, defined 'postmodern constellation', which he used for a foray into the intellectual history of recent times, *Die Postmoderne Konstellation*, Freiburg 1988, pp. 36ff.

2. Friedrich Nietzsche, 'On the Uses and Disadvantages of History for Life' (1873/1874), in *Untimely Meditations*, Cambridge 1983.

3. An allusion to Hegel's remark that the owl of Minerva (identified with the philosophy of history) took flight only as the dusk was falling.

4. Nietzsche, 'On the Uses', pp. 63, 111.

5. See Carl Hinrichs, *Ranke und die Geschichtstheologie der Goethezeit*, Göttingen 1954, pp. 127, 164.

6. Oswald Spengler, *Der Untergang des Abendlandes* (1918/1922), 2 vols, Munich 1973. On the aspects discussed here, see also Detlef Felken, *Oswald Spengler. Konservativer Denker zwischen Kaiserreich und Diktatur*, Munich 1988; and Jacques Bouveresse, 'Spenglers Rache', in Peter Sloterdijk, *Kritik der zynischen Vernunft*, Frankfurt/Main 1987, pp. 356ff.

7. See, for example, Theodor Adorno, 'Spengler after the Decline' (1938), in *Prisms*, Cambridge, Mass. 1981, which in this respect foreshadows some of the ideas that he would later develop in his dialectical critique of the Enlightenment: 'Spengler sees something of the dual character of enlightenment in the era of universal domination' (p. 57).

8. Seidel, p. 199.

9. Peter Sloterdijk has gone furthest in readopting this perceptual tradition: 'The grand HISTORY of old turns out to have been an evolutionary stratagem, which could not reveal itself if it was to remain effective: an active, auto-hypnotic myth. Today this secret has been let out and used so as to take effect. Perhaps HISTORY was just a fairy-tale of the violent might of reality, which paid off so long as its target group could be used to become subjects of the fairy-tale action and to weave their personal histories into HISTORY.' (*Kopernikanische Mobilmachung und ptolemäische*

Abrüstung. Ästhetischer Versuch, Frankfurt/Main 1987, p. 24.) In *Verlust der Geschichte* (Göttingen 1959) Alfred Heuß already analysed the dissociation between an ongoing apparatus for reconstruction of the past and the break in the public coherence of meaning and identity involved in historical understanding – or, in his own terms, between history as science and as memory. Heuß himself lamented this loss of relevance of an elaborated apparatus of historical knowledge, whereas in recent years it has more often been hailed by historians as a release from the fear of catastrophe and the longing for meaning in the public. (See, for example, F.G. Maier, 'Die Eule der Minerva. Endzeit und Historie', *Neue Zürcher Zeitung*, 5 April 1985.) Others such as Michael Stürmer see in this dissociation a void which beckons us to synthesize new – in his case, national – images of history as a propagandistic substitute-meaning.

10. H.G. Wells, *The Time Machine*, London 1895. Cf. Michael Salewski, *Zeitgeist und Zeitmaschine. Science Fiction und Geschichte*, Munich 1986.

11. As well as Stephen Toulmin and June Goodfield, *The Discovery of Time*, London 1965, and Hans-Willy Hohn, *Die Zerstörung der Zeit*, Frankfurt 1984, see Rudolf Wendorff, *Zeit und Kultur. Geschichte des Zeitbewußtseins in Europa*, 3rd edn, Opladen 1985, on Nietzsche (pp. 446ff.) and on the contradictions of contemporary time-consciousness (pp. 617ff.) Cf. Helga Novotny, *Eigenzeit*, Frankfurt/Main 1989.

12. See Ernst Jünger, *An der Zeitmauer*, Stuttgart 1959; and various novels including *Auf den Marmorklippen*, Frankfurt 1985 [*On the Marble Cliffs*, Harmondsworth 1970] and *Heliopolis: Rückblick auf eine Stadt*, Tübingen 1949.

13. Ernst Jünger, *Eumeswil*, Stuttgart 1978.

14. Jünger's image of history followed Spengler in its basic content and its political thrust. In 1932 he dedicated his Right-Hegelian interpretation of mass society, *Der Arbeiter*, 'to Oswald Spengler, who forged the first new weapons after Germany's disarmament'. Quoted from Felken, p. 114.

15. This is Spengler's metaphor for the unhistorical culture of world cities: *Der Untergang des Abendlandes*, vol. 2, pp. 779ff.

16. See Peter Koslowski et al., eds, *Moderne oder Postmoderne?*, Weinheim 1986, and Koslowski's report to the West German Chancellor's Office: *Die postmoderne Kultur*, Munich 1987.

17. An informative collection of essays on the history of postmodernism may be found in Andreas Huyssen and Klaus R. Scherpe, eds, *Postmoderne. Zeichen eines kulturellen Wandels*, Reinbek 1986. On the (invariably eye-catching) appearance of post-modern architecture see Charles Jencks, *The Language of Post-Modern Architecture*, London 1984; and Heinrich Klotz, *Moderne und Postmoderne. Architektur der Gegenwart 1960–1980*, Wiesbaden 1984, and idem, ed., *Post-Modern Visions*, New York 1985.

18. Two German collections of interviews offer an introduction to the French poststructuralists: Peter Engelmann, ed., *Philosophien*, Graz/Vienna 1985; and Florian Rötzer, *Französische Philosophen im Gespräch*, Munich 1986. See also the textual analyses in Jürg Altwegg and Aurel Schmidt, *Französische Denker der Gegenwart*, Munich 1987, and the overview by Günther Schiwy, *Poststrukturalismus und 'Neue Philosophen'*, Reinbek 1985. An influential work of this period was André Glucksmann, *The Master-Thinkers*, New York 1980. Luc Ferry and Alain Renault (*French Philosophy of the Sixties: An Essay on Anti-Humanism*, Amherst, Mass. 1990) vehemently criticize the reception of German philosophy by the precursors of the new thinking, whose main works set the scene around 1968.

19. See Jürgen Habermas: *Die neue Unübersichtlichkeit*, Frankfurt/Main 1985; 'The New Obscurity', in *The New Conservatism: Cultural Criticism and the Historians' Debate*, ed. Shierry Weber Nicolsen, Cambridge 1989; and *The Philosophical Discourse of Modernity*, Cambridge 1987. For a similar position in the field of historical studies, see Hans-Ulrich Wehler, *Preußen ist wieder chic. . .*, Frankfurt/Main 1983. Less authoritative and informative, but all the more embittered, is

Burghart Schmidt, *Postmoderne – Strategien des Vergessens*, Darmstadt 1986. A wide-ranging discussion of the underlying social changes can be found in Johannes Berger, ed., *Die Moderne – Kontinuitäten und Zäsuren (Soziale Welt*, special issue 4), Göttingen 1986.

20. Baudrillard's major book is *L'Échange symbolique et la mort*, Paris 1976. See also the collections *Revenge of the Crystal* and *Fatal Strategies*, both London 1990, and the travel impressions *America*, London 1988.

21. See Marshall McLuhan and Quentin Fiore, *The Medium Is the Massage*, New York 1967; and for a recent evaluation, Hartmut v. Hentig, *Das allmähliche Verschwinden der Wirklichkeit*, 2nd edn, Munich 1985.

22. In *Traverses* 33/34 (1985), pp. 8–16. An English variant appeared as 'The Year 2000 Has Already Happened', in A. and M. Kroker, eds, *Body Invaders: Sexuality and the Postmodern Condition*, London 1988.

23. See Lyotard; or Jacques Derrida, 'Of an Apocalyptic Tone Recently Adopted in Philosophy', *Semeia* 23 (1982).

24. 'The Year 2000', p. 37. Cf. Baudrillard, *In the Shadow of the Silent Majorities*, New York 1983.

25. Gehlen's favourite expression for the specification and petrification of major structures – which, insofar as it is established by the intellect, may also be described as 'cerebralization'. In earlier writers such as Benjamin, the foreground was taken up by the positive aspect of morphological production within a micro-perspective.

26. 'L'An 2000 ne passera pas' [here translated from the German]. Baudrillard's simulated balance of his past in the PCF and in 1968 is supplemented by interesting factual information in Lothar Baier, 'Der Schwindel der Simulation', *Merkur* 40 (1986).

27. Moreover, the advanced vision is that of a woman, Mary Wollstonecraft Shelley: *Frankenstein, or the Modern Prometheus*, London 1818. The power of this image was particularly strong during the thirties depression: see for example Maurice Wormser's book on economic concentration, *Frankenstein, Incorporated*, New York 1931.

28. Max Weber, 'Science as a Vocation', in *From Max Weber: Essays in Sociology*, eds H.H. Gerth and C. Wright Mills, London 1970, p. 139.

29. The following interpretation owes many of its key points to the multifaceted work of the best authority on Max Weber: Wolfgang Mommsen, *Max Weber*, Frankfurt 1974, esp. pp. 97ff., 'Universalgeschichtliches und politisches Denken'. See also Detlev Peukert, 'Die "letzten Menschen". Beobachtungen zur Kulturkritik im Geschichtsbild Max Webers', *Geschichte und Gesellschaft* 12 (1986).

30. See Weber, *Wirtschaft und Gesellschaft*, Tübingen 1922, pp. 758f.

31. Ibid., p. 662. English translation in *From Max Weber*, pp. 215–16, and Max Weber, *Economy and Society: An Outline of Interpretive Sociology*, Berkeley 1978, p. 975.

32. For critical analyses of the further development of bureaucracy, see Arno Bammé et al., *Maschinen-Menschen, Mensch-Maschinen. Grundrisse einer sozialen Beziehung*, Reinbek 1983.

33. For example, the secular consequences of puritanism in setting the norms of the capitalist dynamic. See Max Weber, *The Protestant Ethic and the Spirit of Capitalism*, London 1930.

34. Weber, *Gesammelte Aufsätze zur Religionssoziologie*, vol. 1, Tübingen 1920, p. 204. The reference to the last men is a quotation from Nietzsche.

35. See Mommsen, pp. 44ff., and Weber, *Gesamtausgabe*, vol. 15, Tübingen 1984, esp. pp. 421ff.

36. On the concept and its history, see Lewis Mumford, *The Myth of the Machine*, vol. 1, *Technics and Human Development*, New York 1966/67, and vol. 2, *The Pentagon of Power*, esp. pp. 263ff.

37. Aldous Huxley, *Brave New World Revisited*, London 1958, pp. 11ff.

38. Alfred Weber, for example, who in 1935 had already written an anti-Nazi critique of the world of officialdom ('Kommt der vierte Mensch?', republished in *Haben wir*

Deutschen nach 1945 versagt?, Munich 1979), now extended it to the general danger, originating in the East, of depersonalization as an index of posthistoricity. (*Der dritte oder der vierte Mensch*, Munich 1953). And even Jean Fourastié, one of the most vociferous postwar champions of productivity and growth in Europe, later began to make a forward projection of their human costs into the twenty-first century: *Les quarante-mille heures*, Paris 1965.

39. See Max Horkheimer and Theodor Adorno, *Dialectic of Enlightenment*, London 1979.

40. 'Theses on the Philosophy of History': see below, chapter 6, n. 7.

41. Hans Freyer, *Theorie des gegenwärtigen Zeitalters*, Stuttgart 1955, esp. pp. 66ff. (on the 'completability of history') and pp. 79ff. on 'secondary systems'; and Helmut Schelsky, *Der Mensch in der wissenschaftlichen Zivilisation*, Cologne 1961. Lepenies gives a useful location of Freyer in *Between Literature and Science: The Rise of Sociology*, Cambridge 1988, pp. 340ff.

42. There are similarities here – not so much in the argument as in the sensibility, interpretative gestures and manner of establishing continuity – with the diagnosis that European state-based cultures are sinking into an epoch of 'world civil war', whose centres lie in the revolutionary hegemonies of the USA and USSR but in which 'third factors' might again play a role. Paradigmatic in this respect is Carl Schmitt's 'Die geschichtliche Struktur des heutigen Weltgegensatzes von Ost und West', in Armin Mohler, ed., *Freundschaftliche Begegnungen, Festschrift Ernst Jünger*, Frankfurt/Main 1955, pp. 135ff. See also Schmitt's appreciation of Freyer in 'Die andere Hegel-Linie', *Christ und Welt*, 25 July 1957. In the work of Gehlen's former assistant Hanno Kesting, this became the general theme of an interpretative approach to the philosophical history of the nineteenth and twentieth centuries: see *Geschichtsphilosophie und Weltbürgerkrieg*, Heidelberg 1959. At that time a less prominent National Socialist intellectual, Erwin Hölzle, adopted a similar starting-point for the further dissemination of such ideas: see *Geschichte der zweigeteilten Welt*, Reinbek 1961. This establishment of a national continuity out of the tradition of conservative revolution was a feature of the Cold War period, when it was associated with a fundamental critique of technology in the work of Schmitt and especially Heidegger. Since the mid 1970s it has been reactivated by Ernst Nolte as a provocative historical programme, in *Deutschland und der kalte Krieg*, Munich 1974, and *Der europäische Bürgerkrieg*, West Berlin 1987.

43. Schelsky (p. 41) even refers to the view of Jacques Ellul (*La Technique ou l'enjeu du siècle*, Paris 1954, p. 354) that the 'myth of man' is nothing more than 'a natural secretion of technical progress'.

44. Pierre Teilhard de Chardin, 'The Formation of the Noosphere' (1947), in *Man's Place in Nature*, London 1966. Related essays by Teilhard de Chardin include such titles as 'From the Pre-Human to the Ultra-Human' (1950) and 'The End of the Species' (1952).

45. Pierre Bertaux, *Mutation der Menschheit*, Frankfurt/Main 1963, pp. 59ff: 'Ende der Geschichte'. In a later edition (Frankfurt/Main 1979, pp. 206ff.), he gave Nietzsche and Teilhard de Chardin as the spiritual sources for his prediction of a new man and characterized the mutation in classically posthistorical terms as a loss of the old values, a transformation of the individual into a herd animal ('homo domesticus') within a kind of termite society, and the founding of a society that would be essentially defined by free time, by play (instead of work) and theories of play.

46. Roderick Seidenberg, *Posthistoric Man: An Inquiry*, Chapel Hill, NC 1950, pp. 55ff. See also his *Anatomy of the Future*, Chapel Hill, NC 1961. Seidenberg (1890–1973) was a New York architect who went back to the land in 1937 to Doylestown, Pennsylvania, where he restored old houses and composed his two prognoses. He was on friendly terms with Lewis Mumford.

47. *Posthistoric Man*, p. 21.

48. Ibid., pp. 81ff. Typical of Seidenberg's evolutionary approach is his refusal of the

posthistorical metaphor of an ant colony, on the grounds that intelligent universal organization cannot be grasped in images from the social biology of insects.

49. Lewis Mumford, *The Transformations of Man*, London 1957, p. 123. Mumford further sketched out the ancestry leading up to 'machine-made man' and envisaged the extinction of 'non-adaptable types like the artist and the poet, the saint and the peasant' (p. 121).

50. *Die Antiquiertheit des Menschen*, vol. 1, Munich 1956, esp. pp. 276ff: 'Geschichtliche Wurzeln der Apokalypse-Blindheit'.

51. Ibid., pp. 286ff. Rather like his former partner Hannah Arendt (*Eichmann in Jerusalem*, New York 1964), he referred here to the surprise of defendants in the Holocaust trials that they as persons, rather than the apparatus they served, were being expected to take responsibility. For as parts of a machine, they had not experienced themselves as individual subjects.

52. 'Endzeit und Zeitenende' (first published in 1972), in *Die Antiquiertheit des Menschen*, vol. 2 (1980), esp. pp. 271ff. Using the example of the My Lai massacre, Anders sought to show that in the meantime there was a competition between man within the military machine and the higher destructive power of the more mechanized parts of the apparatus itself, which in the extreme case was acted out against those without any defence.

53. On the discussion opened by Daniel Bell's *The Coming of Post-Industrial Society* (New York 1973), see Lucian Kern, ed., *Probleme der postindustriellen Gesellschaft*, Königstein 1984.

54. See Ulrich Beck, *Risikogesellschaft. Auf dem Weg in eine andere Moderne*, Frankfurt/ Main 1986, pp. 368ff.; and Claus Offe, 'Die Utopie der Null-Option', in Johannes Berger, ed., *Die Moderne*, pp. 97ff.

55. See Henry Adams's autobiography, written in 1906 and published after his death: *The Education of Henry Adams*, New York 1918. The manner and sensibility with which he reached his theoretical observations is described from chapter 25 on. See Kurt Hoffmann's article: 'Henry Adams. Porträt eines konservativen Anarchisten', *Merkur* 218 (1966).

56. Henry Adams, *Democracy: An American Novel*, published anonymously in 1880.

57. For greater detail see William H. Jordy, *Henry Adams: Scientific Historian*, New Haven 1952.

58. See the posthumous collection of Adams's theoretical writings: *The Degradation of the Democratic Dogma*, New York 1919, esp. 'Letter to American Teachers of History'.

59. It may be argued that he was referring here to the already outdated 'law of phases' of the physicist J. Willard Gibbs, who counted as the most eminent natural scientist in America. Adams distinguished between a religious, a mechanical, an electrical and an ethereal or atomic phase, and situated his own era in the transition from the third to the fourth.

60. Carl F. von Weizsäcker, *Die Geschichte der Natur*, Göttingen 1948, p. 39, with an introduction to scientific knowledge about the temporality of nature. For more recent distinctions, see Bernd-Olaf Küppers, 'Entropie, Evolution und Zeitstruktur', in Dietmar Kamper and Christoph Wulf, eds, *Die sterbende Zeit*, Darmstadt 1987, pp. 133ff.

61. On the topicality and uncritical use of such metaphors, see for example the collection of twenty studies of literature: Gunter E. Grimm et al., eds, *Apokalypse. Weltuntergangsvisionen in der Literatur des 20. Jahrhunderts*, Frankfurt/Main 1986. The editors conclude that there are three structural characteristics 'of the modern consciousness of end-time. . .totality, entropy and irreversibility'. On totality see the earlier remarks on the expansion of the 'megamachine'. Otherwise the definitions are quite straightforward: 'Entropy denotes the dissolution of all systems of domination and order. Decay threatens not only political and social order but also custom and morality, religion and world-views, so that intellectual, ethical and religious laws lose their validity. The category of irreversibility, however,. . . is a dismal feature of

the contemporary world situation. Unlike in earlier processes of decline, the machinery now set in motion can no longer be halted.'

62. In a letter to Henry O. Taylor, quoted in Mumford, *The Myth of the Machine*, vol. 2, p. 232., with an effusive note of appreciation. For a more sceptical assessment of Adams's place in American historiography, see Oscar Handlin, *Truth in History*, Cambridge, Mass. 1979, pp. 91f.

63. These discussions from the interwar period are reappraised in Seidenberg, *Posthistoric Man*, pp. 108ff. In opposition to Spengler's and Toynbee's organic theories of cultural cycles, Seidenberg follows Adams in focusing on the expansion of scientific–technological structures in the modern world, and in tackling the value problems associated with the smothering of freedom in systems for the ordering of human intelligence.

64. A useful introduction to psychoanalysis is Alexander Mitscherlich, *Der Kampf um die Erinnerung*, 2nd edn, Munich 1984. Its formative history and implications for cultural theory are examined in Mario Erdheim, *Die gesellschaftliche Produktion von Unbewußtheit*, Frankfurt/Main 1982.

65. Sigmund Freud, *Beyond the Pleasure Principle* (1920), London 1961. The ambitious yet resigned character of this discussion is expressed in the appended quotation from Rückert: 'What we cannot reach flying we must reach limping' (p. 58). Walter Benjamin in particular later made use of this text to distinguish between memory and experience in the theory of reception and history, and this – together with the rise of Oral History – is one reason why it has become widely discussed again today.

66. See especially 'Why War?', Letter to Albert Einstein, September 1932, in *Standard Edition of the Complete Psychological Works*, vol. 22, London 1964.

67. *Beyond the Pleasure Principle*, pp. 43–4. Cf. ibid., pp. 1–2.

68. See Hannes Böhringer, 'Die Ruine im Posthistoire', *Merkur* 406 (1982).

69. *Beyond the Pleasure Principle*, pp. 32–3.

70. Ibid., pp. 49–50.

71. 'Why War?', p. 213.

72. Ibid., p. 211.

73. Norman O. Brown, *Life against Death: The Psychoanalytical Meaning of History* (1959), 2nd edn, Middletown, Conn. 1985.

74. In his first works Pynchon (b. 1938) translated to America the themes of T.S. Eliot's *Waste Land*, and then in 1960 with *Entropy* embraced Adams's historical metaphor from the natural sciences. (See Joseph W. Slade, ' "Entropy" and Other Calamities', in E. Mendelson, ed., *Pynchon*, Englewood Cliffs 1978.) He made his breakthrough with V. (New York 1963) and acquired international fame with *Gravity's Rainbow* (New York 1973).

75. *Life against Death*, p. xvii.

76. Ibid., p. 19.

77. Ibid., pp. 14ff.

78. Ibid., esp. pp. 77ff., 'Instinctual Dualism and Instinctual Dialectics'. The blurring of the mediations of social reality in this abstract dialectic of nature – which paved the way for 'Make Love Not War', all manner of mystical sects and the sympathetic illusion of Flower-Power – was criticized by Herbert Marcuse in an afterword to Brown's later *Love's Body* (New York 1966), a salvationist text consisting entirely of meditative quotations.

79. 'Studies in Anality', in *Life Against Death*, pp. 179ff.

80. See the collection edited by Heinz Ickstadt, *Ordnung und Entropie. Zum Romanwerk von Thomas Pynchon*, Reinbek 1981, especially the translation of Lawrence C. Wolfley, 'Repression's Rainbow: The Presence of Norman O. Brown in Pynchon's Big Novel', *Proceedings of the Modern Language Association* 92, 1977, pp. 873–89.

81. See section II, above.

82. Karl Jaspers, *The Atom Bomb and the Future of Man*, Chicago 1963, p. 289.

83. This also marked the explanatory structure of those who turned against 'an apocalyptic tone recently adopted in philosophy', such as Jacques Derrida in a

previously mentioned text with this title. On the equivalent tone in literature see Gunter E. Grimm et al.

84. This is meant mainly in the literary sense of 'translated', but it is also true of the ideas themselves. See, for example, the central role of the concepts of 'exterminism' and 'megamachine' in the post-Marxist, eco-pacifist writings of Rudolf Bahro: *Wahnsinn mit Methode*, West Berlin 1982, and especially *Logik der Rettung. Wer kann die Apokalypse aufhalten?*, Stuttgart 1987. Starting from the position that 'history is psychodynamics', Bahro focuses his critique on the 'male logos' which is heading for death via patriarchy, natural science, capitalism, the industrial megamachine and exterminism based on the arms drive and ecological devastation. His hopes are centred on a world-wide, invisible church of integral humanity, which he defines by reference to Gramsci's concept of 'new order' – an attempt to counter market-ecological *ordo*-thinking with the constitution of a 'prince of the ecological turn' that remains close to the grassroots.

85. Jeremy Rifkin, *Entropy: A New World View*, London 1985.

86. Ernest Callenbach, *Ecotopia*, Berkeley 1975.

87. Rifkin warns of this especially in *Who Should Play God?*, New York 1977.

88. *Entropy*, pp. 281f.

89. Edward Thompson, 'Notes on Exterminism, the Last Stage of Civilization', in New Left Review, ed., *Exterminism and Cold War*, London 1982. The title is an ironic play on Lenin's *Imperialism, the Highest Stage of Capitalism*.

90. Ibid., pp. 21–2.

91. Michel Serres, 'La Thanatocratie', in idem, *Hermes III. La Traduction*, Paris 1974, pp. 73ff.

92. These urgent gestures, which seem to the publicly committed natural scientist to have become characteristic throughout the world, are represented in Germany by physicists or philosophers such as Robert Havemann (*Morgen. Die Industriegesellschaft am Scheideweg*, Frankfurt 1982), C.F. von Weizsäcker (*Die Zeit drängt*, Munich 1987) and Klaus Michael Meyer-Abich (*Wege zum Frieden mit der Natur*, Munich 1986).

93. When the Federal Republic took part in its first world exhibition – the one held in Brussels in 1957 beneath a giant model of an atom (atomium) – it arranged its own pavilion around this principle of Luther's. The latter also served as the motto, and inspired the title, of the apocalyptic work by the ecologist Hoimar v. Ditfurth: *So laßt uns denn ein Apfelbäumchen pflanzen. Es ist soweit*, Hamburg 1985 – the last chapter of which is entitled 'The End of History'.

4

Recapitulation

Ich weiß nicht, was soll es bedeuten,
daß ich so traurig bin.
Ein Märchen aus uralten Zeiten,
das geht mir nicht aus dem Sinn.[1]
Heinrich Heine

I began this book with an invitation to a tracking of the Zeitgeist, and by now the reader will probably feel confused by our backward and forward movements. Cournot, Nietzsche, Weber, Freud – are they really the contemporary world? And do chains of association add up to history? Let us then recapitulate the highways and byways of our journey. We began with the jump from the right to the left end of the intellectual spectrum which the concept of 'posthistory' executed in the Federal Republic after the 'German autumn'. We then looked for the significance and origins of a diagnosis of the contemporary world that does not disquieten historians alone: namely, that history is over and is disappearing into a future uniformity defined by Gehlen in 1972 as 'movability on a stationary foundation'.[2]

Standard references in the literature led us to Cournot, but we found there neither the concept as such nor the mood of despair that clouded it in the postwar period. On the contrary, Cournot foresaw a modernization of society arising from repression of the instincts by the intellect, such that the dangerous scope for chance in previous history would be overcome. The historicist fixation had no future, and a scientific system would now develop to weigh up the masses. Stable structures would crystallize in a world society which could be anticipated in metaphors from nature and technology. With these three references we began the return journey to the present and – in a fine postmodern flight forward, almost like that of Jünger's anarch – we were able to observe exemplary forms of these particular aspects.

If we consider these three chains of association stored in the intellectual memory – many parts of which are still (or once more) extremely effective regardless of their historical origin – then we can offer a number of more general observations. The contributions made in the period before and after the Second World War are particularly clear and striking.[3] For it seems typical of the first group of authors that they start out from individual standpoints or discoveries and develop far-reaching and fundamental perspectives. The link between them lies not at the level of argument or information, but in intellectual outlooks and coincidences for which certain allusions and codewords continually appear: for example, references to the tradition of Nietzsche and Schopenhauer, as opposed to the Enlightenment. At their centre stands an ambivalent fascination with scientific rationalization, at once urging it forward and presenting it as a danger for the life-forces of the individual. The dynamization and levelling of society tend to produce a lifeless structural compulsion and to mark out progress as decline and exhaustion. If these authors set anything against such tendencies, it is hopes (often desperate) in the vital forces of the individual, in genius, charisma or eros and an ethic of responsibility. Except in the case of Freud, the factors which are to realize such hopes are sought not in properties of each individual within the mass, but in a great individual – perhaps a group or a political or cultural vanguard – who stands out from the mass and guides or controls it. All these authors, without exception, are highly productive and emphatically bourgeois intellectuals, who justifiably include themselves in this kind of individual or leadership group. At the end of the First World War, Thomas Mann presented himself as an example of such an aristocratic member of the educated classes, using the formula 'Ethics, the burgher mentality, decline: they belong together; they are one.'[4]

The contributions from the first decades after the Second World War seem much more heterogeneous in terms of their background in politics and life. Their widely varying intellectual references – chiefly, and more or less explicitly, to Hegel and Nietzsche, but also to Kant, Marx, Spengler, Heidegger, the Frankfurt School, and others – seem to be of only relative importance, perhaps even somewhat arbitrary.[5] What are really decisive are two other factors.

First, these authors see themselves facing anonymous structural processes before which individuals feel so powerless that they endow them with omnipotence and, without detailed argument, authenticate them through a grid of allusions and metaphors. These processes are endowed with properties such as independence, prominence, dynamism, irreversibility and a capacity to dissolve cultural values in non-temporal randomness. Permanence is thus accorded to the now independent structures of 'secondary systems' (Freyer) – a departure

both from prewar conceptions of end-time and from the contemporary
theme of the possible self-annihilation of the human species or its
environment.[6] In this way subjectivity, contingency and perceptible
reality come to disappear.

The second factor is a variant of that melancholy mood and posture
which Wolf Lepenies has scored in as the individualist contrabass of the
history of bourgeois society.[7] Its specificity seems to be the shrill tone in
which depression has come on the market since the Second World War
– either in an imperiously dismissive set of gestures, or in a flood of
images pouring out of a shattered conceptual system. Subjective disappointment can here turn outward and assume a high intellectual
'profile' because it knows that large parts of its generation have gone
beyond it in their sensibility. Most of the authors in question no longer
see any chance that a great personality or a vanguard can change
human relationships; but that is the viewpoint from which they see
these relationships.[8] They draw up no new perspectives for action, but
bemoan the irrelevance of the old. Most of them recoil from measuring
the play left for mass subjectivity within the new structures, because for
them self-perception within that mass is inconceivable. Where the
guiding individual or vanguard no longer operates, they can see
nothing at all in operation. Bourgeois prophets of the Right as well as
the Left declare history to be finished.

This should remind us that the questions we posed before turning to
Cournot have not yet been tackled. What history is finished? Within the
concert of voices telling us of the limits of twentieth-century bourgeois
society, who are the prophets who actually say that 'history' is over and
that we can longer expect anything significant to happen? Finally, what
has all this to do with historians? These questions will have to be taken
up and answered at the end.

In order to prepare ourselves for this task, we must first look into the
imagery now current in the evolution of posthistory itself. Let us then
take two metaphors of the relationship between individual and history:
one from the classical philosophy of history, and one from contemporary literature. These distinct searches will meet up around the time of
the Second World War, when they are concretized in images of
movement which seizes, carries along and threatens to engulf the
individual subject, or which encounters attempts to bring it to a halt.
Hopefully, given the dearth of substantive formulations about 'posthistory', these images will be seen to contain more complex interpretative
material. This time I shall not tear thematic fragments from their wider
framework, but on the contrary shall try to trace pieces of literary text
back to their contexts (complete with references).

In the first case we shall take Hegel's man riding on horseback – an epoch-making event and metaphor for the breakthrough of a historical philosophy – and then pursue it through one major strand in the twentieth century. This 'left-wing' interpretation, originally within a certain Marxist tradition but also influenced by Heidegger, was then itself thrown into question by history in the period of the Second World War. In the second, contrasting case – Ernst Jünger's *Waldgang* (Forest Way) – a topos for the sheltering of the individual from power in posthistory will be followed through in contemporary literature to the context in which it emerged. We shall again find ourselves in the period of the Second World War, but now it will be a 'right-wing' reading of the age in which the history of life is treated by prominent intellectuals of the 'conservative revolution'. Finally, we shall consider two European intellectuals in the situation of their time, which corresponded to the 'forest way' topos and within which they developed the modern idea of an exit from history. One was a former socialist theorist and politician from Belgium, the other, an ex-fascist journalist and later liberal theoretician from France, both of whom covered parts of the common route in the world economic crisis and the experiences of collaboration and exile. A whole series of confusing references will thus open up for us, but we shall also become aware of a specific type of intellectual, combining both political and theoretical labour, who may be provisionally and rather loosely described as 'voluntarist Hegelian'. Characteristic of the general demand for meaning in those times, this type has left behind a similarly general interpretation of its failure as an exit from history in general.

There was a dense network of encounters and relations between German and French intellectuals – from the Popular Front through the years of collaboration and liberation up to the Marshall Plan. Nearly all the main actors whose metaphors of history we are considering here met and kept in touch with one another, regardless of their political positions. They were a class-for-itself and, in the postwar period, formed a kind of underground school that cut across factional boundaries.[9] The reader is therefore advised to keep in mind the grid of names that will follow in the text and notes – including those in the remarks in chapter 6 on Benjamin's 'angel of history', who stands out particularly sharply from a text on the concept of history that is generally rich in imagery. This text too should be set against a background of Franco-German intellectual relations in Paris in 1940, but it sketches a conception and assimilation of history that are different from the typical posthistory diagnosis. It does not involve a broad, sweeping perspective, but focuses on the small scale, on the individual and the experience of recollection. It could thus refer to degrees of freedom that are denied in the posthistory diagnosis, except that the story of its later influence – moving beyond a very narrow circle only at the time of the student movement – almost irresistibly pressed the meaning of the text into a posthistorical framework. Just as its metaphors prove on close examination to be less ambiguous than its interpreters, the words themselves resist the readings of disenchanted intellectual activists; rather, they point again towards the modest alternatives of historical perception and orientation which open up for those not blinded by fantasies of grandeur.

Notes

1. 'I don't know what it can mean that I am so sad at heart. A tale from times of old won't go out of my head.' Heine, 'Die Heimkehr', *Werke*, West Berlin 1963, p. 83.
2. Arnold Gehlen, 'Ende der Geschichte?', in idem, ed., *Einblicke*, Frankfurt/Main 1975, p. 122.
3. The main focus here has been on European contributions. American authors of the fifties such as Seidenberg, Mumford and Brown are at once late and early by comparison: that is, they join up European discourses of the early and late twentieth century against a background of the rise of the United States as a superpower and world cultural model. In their case, the exit from history appears less as an experience of loss by intellectual elites than as a critical programme of an alternative culture.
4. Thomas Mann, *Reflections of a Nonpolitical Man* (written in 1917), New York 1983, p. 74. Translation modified. In this chapter on the 'burgher mentality' [*Bürgerlichkeit*], the self-image of this class – including its specifically German formation and its references to Schopenhauer, Wagner and Nietzsche – is concentrated as in a burning-glass.
5. It seems to me that the merit of Henri Lefebvre's *La Fin de l'histoire* (Paris 1970) – which did not enter into the discussion in Germany at least – was that after 1968 it placed the fading references to the philosophy of history of Hegel, Marx and Nietzsche, and prepared the ground for perception of the historicity of everyday life.
6. It is striking that in most cases – Günther Anders and Michel Serres are exceptions – the procedural structures appear as a stable and unopposed occupation of the world by the industrialized countries. In other words, it is rare that any alternatives figure in such thinking: whether those which stem from other countries in the world, or those which entail physical annihilation, or those which (as in the previously quoted reflections of Brückner) assign to the individual significant room for theoretical or practical revolt. For their part, the 'right-wing' contributions (Gehlen, Jünger et al.) assume that the old European traditions will remain in currency, even after a major catastrophe.
7. See Wolf Lepenies, *Melancholie und Gesellschaft*, Frankfurt/Main 1969 – a work which actually ends with an investigation of Gehlen's ideas of posthistory and cultural crystallization. See also his 'Bastelei im posthistoire', in Martin Jürgens and Wolf Lepenies, eds, *Ästhetik und Gewalt*, Gütersloh 1970.
8. In 'Ende der Geschichte?' (p. 117) Gehlen expresses this sensibility when he speaks of the 'great historians' of Antiquity: 'One has to stand above in order to see something.'

And their themes are the finality of the really great victories, an obituary of what is lost and some insight into the full-blown decline.'

9. Examples would be Carl Schmitt's Ebrach Circle in the Federal Republic, or Alexandre Kojève's conveying of Hegel and Heidegger to France.

5

History, Destinies and the Resurrection of the Lord: Metaphors of the Impact of History

I HEGEL'S MAN ON HORSEBACK

The Achilles' heel of the philosophy of history is the present. Prophets looking forwards or backwards subsist on the vagueness of their reference to reality, and thus on the scope for interpretation bound up with the inevitable contraction of meaningful expression. The present, however, contains the allure of concreteness. The best-known illustration of this is probably Hegel, who at the peak of his career glorified the Prussian state in the period of reaction as the fulfilment of history, but who in his youth had sympathized with the French Revolution.[1] Since he managed to keep his dialectical system so general and flexible that both parties – at least in Germany – could feel expressed within it, the history of its influence would be long and diversified. Between the two poles, when he had just completed in Jena the *Phenomenology of Mind* as the first systematic presentation of his historical philosophy, the concrete allure of the present closed in on him. Or, to be more precise, it rode past him in the shape of Napoleon, whom he saw then as the extender of the achievements of the French Revolution. On the eve of the Battle of Jena he wrote to his mentor: 'I saw the Emperor, this world-soul, ride through the town on a reconnoitre. It is truly a wondrous experience to behold such an individual, concentrated at one point, sitting on a horse, spread over the world and assume mastery of it.' And after noting the Prussian retreat, he continues: 'Such advances, from Thursday to Monday, are possible only for this extraordinary man, whom it is impossible not to admire.'[2]

Not for nothing is this observation about the world-soul on horseback so well known: it shows not only Hegel's political interest and fascination with power, but also the person whom he then considered to be the vanguard of the world spirit. If reason adhered to history itself, it had to change horses at the latest after Waterloo. It is thus not surprising that Hegel – who then felt the world-soul becoming conscious of itself in his own thoughts and later took the calibre of Europe as 'the end of history per se' – should have been eager to move from the south to the rising centre of power in Berlin ('an inherently greater focal point') and praised its reality as rational. This transfer certainly contributed to the fact that Hegel's influence remained limited outside Germany, until his dialectic was methodically internationalized through the mediation of Marxism.

At any event, this mediation – as well as the anecdote about the world-soul on horseback – was significant for the interest in Hegel that developed for the first time in France in the middle of this century. This new conjuncture began with a modest series of lectures on Hegel's *Phenomenology of Mind* at the Paris École Pratique des Hautes Études, which was attended between 1933 and 1939 by future celebrities of the French postwar intelligentsia.[3] The lecturer was a Russian exile, Alexandre Kojève (actually Kojevnikov, 1902–1968, a nephew of the painter Kandinsky). Having been confronted with the force of Marx's and Hegel's theories of history during the October Revolution, he tried in vain to discover more about them while studying philosophy in Germany in the 1920s. Instead he learnt Sanskrit and Chinese and received a doctorate under Karl Jaspers for work on a Russian philosopher of history and religion.[4]

'I tried to read Hegel,' he said later. 'I read the *Phänomenologie des Geistes* four times from beginning to end, giving myself up to it completely. I didn't understand a word.' After Kojève moved to Paris in 1930 and lost the financial support of his uncle, he was invited to give a course of lectures on Hegel. 'I accepted. I read the *Phänomenologie des Geistes* again, and when I came to Chapter IV I realized that it was referring to Napoleon. I began my lectures. I prepared nothing in advance: I read and commented, but everything that Hegel said seemed to me evident. Yes, it gave me an extraordinary intellectual pleasure.'[5]

Kojève's audience, according to Bataille, was 'breathless, riveted, . . .continually bowled over, pounded, thunderstruck'.[6] Kojève was a 'very talented story-teller', to quote the recent assessment of a French historian of philosophy who traces the vicissitudes of the dialectic in France back to the October Revolution and this series of lectures. In the commentaries, 'the austere Hegelian *Phenomenology* turns into a kind of serialized philosophical novel, where one dramatic scene follows another; picturesque characters come face to face, reversals of situation keep up the suspense, and the reader, avid to know the end of the story [*la fin de l'histoire*], clamours for more'.[7] Kojève displayed an astounding political intuition and range of positions. At the same time that Kojève was giving the Hegel lectures, Henri Corbin was translating Heidegger's *Being and Time* and interpreting it in the next-door auditorium, and the two of them worked together on a translation from German of Hendrik de Man's anti-Marxist programme for an idealist socialism: *The Socialist Idea*. Kojève himself was influenced by Heidegger, but he – the refugee from Russia of 1920 – also counted himself a Communist at the time of the Popular Front in France. Thus, if he fascinated his listeners so deeply with his austere material, it was because he brought to Hegel's text a version of Marxism, an anthropological reduction drawn from Heidegger, and an updating of history, the final interpretation being as bold as it was elegant. I can do no more here than indicate the broad lines of his approach.[8]

Kojève started out from section B.IV.A of the *Phenomenology*: 'Independence and Dependence of Self-Consciousness: Lordship and Bondage' – which seemed especially important to him, as it did to Marx. To this text, which treats 'recognition' as a prerequisite of human self-consciousness, he brought four philosophical-anthropological premises expressed in Heideggerian language: (1) 'being-there' [*das Daseiende*] reveals itself in words and (2) man 'negates' (appropriates or changes) it through his desire-driven action; (3) desires are reciprocal up to death or submission, when (4) human inequality establishes itself insofar as there can be a victor and a vanquished. The master is thus the one who stakes his life in a struggle between men for prestige, while the slave is he who submits out of fear of death and is thereby compelled to work for the master. Insofar as the master is recognized, he enjoys self-consciousness and becomes a man in 'the true sense of the word'. But he achieves no more. The activity of the slave – who, by being forced to work, rises above his animal instincts and so becomes human too – directs itself to nature and changes it through the objectification of his imposed labour. That is the precondition of history, which consists in struggle and labour.

As relations of domination became general in the Ancient world, the masters came to assume the mediated form of citizens. However, this tended to blur the distinction with slaves – which manifested itself in the spread of their religion, Christianity. The citizens, these slaves without masters, continued to labour, not for a master but also not for themselves (which would have meant their sinking into instinctual animality) – rather for the state and private property as such, for capital. In the *ancien régime* mastery or lordship thus outlived its time and became replaced by the civil society of private producers, whose generalization at the level of the state produced the 'world-soul'. In its world empire the individual recovered himself, externalized religion could be brought back home by the philosophical spirit in the identity of God and man, and the social dialectic came to a standstill. Kojève thus joined together beginning and end of this train of thinking:

> And universal history, the history of the interaction between men and of their interaction with Nature, is the history of the interaction between warlike Masters and working Slaves. Consequently, History stops at the moment when the difference, the opposition, between Master and Slave disappears. . . . Now, according to Hegel, it is in and by the wars of Napoleon, and, in particular, the Battle of Jena, that this completion of History is realized through the dialectical overcoming [*Aufheben*] of both the Master and the Slave. . . . It is because Hegel hears the sounds of that battle that he can know that History is being completed or has been completed, that – consequently – *his* conception of the World is a *total* conception, that his knowledge is an *absolute* knowledge.[9]

And this brings us back to the world-soul on horseback, who rides ahead of the world spirit. In Kojève's reading of Hegel, history had come to an end with Napoleon and humanity had since been living in a posthistorical condition where it fully accomplished the qualitative change. The history of Hegel's man on a horse was not, of course, finished, as could be seen from the resonance of the Popular Front in France, just as the Stalinist show-trials were reaching their climax in the USSR. At this time Kojève – who, as we have seen, considered himself a Communist – delivered a lecture to sociologists on *les conceptions hégéliennes*. One of the organizers reported:

> This lecture made us all speechless, both because of Kojève's intellectual power and because of his conclusion. You will remember that Hegel spoke of the horseman who announced the end of history and philosophy [sic!]. For Hegel this man was Napoleon. Kojève told us that day that Hegel had seen something correct, but had miscalculated by a century: the man of the end of history was not Napoleon but Stalin.[10]

Stalin, be it noted, not the October Revolution. For Kojève also sought to be faithful to Hegel in asserting that only terror can be effective in the society of equals, which recognizes itself in the institution of universality – that is, through the establishment of a state rising above the social.[11] He maintained this justification of Robespierre both before and after 1937.

The working Bourgeois, turned Revolutionary, himself creates the situation
that introduced into him the element of death. And it is only thanks to the
Terror that the idea of the final Synthesis, which definitely 'satisfies' Man, is
realized. It is in the Terror that the State is born in which this 'satisfaction' is
attained. This State, for the author of the *Phenomenology*, is Napoleon's
Empire.[12]

After the Second World War, when a philosophy commission of the
French Communist Party charged Kojève with 'revisionism of a fascist
character',[13] Stalin dropped out of the picture, and the end of history
was again moved back to Jena. According to Fetscher, who does not
give any more details, Kojève joined the French Resistance during the
war. Afterwards he took up a high post in the French foreign economic
affairs administration, secured for him by a former student, Robert
Marjolin, who now occupied key positions for the development of the
European capitalist economy within Jean Monnet's planning authority
in France, the Marshall Plan administration and the directorship of the
OECD. Kojève remained there until his death in 1968 – further
evidence of his talents and versatility, although at the same time he
continued to call himself a Marxist.[14]

In a footnote to his lectures written in 1946, at a time when an all-
party Resistance coalition assured France's membership of the victorious anti-Hitler alliance, Kojève explained his view of the end of history
by reference not to the present reality of Stalin's Russia but to Marx's
perspective of a future 'realm of freedom'. It was historically optimistic
in its evocation of the 'world myth' of industrialization,[15] but philoso-
phically despondent in its focus on the coming animalization of humanity in conditions of peace and abundance (that is, without struggle and
labour).

The disappearance of Man at the end of History is thus not a cosmic
catastrophe: the natural World remains what it has been throughout
eternity. Nor, then, is it a biological catastrophe. Man remains alive as an
animal who is in *harmony* with Nature or Being as it is given. What
disappears is Man properly so called – that is, Action which negates the
given, and Error, or more generally the *opposition* between Subject and
Object. In fact, the end of human Time and of History – that is, the final
annihilation of Man properly so called or of the free, historical Individual –
simply means the cessation of Action in the strong sense of the term. In
practice this means the disappearance of wars and bloody revolutions – and
the disappearance of *Philosophy* as well. For if Man no longer changes
himself in any essential respect, there is no longer any reason to change the
(true) principles underlying his knowledge of the World and of himself. But

all the rest can continue indefinitely: art, love, play, etc. – in short, everything that makes Man *happy*.[16]

In 1960, in his only addition to the second edition of the *Introduction*, Kojève spelt out the only thing that remained to be said: the 'post-historical animals of the species *Homo sapiens*' would not be happy but simply contented by definition, because the Logos – the quest for discursive wisdom and this wisdom itself – would also disappear. Instead the posthistorical animals would 'respond with conditioned reflexes to sound or sign signals'. Moreover, Kojève reported that shortly after composing the above text – that is, in 1948 when the European Left was breaking in two at the peak of American supremacy – he realized that Hegel had been right and history had come to an end with the Battle of Jena. Now 'the American way of life was the one fitted to the posthistorical period'.

> What has happened [since the Battle of Jena] has been no more than a spatial extension of the universal revolutionary power actualized in France by Robespierre–Napoleon. From the genuinely historical point of view, the two world wars with their train of minor and major revolutions have merely brought the backward civilizations of outlying provinces into line with Europe's (actual or potential) historical positions. If the sovietization of Russia and the communization of China are more and other than the democratization of Imperial Germany (through the detour of Hitlerism) or Togo's new independence or even the self-determination of the Papuans, this is only because the Sino-Soviet updating of Robespierrean Bonapartism compels post-Napoleonic Europe to speed up the elimination of the numerous, and more or less anachronistic, after-effects of its pre-revolutionary past.[17]

This account of Europe's modernization in the image of America makes it sound almost like the Stein-Hardenberg reforms that followed the Treaty of Tilsit in 1807. And indeed Kojève – who, as we have seen, worked at the planning headquarters of the modernization programme – now seems to have switched his world spirit on horseback and, metaphorically speaking, to have made his move from Jena to Berlin. Hegel too had hopes that in Berlin, in place of 'the precarious function of lecturing in philosophy', he might 'turn to and be needed for another activity'[18] – hopes which evidently came to nothing. Kojève proved more dexterous, and even kept his self-assurance by disparaging the historically given object of his adaptation:

> One can even say that, from a certain point of view, the United States has already reached the final stage of Marxist 'communism', since, in effect, all the members of a 'classless society' can already appropriate whatever

appeals to them, without working more than they feel like doing. [During trips to the USA and USSR between 1948 and 1958, he gained the impression] that the Americans play the part of Sino-Soviets become rich, because the Russians and Chinese are still just poor Americans.[19]

This attitude was perfectly in harmony with German theorists of posthistory such as Ernst Jünger, as well as with Carl Schmitt's appreciation of the East–West conflict. At least, Kojève's final shift in his end-of-history posture must be interpreted in the light of his contacts with these background figures of the cultural history of Adenauer's Federal Republic – even if he himself pointed to the importance of other experiences.[20] A year later, on a trip to Japan, his philosophical tourism uncovered an alternative to the posthistorical one-way street of American animalization. Once again Kojève proved to be a trend-setter for the intelligentsia, with a kind of aesthetic simulation of lordship after its historical demise. In this version, the posthistorical animal might save its human character by detaching forms from contents and living in accordance with 'totally formalized values'. Posthistorical existence had an 'as if' form,[21] which Kojève thought he could discern in the samurai tradition of the Japanese upper stratum. He therefore proclaimed the Japanization of the West as the way of avoiding man's decline into posthistory.

> But despite the persistence of social and economic inequalities, all Japanese without exception are now in a position to live in accordance with totally formalized values, devoid of any 'human' (in the sense of 'historical') content. At the extreme, therefore, every Japanese is in principle capable of carrying out a completely 'gratuitous' act of suicide, out of pure snobbism . . .which has nothing in common with risking one's life in a Struggle waged according to 'historical' values with a social or political content.[22]

This tourist fantasy, in which snobbism appears as the chance remaining to man 'properly so called' since the Battle of Jena, shifted the discussion of 'posthistory' into the realm of the aesthetic.[23] At the same time it described the anthropological self-understanding of Ernst Jünger's 'anarch', whom we have already briefly met between Nietzsche and Baudrillard.

II Jünger's Forest Way

In the first section of this chapter, we have followed the updating of Hegel's purported end of history and its multiple reinterpretations before and after the Second World War by a highly individualist Left-

Hegelian influenced by Heidegger. Like Hegel he sought for reason in history – which now exposed him to sudden changes of direction and allowed him to transfer his identification with the empire of slaves to the model of an aesthetically simulated master-life devoid of slaves. This model in turn resembles the 'anarch' in Ernst Jünger's late, posthistorical novel *Eumeswil*.[24] In this section, we shall be concerned not with a tradition of influence but with the presuppositions of a multilayered metaphor, its antecedents, parallels and variations. A consideration of Jünger's imagery may thus provide us with more complex self-expressive material than we find in the reproachful or mostly defensive articles of the postwar period – those, that is, which rise above the prevailing silence of the generations concerned.

Here we shall meet again the figure of a mid-century intellectual, at once committed and distant, who does not have the restricted charismatic following of a Kojève, but rather makes a literary impact on a mass scale. Jünger's accounts of his experiences in the First World War[25] had the same kind of meaning for the Weimar Right that E.M. Remarque's *All Quiet on the Western Front* assumed for the Left, and in the 1950s he was, after Thomas Mann, the most widely read author of serious prose in West Germany.

The Adventure of Power and the Myth of Nature

In the final chapter of *Eumeswil*, 'Vom Walde' [Of the Forest], Jünger distinguishes the theory of the 'anarch' from that of the anarchist.[26] Whereas the latter turns against the power structures in society and thus remains imprisoned by them, the former distances himself from these structures altogether so as to shelter from danger while moving within them. For this highly individualist Right-Hegelian associated with Heidegger,[27] whom the literature describes as a 'dandy' or 'adventurer',[28] the ideal is to restore inner freedom as compensation for a lost sociality. It is realized by an 'as-if master', a military man who in civil life is a waiter and historian working for a petty military dictator, in a posthistorical future where everything has yet remained the same.[29] He has overcome his fear of death, not to subject another to exploitation, nor out of boredom, but so as not to be subjugated himself and, if necessary, to forestall unreasonable demands going beyond his military zeal, which he manages to evade and *in extremis* will refuse through suicide. The experience for which he strives is to be master of himself, to move unfettered at all levels of the hierarchy, satisfying his curiosity about the dictator's milieu, and in return he will perform all services except those that require him to share responsibility

The uncommitted opportunism of the anarch presupposes an un-
changeable society, in which no change is worth the effort because it
could only replace the satraps of one despot with those of another,
without altering the structure of the 'social protectorate'. We are not
told how the anarch has been drawn into the kitchen cabinet of
provincial despotism.[30] All we are given is a noble cover-fantasy: 'The
anarch can approach the monarch without inhibitions; he feels himself
an equal even among kings.'[31]

At a certain point, however, the changing fortunes of the empires
which rule the masses make life dangerous for those in the vicinity of
the despot, without offering the enticement of a winnable struggle. And
so the anarch makes off into the forests. The forest way spares him the
risks of existence – which otherwise would force him to accept the
demands of collaboration or to defend himself against them out of self-
respect – and replaces them with a kind of self-chosen social death. Or
rather we should say the appearance of death, for its meaning lies in the
hope that it will be limited in time. The anarch has engaged in survival
training to prepare for the forest way, so that he can wait there until the
next despot has established himself and then re-emerge with greater
self-assurance. In the forest he builds up strength, because he has to
fend for himself and is close to the non-historical being of nature. More
than in the feuding of empires, he has here the prospect of an absorbing
struggle: for people rarely lose themselves in the forest, and tracking
operations by the rulers soon thin out. The forest way of the anarch
from Eumeswil, moving just ahead of a suicide squad that foreshadows
the despot's collapse, is freely chosen, skilfully calculated, valiantly
implemented, and marked by natural innocence.

The Roulette Wheel of History

Things were not always so. After the Second World War, the forest way
became a repeated topos in Jünger's work. One of his first postwar
essays was given over to it, and there he still stuck to its Nordic roots:
'The forest way followed a case of ostracization; a man thereby
expressed his will to prove himself through his own strength.'[32] In its
origins, then, the forest way was not freely chosen but involved a
suspension of capital punishment for a trial by ordeal. 'Homicide was
usually what preceded the ostracization.. . .' In the legal system taken
up by Jünger, the ostracized person deserved to die because he had
caused someone else's death; but since it was not clear that he had
meant to do this, the legal community held back from execution and,
by excluding him from its protection, left him to the company of

wolves. The forester is thus no longer a legal subject and resumes his bare existence in confrontation with nature. Only by passing this test can he demonstrate his human character.

For this intellectual who did not want Auschwitz, but whose earlier cultural practice implicated him in its determining nexus, the choice of imagery and the underlying message seem clear enough. Such an intellectual must now go into internal exile and refrain from public cultural activity. The image would be transparent, however, only if we did not actually read it – in Jünger's seventh published work in the six years following 1945, or the seventeenth since 1933. Evidently we are not dealing here with ostracism (nor exactly with a forest-dweller) – at least not if the word still has any meaning, that is, if it can be distinguished from others. But the author himself took away this meaning by an act of generalization. If I had quoted in full what he had to say about homicide, we would already be aware that he considered everyone and no one to be guilty of it, at least potentially, although many did not yet realize it. History turns with the speed and randomness of a roulette wheel. Here is the whole quotation:

> Homicide was usually what preceded the ostracization, whereas today this usually strikes people automatically, as in the spinning of a roulette wheel. [And the examples can be whatever you like:] For ostracism arrives suddenly, often as from a clear sky: You are a red, a white, a black, a Russian, Jew, German or Korean, a Jesuit, freemason and at any event much worse than a dog.[33]

Why is the colour brown, as in brownshirt, missing from the list? One can think of many possible reasons: for example, that the author saw a difference between denazification and the extermination of the Jews – which is rather unlikely[34] – or that omission of the most obvious is a clever touch based on the assumption that the reader will not fail to make the transference. I suspect the reason was different. Jünger did not see brown as his main problem, and when it was made a problem for him, he had already put it to one side, having found (or retained) a following that bore him out. Then there is the clear sky from which the ostracism flashed down, not for the years of 'catastrophe' but for a blatant discrepancy between high-pitched expectations and negative personal experience. The clear sky must be the one of enthusiasm for the national revolution of 1933, after which he kept away from the regime because he had taken it for something else and now felt fear and intolerable pressure – although he did remain a much published author in great demand. If we set this together with Jünger's arbitrary definition of groups targeted for elimination, we can see a failing grasp both

of himself and of history. While he blots out his own complicity in the
creation of the totalitarian state, his imagery frees it of blame for the
fate of its victims. In reality, however, they were not found guilty of
homicide and then ostracized, but were seized by the state without any
objective grounds and then liquidated. No forest way was offered to
the Jews. The image which at first seemed so accurate in personal terms
proves, through generalization, to be a historical deception. The forest
way was supposed to mark a retreat into Being and a renewal of human
self-consciousness, but on closer inspection it is a flight into mere
existence [Dasein] and a defence against more precise historical
self-awareness.

The Age of the Titanic

In order to unravel the connection between the forest way and posthistory, we must look a little more closely at Jünger's range of metaphors,
in which kindred biographies are also of some relevance. I shall
therefore take four paradigmatic intellectuals from the period of
fascism: the legal theorist Carl Schmitt, the philosopher Martin Heidegger, the psychologist and Belgian politician Hendrik de Man, and the
French journalist and political theorist Bertrand de Jouvenel.[35] They
were all, like Jünger, prominent figures in their various fields; all took
part in the struggle against Marxism and liberalism in the 1920s; all
worked intensively for a certain time with the fascists; all subsequently
took the forest way, withdrew from public commitments or from public
life in general, and lived in the country, in mountain retreats or in a neutral
foreign country; and all saw themselves as opposed to Hitler by the end
of the war at the latest, but were treated as collaborators by the Allies
or their own compatriots and could never, or only after some time, take
up their former public activity. It is interesting that they used their
'forest way' not so much for studies of nature as for a historical
reinsurance with the pre-modern legacy,[36] and first returned to public
life with their particular variant of Jünger's Waldgang.[37]

It is not only the subjective experience of these writers that will help
us in our tracking of posthistory, but also their coding of the external
world from which the forest provided shelter. After Jünger's attempt to
switch from history to myth, we should no longer be surprised that,
apart from an occasional allusion, they make no concrete reference to
the Third Reich. Jünger's own image for the 'historical world in which
we find ourselves' was a symbol taken from religious history which,
since Antiquity, has also stood for the state: namely, a ship. In his case,
however, it is a ship that has sunk: the Titanic.[38]

Here light and shadow stand in sharp contrast: the hubris of progress collides with panic, extreme comfort with destruction, automation with the disaster that appears as a traffic accident. In reality, growing automation and fear are very closely connected, since man is limited in his decisions by technological alleviation. This leads to many kinds of convenience. But inevitably the loss of freedom must also increase. The individual no longer stands in society as a tree in the forest, but resembles a passenger in a fast-moving vessel whose name might be *Titanic* or also Leviathan. So long as the weather is good and the outlook agreeable, he hardly notices the condition of lesser freedom into which he has fallen. On the contrary, a certain optimism appears, a dizzying sense of power. But that changes if fire-spewing islands and icebergs come into view. Not only does technology then cross from convenience into other spheres, but the lack of freedom also becomes visible – whether in the victory of elemental forces, or in the fact that individuals who have remained strong exercise an absolute power of command.[39]

The image displays an object of fascination for the author, whose wide-ranging collector's interest (mainly in insects) extended to books about shipwrecks.[40] As Hans Blumenberg has shown, the 'shipwreck with onlookers' is a metaphor which, in the history of Europe since Antiquity, has repeatedly evoked the dangers to life, the joy of survival, the collapse of certainties, and the attempt to gain a distance from history.[41] The English luxury liner which collided with an iceberg on its maiden voyage in 1912 is an arresting image of the historical world. However, there still seems to be an onlooker who stands like a tree in the forest – and so we are not necessarily all at sea, or there is some land even at sea. Somewhat later Jünger felt provoked to extend his mythological range still further:

> Sea voyage and forest – it may appear difficult to combine such distance in the picture. But the contrast is well-known in myth: Dionysus, for example, having been abducted by Tyrrhenian sailors, had ivy and grapevine grow over the tiller and shoot up the mast. From this thicket sprang the tiger who ate up the pirates.[42]

One is immediately fascinated by the prophetic violence of these images, composed three decades before the emergence of the peace and ecology movements. Yet they also have a number of striking barbs. Hobbes's embodiment of the Absolutist state was certainly no longer the crocodile-like beast of the end of time from the Book of Job, but can the Leviathan really be a fast-moving vessel? Is the sinking of the ship above all a deprivation of liberty? Is mass resistance going on below decks? Are Hitler and Stalin the 'individuals who have remained strong'? Or, on the other hand, are the captains of world civilization

the kidnappers and pirates from whom we shall be delivered by the
monster from the German forest? To be sure, these may be all-too-
boring interpretations of dense prophecy. But the number of fracture-
points shows that two images have here been pushed into each other.
The staged anti-totalitarian critique will not fit the basic model of
cultural criticism directed against the Anglo-American type of industrial society, which is supposed to be steaming into an imponderable
crisis on its way to world civilization.

Land and Sea

In the 1940s, we find in Jünger's friend Carl Schmitt both the separation of these two images in *Land und Meer* [Land and Sea][43] and
their superimposition in the image of the ill-starred ship that he used
after 1945 in a work of self-vindication. This brilliant fighter against
liberalism and the Weimar Republic had been crown jurist under the
pre-1933 presidential regime, but despite some depressing early con-
cessions – such as his article 'The Führer Defends the Law',[44] written
after the massacre of the SA leadership and conservatives of his own ilk
– he had been unable to maintain that rank for long in the Third Reich.
During his period of retreat, he turned his attention to international
law and its historical – or, to be more precise, historical–ontological –
presuppositions.[45] In his view at that time, there was a world conflict
between the force for peace of continental absolutism (land) and the
insatiable benefaction of seafaring imperialists (sea). In 1939, when
Britain was still seen as the main rival, he suggested that the two sides
should consider their geopolitical requirements, divide the world into
spheres of hegemony and prevent the Americans from intervening in
Europe.[46] After the war, he argued that the same imperialist compromise should be struck before the attack by the continental empire
finally took place; it represented that longing for the peaceful power of
a European order which went back to early modern times, and of which
he was the last representative. Now, however, the victorious anti-Hitler
coalition was bent on a new paradigm: the 'unity of the world'.[47] The
restless maritime spirit was incapable of peace – that is, of stabilizing
itself through state instruments – and would therefore perpetuate the
'world civil war'.[48] This war was rooted in the world-wide extension of
the English-based industrial revolution, together with the social resistance
to the state in the French and (geopolitically more significant) American and Russian Revolutions. In contrast to Jünger,[49] Carl Schmitt
did not see the Cold War of the 1950s as the expression of a recurrent
East–West conflict, nor did he think that its frontlines could be either

dissolved or stabilized in the context of the world civil war. Only when he further developed the historical ontology of land and sea, and understood that the Soviet Union and the United States had eclipsed the old German–British opposition, did he gain a fresh perspective. He then looked forward to the overcoming of this bipolar unity through the new weight of state domination – that is, through the new regional 'land empires' of China and India. This, he hoped, would limit the intertwining of the world civil war with the imperial interests of 'the sea', and restore to the world that 'multiplicity' in which – let us add – Germany would again be one centre. To change his position was never a problem for the legal theorist with a historical bent, but he did try to adjust his vision to the course of things:

> Historical thinking refers to unique situations and thus to unique truths. The truth of polar oppositions is eternally true – eternal in the sense of an eternal return. A historical truth, on the other hand, is true only once. . . . The uniqueness of historical truth is the age-old arcanum of ontology. . . . Historical reality, however, involves the emergence at certain times of peoples and groups who are capable of historically effective action, who take and divide the earth in friendship and amity and graze and busy themselves on their part of it.[50]

In the land–sea opposition the elements were clearly differentiated, and the author knew where he stood: on the land. But now the fronts have become blurred in the raging of a world civil war in which he feels trapped, but from which he also expects liberation. Thus, the images are again superimposed in projections of the subjective historical experience of the intellectual. In *Ex captivitate salus*, written in 1947 when he was still in Allied detention, Schmitt took up Hermann Melville's *Benito Cereno* from 1855.[51] Here the captain of a slave-ship in distress, a Spanish aristocrat, is forced by mutinous slaves who have killed his officers to remain in technical command under their terrorist rule. This is so skilfully managed that, even when they meet an American navy ship, the slaves' prisoner has to feign order and harmony before its rather naive crew, until he finally takes advantage of tumultuous fighting between the marines and the rebellious slaves to leap into the American ship.

The story is actually more fascinating than its metaphorical exploitation, which does, however, throw light on the striking fractures in Jünger's comparison of modern civilization to the *Titanic*. The intellectual (or aristocrat of the mind) is the one who should command within the European order. But if this breaks down in times of crisis and is replaced by mass terror, he becomes a tragic figure and even has to act outwardly as if he were still responsible – that is why he can be misperceived as a collaborator. The eventual liberators, however, represent a society of equals which tends to produce the same mass revolt in crisis, and which did in fact originate in such a revolt, unrestrained by traditional forms of rule. The rescued captain, seeing no way out and reeling from his apocalyptic experience, retreats into the cloister, into the safety of the Eternal. In other words, he becomes a forest-dweller. In Melville's tale, of course, the aristocrat dies there after a few months, while the compromised would-be captains go on writing and writing. The first piece that Carl Schmitt published after his release in 1949 was a pathetic appeal to the new Federal government, in which he called for an amnesty to draw a line under the 'world civil war'.[52] As things stood, the author of this article – who spoke anonymously in the shape of Zeus – could have meant by 'world civil war' nothing other than denazification and the prosecution of Nazi crimes.

Passage de la ligne

Immediately before *Waldgang* and as a justification of it, Ernst Jünger published a short essay 'Über die Linie' [Across the Line] in the Festschrift marking the sixtieth birthday of the denazified and compulsorily emeritus professor Martin Heidegger.[53] The man so honoured, who recovered his chair a year later, paid Jünger back by contributing to his own Festschrift in 1955 another piece sensitively titled 'Über "die Linie"'.[54] At the first opportunity Jünger then answered him with 'The End of the Historical Age'.[55] The public exchange between the field-walker and the forest-walker[56] thus began with the existential crisis following the collapse of the Third Reich and ended with the dawning of posthistory. For Jünger, this would make possible a new 'Third Reich', now, of course, an empire of love and spirit, such as Joachim of Fiore foretold in twelfth-century prophecies that did not come true either, but which – as postmodern readers of Umberto Eco's *The Name of the Rose* will know – was fervently awaited by many.

We might say of the exchange between Jünger and Heidegger what the latter wrote in 1950 for *Holzwege*, a collection of his works from the forest years: 'Wood is another name for forest. In the wood are paths which are usually grown over and suddenly end in the Unfrequented. They are called paths in the wood [*Holzwege*]. Each one runs separately, but in the same wood. It often appears that they are the same. But it only appears to be so.'[57]

Jünger's 'Über die Linie' treats of 'crossing the prime meridian'

[*Nullmeridian*], a rather lurid image, in the tradition of 'land and sea',[58] for the personal and historical situation of those small elites who lent their talents to the rise of fascism and were driven into isolation by the rigours of nihilism. In his war diaries he called it simply the zero-point [*Nullpunkt*] – that is, the hope of overcoming his nihilism through daily reading of the Bible.[59] But the 'meridian' image stretches this into an epochal zero-point and thus evokes the metaphysical opportunism of the bourgeoisie in the so-called Zero Hour.[60] The withering of values and responsibility in Jünger's own distinctive nihilism is projected on to the culture as a whole, so that 'atrophy' appears as the sign of the epoch. But he also bewails the disenchantment of the world and holds the masses to blame for the fact that they have no religious or other metaphysical commitment. As the sea is barred to him and is anyway less appealing since the fate of the *Titanic*, the crossing leads into the forest. There he seeks the proximity of Being, but also a hiding-place. For in the age of massification one can expect no more than another despotism, and the transition crisis holds dangers precisely for those who at first lent their voice to the previous regime, given that this is inevitably better documented than their disappointment and intellectual aloofness. Martin Heidegger was a notable case in point: he had been regarded in the late twenties as the new thinker of the historical world and had wanted to make himself its spiritual leader in 1933; his self-exoneration through a retreat from that world into fundamental principles therefore makes him an interesting and more far-reaching variant on Jünger.

Excursus: Leading the Leader

Heidegger became known in the late 1920s through his major work *Sein und Zeit* [Being and Time], which sought to grasp the meaning of Being in thought that focused on the individual subject ('authenticity') and counterposed it to superficial attributions of meaning by the public (the 'they').[61] Working among professors erudite in the history of philosophy, he made an attractive and educational impact as a teacher.[62] Although he adopted a dismissive stance towards Weimar public life, he did not yet take part in political activity. But when Hitler came to power in 1933, he accepted the rectorship of the University of Freiburg and hoped to shape the 'national revolution' throughout the higher education sector in Germany.

Habermas has shown how, in the medium of the 'national revolution', the significance of Heidegger's philosophy – which may previously have been rather problematic, but could be and actually was

discussed on a broad scale – discreetly shifted from the individual to the
collective. The covert Christian existentialism thus passed over into
national fanfares for the 'new paganism'.[63] A debate has recently
developed around this turn which, in view of Heidegger's world
reputation as a philosopher, cannot avoid the question of whether his
work can be divorced from his personal history.[64] A provisional
answer might be as follows. Heidegger's involvement with the Nazis
did not follow necessarily from *Sein und Zeit*, but nor did that work
stand in the way.[65] Its author belonged to an upwardly mobile class of
intellectuals who wanted to put 'philosophy back in the dominant
position';[66] at the same time he stood within the tradition of anti-
Weimar Catholic provincialism, though at first from a position of
private apoliticism. Hitler's 'national revolution' then provided the
medium in which the original culture and the aspirations of intellectuals to dominance could be fused with Heidegger's timely work,
which required only slight but momentous modifications. Given this
openness of his work, which became a dependent variable through the
short-circuiting of individual biography and History, there is something obsolete about the current question, whether the person should
be located within the necessary outcome of his work, or whether the
work should be separated off from the foibles of its author.[67]

In a programmatic address, Heidegger once called for 'spiritual
leadership' of higher education, a reorientation of academic freedom
through commitment to the national community ('labour service',
'armed service' and 'knowledge service'), and a new spiritual *Volk*-
world as the guarantee of the people's greatness and 'the power that
most deeply preserves [its] strengths, which are tied to earth and
blood'. 'For it necessitates that the constant decision between the will
to greatness and a letting things happen that means decline, will be the
law presiding over the march that our people has begun into its future
history.'[68]

With basic existential concepts of resoluteness or will to self and
greatness, as well as struggle as the cardinal principle of life, Heidegger
sought to make his philosophy the spiritual programme of the political
movement and – as Jaspers scornfully observed – 'to lead the leader'.[69]
In contrast to the many opportunist moves of the time, Heidegger's
addresses were meant to be taken seriously, and all the harsher was his
realization that his leadership was not recognized in higher education,
let alone in the country at large. Indeed, within a few months 'the old
and the new' in university politics were joining forces 'to paralyse my
efforts and to finally get rid of me'.[70] He then pulled back, but without

making any visible break. He continued to teach, remained in the NSDAP he had joined in 1933, published his philosophical work, and removed the dedication to his Jewish teacher Edmund Husserl from the 1937 edition of *Sein und Zeit*; he also participated in government advisory circles and drew up anti-semitic reports. It should be said, however, that he was more radical-national than racist, and that was one reason why Alfred Rosenberg – the racist ideological apostle of the new regime – would brook no competition from him.

Decline into Profundity

Heidegger never wavered in his determination to seal his own greatness – first as a philosopher, then as a theoretically sound cultural politician, and finally as a solitary sage – and his own apologists see this as the innermost driving-force of his commitment to National Socialism.[71] Even in 1945, when he had been relieved of his post by the occupation forces, he wrote to his university that it did not matter if he had to wait; the problem was more whether Germany's young people and the intellectual situation could wait[72] – apparently for him. His flair for cryptic language-games led him to reclaim from the 'decline' [*Untergang*] a perspective of, as it were, a subterranean forest way [*unterirdischer Waldgang*]. 'Everything now points to ruin,' he wrote in summer 1945 to a like-minded colleague. 'However, we Germans cannot go under, because we still have not risen; hence, we must persist through the night.' And already in winter 1944 he had written in a friends' guestbook: 'Decline is not the same as death. Every decline remains secure within the ascent.'[73]

Decline, taking place in the crisis of historical phenomena, leads through a zone of darkness. Where the author's historical existence is compromised, he seeks to detach from it the reflexivity of his alter ego – that is, of his reputation-making work *Sein und Zeit* – so that he can preserve his reputation and use its shade for a highly stylized private existence that will remain constant or grow in intensity. This tactical retreat from history and politics is intended to preserve spiritual leadership through self-exoneration. Whereas Heidegger's collision course with Weimar culture might be understood as a 'longing for firmness and solidity',[74] his critical student Karl Löwith, with a characteristically delicate note of scepticism, has attributed the so-called turn or reversal to a 'craving for the loss of solidity and resoluteness',[75] and thus also to a flight from his own responsibility.[76] This led to writings which consistently changed the meaning of his major work – as if his investigations had essentially focused not on *Dasein* but on Being as the presupposition of thought – and which commended the thinker as one who lived in the proximity of Being and bore witness to its history.[77] In the new passage, where hyper-German verbal play seems to be depoliticized and naturalized through references to forest and field, this Being appears as a 'clearing' on whose margins man 'exists' – that is, stands out – with his back to the forest.[78] From this position all historically concrete interaction, responsibility and communication vanish into a 'destiny' which, at best, can be moderated through abstention. Instead he thinks he can glimpse a new epoch in the history of Being, which will replace the self-certainty and technological assurance of modernity.[79]

Now, it is not so easy to imagine proximity to Being as a profession, living off revelations or abiding in meditation. But we already know enough to understand that the philosophical hermit, whom 'the inexhaustible strength of the Simple' had endowed with new authority, was in a position to take up the new central perspective on Being, or Nothingness.[80] In dark, stilted prophecies, the writer who had forgotten human existence [Dasein] taught that the contemporary world displayed the worst forgetfulness of Being [Sein] or, more simply, of salvation; but that out of the history of Being came the expectation of the coming God. For salvation he looked to the Alemmanic; the völkisch dimension had faded in a more restricted homeland. But in a deeper sense, the German people was still the one chosen by Being. America and Russia

> are metaphysically the same, namely in regard to their world character and their relation to the spirit. . . . We are caught in a pincers. Situated in the centre, our nation incurs the severest pressure. It is the nation with the most neighbours and hence the most endangered. . . . If the great decision regarding Europe is not to bring annihilation, that decision must be made in terms of new spiritual energies unfolding historically from out of the centre.[81]

Despite many points in common, Heidegger does not care for Jünger's hope of speedily crossing the prime meridian of nihilism so that the small elites of the conservative revolution can feel some metaphysical forest ground under their feet. With the dominance of technological–industrial civilization on a 'planetary' scale, which Jünger described in Der Arbeiter and Nietzsche in The Will to Power, and which for Heidegger is 'the final phase of nihilism [as] a consolidated normal state', Jünger's line becomes 'unusually broad' or 'not yet at all visible at the end'.[82] Not for the first time Heidegger felt pulled or enticed to the mountains, where he could think of man as the 'shepherd of Being'.

By contrast he suspected that Jünger's crossing of the line was merely an individual flight which, as the language showed, participated in the metaphysics of nihilism. The priest of the coming God – whose kingdom might be built out of awareness of the technological menace, if it was not buried in an atomic catastrophe – gingerly took apart the voluntaristic appeals of individualist mythology ('easy to read but difficult to think'). The meaning of the forest way was not an escape from the worker's realm of necessity into a dreamworld of freedom where history still repeated itself for a few (in real life, ever fewer) aristocrats. Rather, it was the peace of listening to the signs of a new eon in the history of Being, which would not be independent of human technological dispositions but, in one way or another, would be accompanied by the materialization of technological dangers. In conclusion he referred Jünger to Nietzsche's mental derangement – as a warning of collapse or a limit of nihilist thought – and took his leave with a quotation from Goethe about the danger of worn coins and 'sacred testimonials' in spiritual interchange.[83]

We do not know whether Heidegger was satisfied with the response of the man so rebuked. At any event, Jünger took the greatest pains to ground his announcement of posthistory on his own interpretation of the history of Being: that is, to define it as a conjuncture in the Earth's history that pointed towards the end of human history.[84] In this presentation of Jünger's whole understanding of history,[85] the perspective of a possible mutation of humanity encompasses all his earlier themes,[86] at the core of which lies the opposition between 'worker' and 'forest-dweller'. On the one hand the mass society, in which fascism, bolshevism and Americanism are deeply joined together, is unworthy of life and is steering the planet towards catastrophe. On the other hand, the self-ennobling small elites take on through asceticism the freedom which is alone capable of history – but instead of continuing to use it, they engage in an aesthetic updating of myth whereby all history (repeating itself à la Spengler) is experienced *in nuce* in their own life-history. Here we find ourselves almost back with Kojève's final stance.

Postscript on Forest and Reality

Jünger's metaphor of the forest way has a further level of meaning: the level of the real world. In the Second World War, the historically typical form of the forest way was to go over to the Resistance movement, as we can see from the French use of the term *maquis* (the characteristic shrub formation) as a collective term for the partisan groups operating in rural regions of central and southern France.[87] Forms of life and

struggle typical of 'small elites' were then present throughout German-
occupied Europe. But such groups were not composed of hermits
practising self-awareness and survival training; they were regular
formations which, whenever possible, tried to link up with the underground in the cities and engaged in a historic struggle, however one
may assess the effectiveness of their contribution to the victory over
fascism. Although they were mostly in flight from the occupation
troops, their goal remained that of the national, and above all social,
liberation of their societies.

The heroic element in Jünger's metaphors thus draws a contrary
meaning out of the experience of his time.

III De Man's Current

Now and then, a reality did appear which corresponded to Jünger's
forest way. The one who would most clearly seem to have lived it was
the aristocratic socialist Hendrik de Man, whose own story reads in
detail like a model for the more cynical and romantic hero of Jünger's
novel.[88] Between 1941 and 1944 de Man lived in an isolated mountain
hut in the Haute-Savoie region of France, and at the end of the war he
fled to Switzerland. There he wrote a book from which the former
conservative revolutionaries in West Germany derived the concept of
'posthistory',[89] although they apparently wished to conceal its prov-
enance in an ex-Leftist and collaborator. Or were there other reasons
why they avoided mention of him?

Biographical Note (1)

As he is still little known today, a few words on de Man's biography
might be useful. Hendrik de Man (1885–1953) came from a mer-
chant's family in Antwerp, became an anarchist at an early age and
then a Marxist, studied history in Leipzig where he received a doctorate
under Bücher and Lamprecht, and worked on the Social-Democratic
Leipziger Volkszeitung until 1910. After a year in England he became a
Socialist Party official in Belgium and a spokesman of the Marxist
opposition. Although a pacifist, he volunteered for the army after the
German invasion in 1914 and was made an officer. In 1917 he joined a
government delegation to Russia – an experience which, together with
a longer stay in America, convinced him of the necessity of democracy
for socialism and brought to a complete end his radical-left phase. In
the 1920s he lived in Germany, teaching at the Labour College in

Frankfurt and later lecturing on social psychology at the University. Among his writings were a critique of the role of Marxism as a substitute religion for rising Party functionaries, and an early study in industrial sociology.[90]

In 1933 de Man returned to Belgium and was appointed spokesman of the Socialist Party for a joint study-group with representatives of capital, which was to develop proposals for economic planning to overcome the crisis. Although this 'labour plan' collapsed, it made its author known as the advocate of a socialism that sought to rise to the challenge of fascism and the Popular Front in Europe. In addition to becoming Party chairman, he served several times as finance minister and adviser to the King, who in light of the First World War experience sought a policy of appeasement even after Munich. In fact, de Man remained at his side after the capitulation to the Germans, whereas the majority of the political class went into exile. In 1940, hoping that the Germans would allow some room for an independent policy in Belgium, he fused the political trade unions into a single, non-political formation, and set his sights on the development of reform socialism in Europe after it had been united by Hitler.

When de Man's solo effort in Belgium proved increasingly unsustainable, he ended further collaboration and withdrew to an alpine hut where he could forget the political–intellectual maelstrom. Indeed, he plunged so deeply into historical research about an early capitalist from the Hundred Years' War that on more than one occasion he dated a letter 1444 instead of 1944.[91] The tough, militarily self-disciplined bachelor remained completely alone on the mountain, only rarely travelling down to Brussels or Paris: he took pleasure in nature, kept his own household and – as he later wrote[92] – lived in a trance-like fatalism carried over from the extreme loneliness of the collaborationist period, eventually finding himself between the *maquis* and their pursuers. He fled to Switzerland before the Liberation, and was not handed back in 1947 when he was condemned in absentia to twenty years' imprisonment for his collaborationist activity. He married in 1948, lived in the Bernese Oberland, published three more books and was killed in a road accident in 1953.

Disappearance of the Dinosaurs

It will probably come as no surprise that de Man's own account of his life draws again on the code of the forest way, though with obvious differences. After asserting his faith in socialism and recognizing his own mistakes and disappointments, he attempts to defend himself in

concrete terms and argues that the workers' movement, in the course of
a century, has achieved fundamental material and cultural improve-
ments in the proletarian condition. Then he suddenly interjects:

> The tragic moment arises from the possibility, if not probability, that the
> ship itself, whose between-decks passengers are better accommodated and
> nourished than before, will soon go down with all hands. At the moment,
> however, it seems to be swept along by a spiral current which is approaching
> its centre at an accelerated tempo that betrays the fast-increasing proximity
> of a final catastrophe.[93]

Again a ship in danger of sinking. But this time what is at stake is not
the captain's freedom or the life of the better ranks on deck; the beast
from the depths no longer lurks between decks. In fact, de Man rejoices
that the passengers there enjoy better accommodation and nourish-
ment. Nor does the ship face an iceberg, that primitive, crystalline force
from the deep which can sink it all by itself. It is true there are
turbulences, but the real problem is the poor navigation. And that is
again due to a misunderstanding between intellectuals and the masses:
not in the sense that intellectuals are kept in chains, but that they lack
something. In other words, the small elites are cut off and too reduced
in numbers: they can no longer get things under control. It is not as if
the masses are cunning and brute-like or are using terror to make the
grandees of old Europe into their puppets. Rather, they are organized in
too large units and thus – irrespective of their character – display an
inertia that is disastrous for the steering of the ship.

> Above a certain dimension things and people, which a will seeks to guide
> from above, become more or less uncontrollable. A decisive role is therefore
> played by that mysterious collective power which can best be compared to
> the inertia of a solid body. . . . Our epoch reminds one of the picture that
> paleontologists present of the disappearance of the dinosaurs towards the
> end of the Tertiary – gigantic bodies with tiny brains that proved incapable
> in the end of adapting the beasts to changed conditions of life. The
> gigantism afflicting our epoch has assumed much more complex and subtle
> biological–social forms, but the evil is essentially the same: failure of the
> guiding apparatus.[94]

This problem of guidance and organization has the result that 'even the
capitalism–socialism antithesis' loses 'its fundamental conceptual
significance'.[95] De Man does not know what can be done about this
socio-cultural delusion of grandeur that binds the systems together. As
a self-styled loner, he was always defeated by it, even when he occupied
a leading position and precisely embraced corporatism as a solution to
the crisis. Given this lack of orientation, which made sensitive contem-

poraries dizzy, he now introduced the hypothesis of 'posthistory' with an appeal to Jouvenel and Cournot,[96] distinguishing it from the state of exhaustion in Spengler's doctrine of cultural cycles.

Two arguments therefore remain for the case that we are entering 'extra-historical time' – one evolutionary and one historical. First, in the dinosaur image of a petrified megamachine, the culture that bears it has come to the end of its archetypal significance: 'The alternative then, in biological terms, would be either death or mutation.'[97] Second, the science of history establishes meaningful cause-and-effect relationships that bear upon the fate of humanity, so that 'historical events can be measured by the yardstick of human goals and powers'; if such relationships can no longer be demonstrated, 'the course of the world [falls]. . . outside the framework of history'.[98]

Such arguments – which, in comparison with those previously mentioned, are essentially more rational and cautious – cannot satisfactorily explain the lack of any way out in de Man's prognosis. For the first argument could be countered by a programme that made room for smaller units and greater curbs on violence, a policy of mass subjectivization and decentralized decision-making. Or would that already be social mutation? As to the historical argument, it focuses on the collapse of individuality in the steering of large systems, and thus on a yardstick that is too narrow for 'human goals and powers'. Precisely in de Man's more rational command of thought, we can measure how strongly the hopelessness of the posthistorical perspective is bound up with the presumption, tragedy and decline of educated middle-class individualism in the political practice of the wartime years.

This will become strikingly clear if we examine the final reference, where de Man invokes that sensitive mind who for the first time has expressed the idea of a dawning extra-historical period: namely, Bertrand de Jouvenel. For here we again come across a paradigmatic intellectual, political border-crosser and 'forest-dweller', who was actively involved in fascism and collaboration but was also reported to have been hunted by the Gestapo; who escaped from France to Switzerland a year before de Man and brought out there – with the same publishing house that produced de Man's book on the years of collaboration[99] – a major work, *On Power*, that he had written in the period of seclusion.[100] The two men had known each other since the early 1930s, when de Man's corporatist 'labour plan' was seen as the herald of a European planned economy beyond communism and fascism. At that time Jouvenel, as well as Kojève and his later boss Robert Marjolin, was among the intellectuals from various fractions of the centre-Left who preached de Man's message in France.

Biographical Note (2)

Here too some biographical information might be useful.[101] Bertrand Baron de Jouvenel des Ursins (b. 1903) was the son of a well-known liberal publisher, diplomat and senator in the Third Republic, and a mother who came from a family of Jewish industrialists. After his parents divorced, the novelist Colette became his stepmother. He studied mathematics, law, biology and economics, and in the 1920s mixed with the right wing of the Left as a forceful author of syndicalist and planning-oriented appeals for an overcoming of the crisis. From 1928 to 1932 he tried by means of a Youth Manifesto to win the left-liberal Radical Socialist Party, of which he was a member, to the cause of a 'New Deal'. But the attempt proved unsuccessful. In the 1930s he made a name for himself as a journalist, especially as a foreign correspondent: he published a major interview with Hitler on 21 February 1936,[102] but also conducted one with Mussolini in Rome (where his father had been ambassador) and sent reports from the civil war in Spain.

In spring 1934 the PCF leader and deputy chairman of Comintern, Jacques Doriot, was unable to win support in Moscow for his early advocacy of a Popular Front line and was expelled from the Party in June. He then went on to found the left-fascist Parti Populaire Français, which Jouvenel joined in 1936. He became editor of the new party organ,[103] and was a member of the Politburo for half a year in 1938. After the Munich Accord, when Doriot developed into a pioneer of collaboration, Jouvenel seems to have distanced himself from the movement; he volunteered for the infantry around the time of the German attack. Nevertheless, under the Occupation he was a leading and active collaborationist publicist,[104] and some time passed before he withdrew – in a noble variant of the forest way – to take up historical studies on his family's estate in Corrèze. There he is reported to have made contact with the Resistance, and with the Gestapo on his trail he left France in 1943.

Jouvenel subsequently worked for newspapers in Lausanne and Geneva, and some of his series of articles – on the socialist experiment in Britain or the Marshall Plan, for example – were also published in book form. In a further shift he then became a spokesman for a certain kind of Western neo-liberalism, as well as a theoretician of pure politics. After numerous guest professorships in England and the United States,[105] he founded a society whose conferences and information services familiarized the French elite with the philosophy and methods of US management, and which also built up a French futurology.[106]

After the success of some further works on political theory and economics,[107] which increasingly took up questions of qualitative growth and ecology, he became a professor in Paris and was showered with international honours and offices, including membership of the Club of Rome.

The 'Social Protectorate'

Jouvenel has sometimes been compared to de Gaulle, as a man 'from before yesterday and after tomorrow'. The basis of this reputation was laid with his twelfth book, *On Power*, the fruit of his forest way, which was first published when he was forty-two years old. This wide-ranging historical essay follows the growth of state power or the 'Minotaur' – 'masked' in the *ancien régime*, 'unmasked' in bourgeois society and 'ubiquitous' in the mass age – and analyses it in terms of the decline of particular liberties.[108] In the tradition of Tocqueville he sees the French Revolution not as an emancipation of society from the absolutist state, but on the contrary as the social centralization of a potentially terrorist state power set against the traditional spaces of freedom (of the aristocracy).[109] In this view, the mimetic power of the attacker over the attacked partly explains the totalization of all the societies that took part in the Second World War, but the abuse of power was essentially consolidated through the twentieth-century rise of the welfare state, and the strengthening of the police and the means of state education and propaganda.[110] In this way the state has become a machine to which all individuals are chained by material interests, fear and ways of thinking, so that they bring upon themselves the loss of freedom. 'Where the idea comes from that men hold despotism in detestation, I do not know. My own view is that they delight in it.'[111]

For Jouvenel, then, the danger of a 'social protectorate' weighs upon all regimes, because they already dispose of the necessary apparatuses and it is in the nature of the masses to give themselves up to sweet slavery. Hitler and Roosevelt, though not to be equated with each other, are the two main examples of this twentieth-century trend.[112] Now, when de Man quoted Jouvenel as the herald of posthistory, he was probably referring to this image of *Gleichschaltung* by the machinery of power. But had Jouvenel himself not sought the introduction of a planned corporatist economy in France, according to the successive formulas of Roosevelt, de Man and eventually the fascists? We do, in fact, find the current with which we are already familiar from de Man – but now there is no more talk of navigation:

> Every people is today being swept along on the same current, though not all at the same rate, towards the social protectorate. The interests which uncertainty has frightened, the reason which disorder has offended, the feeling which misery has revolted, the imagination which the vision of future possibilities has inflamed, all these call with one voice for a manager or lawgiver.[113]

The rhetorical flourish, sweeping us along into a magnificent analysis full of ideas, tends to make us forget whether the description of evil is also concerned to find a basis on which things could be made better. In this soaring passage everything concrete is lost in an anonymous current, and on closer inspection only the 'frightened interests' have a bearing on society; the rest is autobiography, of himself and his kind. Why must it remain so general? In an open historical situation it would seem that error was always excusable, however terrifying the counsel may have been. Perhaps the error was not so general after all, but could be identified much more precisely? But against it flowed the current in which the intellectual shifted from one radical faction to the next.[114] In each one he found a greater hearing and reputation, although in retrospect they were all of a piece with the logic of intensification of the author's powers and concepts. That is how things must have seemed after the bloody disturbances in February 1934 involving right-wing radicals, when at the age of thirty-one he broke off his attempts to win the centre-Left to a programme of state intervention, launched his magazine *Lutte des Jeunes* (as an alternative to class struggle) and announced 'My Five Points':

> 1. The crisis can be overcome and the welfare of the working classes can be assured through simple measures of economic planning.
> 2. Economic planning presupposes the authority of a ruling class which does not strive for its own advantage but is competent and aware of its responsibilities.
> 3. Such a ruling class does not exist. Therefore economic planning is not feasible; therefore capitalism must be smashed.
> 4. Capitalism can only be smashed by a dictatorship, which can only be established by a revolution.
> 5. At the present hour the forces capable of achieving such a revolution are scattered and divided. Our task is to give them shape.[115]

Two years later, in the face of the Popular Front, he opted for a mass fascist movement and lent his undeniable talents to that end. Eight years after that, he again climbed into the ring (which he had really never left) and went down in an exhibition bout with the 'Minotaur' – as he called the twentieth-century welfare-state Leviathan – in which he concealed his settling of accounts with fascism. Then, just as fascism came to an end, he produced the most wide-reaching historical analysis that traced it back to 'magical gerontocracy' and forward to the exit from history – quite a record. At the end of his study he could say: 'we have done what we set out to do. We aimed at explaining the successive stages of Power's growth and its monstrous efflorescence that is now before our eyes. The inquiry is finished, the dossier is complete, the reasons have been made good and the consequences foreshadowed.'[116] Bravo, bravo!

On Power has long been considered a classic of political theory – whether rightly or wrongly is an open question. There can be no doubt that, in the epoch of fascism, Jouvenel belonged to that cream of the intelligentsia with whose expressions we have been concerned in this chapter because they went on to diagnose posthistory. The point is not at all to belittle these intellectuals – but, on the contrary, to gain the clearest possible insight into their characteristic surplus of energy and need for self-importance. It was that which so attracted them to the heroic act of violence and made all cats appear grey; that which ruled out self-analysis and allowed their motor activity to continue, even if they eventually fell back on 'their lasting certainties' and traditions, on metaphysics, nature, pure Being or some other basic source, and even if they saw before them only the inscrutable mirage of an anthill reaching to the edge of the horizon, Gehlen's 'motion on a stationary basis'. Here lies the literally reactionary character of these fruits of the forest way. And all this can be perceived in the most personal passage from Jouvenel's work, which might suitably round off our canvas of encounters with history. It comes not in the Preface but towards the end, twisting the experience of the radical collaborationist intellectual into its opposite, as if the 'worldly wisdom' of his aristocratic descent had protected him amid his various enthusiasms.

> How infinitely fair and healthy men could be, would they but cease to be the slaves of habit and the playthings of chance! And what a welter of a world is this in which children who were conceived in inadvertence grow like wild grasses, in which towns spread as greedy speculators direct, like blind animals sprawling in their own excrement! I pity the man who has never experienced the noble temptation to play the gardener to this disorder, to build Cities of the Sun, which shall be peopled by a nobler race. But there is in these visions a danger. Men whose stock of knowledge is small find them intoxicating and may be readily convinced by them that the happiness of a continent requires the complete suppression of fermented liquors, or, worse still, the extermination of an entire race whose blood is deemed impure. Only a man who has himself gone in search of truth knows how deceptive is

the blaze of evidence with which a proposition may suddenly dazzle his eyes.
. . . In the absence of this intellectual realization of the limits of knowledge,
the worldly wisdom of ancient aristocracies may often shield us from the
various enthusiasms which, in their desire to be constructive, come near to
being incendiary. Everywhere, however, it happens that the handling of
public affairs gets entrusted to a class which stands in physical need of
certitudes and takes dubious truths to its bosom with the same fanaticism as
did in other times the Hussites and the Anabaptists.[117]

Notes

1. Jürgen Habermas explains the inner motivation of this opportunism as the aporia
   of an individualist philosophy of consciousness, since it required the historical
   dialectic to be transcended in a supreme political figure. *The Philosophical Discourse of Modernity*, pp. 1f.
2. Hegel to Niethammer, 13 October 1806, in G.W.F. Hegel, *Weltgeist zwischen Jena
   und Berlin*, ed. Hartmut Zinser, Frankfurt/Main 1982, p. 58.
3. These included Raymond Aron, Georges Bataille, André Breton, Pater Fessard,
   Jacques Lacan, Robert Marjolin, Maurice Merleau-Ponty and Raymond Queneau
   (who, together with Bataille and Lacan, seems to have been Kojève's favourite
   student). After the war the lectures were written up and published as *Introduction à
   la lecture de Hegel*, Paris 1947. For a partial English translation, see *Introduction to
   the Reading of Hegel*, trs. James H. Nicholls Jr, ed. Allan Bloom, Ithaca, NY 1969.
4. On Kojève's connections and previous history, see Michael S. Roth, *Knowing and
   History: The Resurgence of French Hegelianism from the 1930s through the Post-
   War Period*, Princeton 1988, and 'Natural Right and the End of History: Leo
   Strauss and Alexandre Kojève', *Revue de Métaphysique et de Morale* 3 (1991).
5. Interview with Gilles Lapouge (May 1968) on 'Hegel, the End of History and the
   End of Philosophical Discourse', translated here from Jürgen Siess, ed., *Vermittler.
   Deutsch–französisches Jahrbuch 1*, Frankfurt/Main 1981, pp. 119ff.
6. Quoted by Jean-Luc Pinard-Legry, 'Alexandre Kojève. Zur französischen Hegel-
   Rezeption', in ibid., pp. 105ff., and in Bernd Mattheus, *Georges Bataille. Eine
   Thanatographie*, vol. 1, Munich 1984, pp. 232ff., which contains one of the few
   photographs of Kojève as well as Bataille's recollection of the time when Kojève
   spoke of the impotence and omnipotence of death. (See Bataille's essay on Kojève,
   'Hegel, la mort et le sacrifice', *Deucalion* 5/1955.) For the rest of this section, see
   also Iring Fetscher's introduction to the German edition of Kojève: *Hegel. Eine
   Vergegenwärtigung seines Denkens*, 2nd edn, Frankfurt/Main 1975; Traugott
   König, 'Die Abenteuer der Dialektik in Frankreich', in *Fugen. Deutsch–franzö-
   sisches Jahrbuch für Text-Analytik*, Olten/Freiburg 1980, pp. 282ff., in which
   Kojève's translator gives the two commentaries on 'post-history' that were not
   included in the German edition; Peter Geble, 'Die Macht des Subjekts nach dem
   Ende der Geschichte. Zu einer Kontroverse zwischen A. Kojève und G. Bataille' in
   Kamper/ Taubes. On Kojève's significance for Lacan, see Elisabeth Roudinesco,
   Jacques Lacan & Co. A History of Psychoanalysis in France 1925–1985, London
   1990, and cf. Nobert Bolz, 'Der ewige Friede als Farce. Zum Horizont der
   "Posthistoire" ', in Hartmut Schröter and Sabine Gürtler, eds, *Ende der Geschichte
   (Parabel vol. 5)*, Münster 1986. Kojève's work and impact are discussed in Vincent
   Descombes, *Modern French Philosophy*, Cambridge 1980, pp. 11–54. More
   guarded in its judgement is Bernhard Waldenfels, *Phänomenologie in Frankreich*,
   Frankfurt/Main 1987.
7. Descombes, p. 27.
8. Kojève's book contains two summaries [the English translation only one, on pp.

31–70] which, unlike Hegel's original text, are accessible to the lay reader. For a critique of both, see Reinhart Klemens Maurer, *Hegel und das Ende der Geschichte*, Stuttgart 1965, pp. 139ff.

9. Kojève [English], pp. 43–44.

10. Interview with Roger Calliois, quoted in Geble, p. 26. Calliois reproached Kojève with the fact that his legitimation of Stalinism had blunted its early critique by, in particular, the Socialisme ou Barbarie group (of which Lyotard had also been a member). See the account of the group's positions by its spiritual director Cornelius Castoriadis: *Sozialismus oder Barbarei*, West Berlin 1980. On Kojève's talk at the Collège de Sociologie on 4 December 1937, see also Pinard-Legry, pp. 110f. During the last years of his exile Walter Benjamin was in touch with this small but intellectually influential circle through his friend Georges Bataille.

11. Descombes (p. 14) speaks of a 'terrorist conception of history' and follows it through in the later history of the French intelligentsia.

12. Kojève [English], p. 69. Cf. *The Phenomenology of Mind*, BB.VI. (Spirit) B. (Spirit in Self-Estrangement) III. (Absolute Freedom and Terror). [*Postscript 1992*: This central element in Kojève's bloodthirsty account of the formation of homogeneous social and political structures in the modern world is completely omitted in Francis Fukuyama's rather laborious reenactment, *The End of History and the Last Man* (London 1992). Instead one has the impression of a kind of bandwagon operetta, in which the latest world model – the combination of consumer capitalism and liberal democracy – peacefully travels the globe and vanquishes the evil empire. *L.N.*]

13. Quoted by Fetscher in the German edition of Kojève's *Introduction*, p. 299, which also relates that Communist philosophers later reclassified him in more friendly terms.

14. During this period he also wrote works on Kant and tyrannies, and three volumes on the pre-Socratics that were to have been part of a comprehensive introduction to the history of philosophy, and which have been published since his death.

15. This made Kojève interesting for those who interpreted history since the French Revolution and especially after the Second World War in terms of a 'world civil war', as was the case with circles around Ernst Jünger, Carl Schmitt and others in West Germany. See Hanno Kesting, *Geschichtsphilosophie und Weltbürgerkrieg*, Heidelberg 1959, p. 304. Reinhart Koselleck was advised by Carl Schmitt to visit Kojève, but he was disappointed by what seemed to him Marxist monologues. (Personal communication.)

16. Kojève [French], pp. 434–45. He ended this note with the remark that Marx had the same perspective. But in reality the similarities are stronger with Nietzsche's idea of the last man in Zarathustra's Prologue: ' "What is love? What is creation? What is longing? What is a star?" thus asks the Ultimate Man and blinks. The earth has become small, and upon it hops the Ultimate Man, who makes everything small. His race is as inexterminable as the flea; the Ultimate Man lives longest. "We have discovered happiness," say the Ultimate Men and blink.' *Thus Spoke Zarathustra*, Harmondsworth 1961, p. 46.

17. Kojève [French], p. 436.

18. Franz Wiedmann, *Hegel*, Reinbek 1965, p. 60.

19. Kojève [French], pp. 436–7.

20. Already in the late thirties or early forties, Carl Schmitt made contact with the Kojève circle in Paris through a French student or his friend Ernst Jünger. And as early as 1932 both of them were in touch with Leo Strauss. From 1955 they were in correspondence with each other. The date of their first meeting is not yet clear, but at the latest it would have been in 1957 when Kojève gave a lecture at the Rhein–Ruhr Klub in which he distinguished between American development aid or 'donor-colonialism' and the 'taker-imperialism' of the old European powers.

21. This formulation stems from the Jewish philosopher of religion Jacob Taubes. In *Ad Carl Schmitt. Gegenstrebige Fügung*, West Berlin 1987, p. 24, he recounts how the future leaders of the student revolt listened with bated breath to Kojève's lecture in

Berlin in 1967, where he explained that 'history has now come to an end and can only be repeated in the form of an "as if" ', and advised that the most important thing which could be done now was to learn Greek. From Berlin Kojève travelled to Plettenberg to see Carl Schmitt, the only person in Germany with whom he considered it worthwhile to enter into dialogue.

22. Kojève [French], p. 437.

23. See Jacob Taubes, 'Ästhetisierung der Wahrheit im Posthistoire', in Kamper/Taubes, also in *Festschrift Margherita von Brentano*, West Berlin 1988. Taubes here links Kojève's remarks with Heidegger's 'Die Zeit des Weltbildes' (in *Holzwege*, Frankfurt/Main 1950) and Odo Marquard's 'Kant und die Wende zur Ästhetik', in *Zeitschrift für philosophische Forschung* 16 (1962), pp. 231–43 and 363–74. In doing so, he poses the central question of the Kamper/Taubes collection concerning aesthetics and posthistory, and thus the connection between the discourses of posthistory and postmodernity.

24. Jünger, *Eumeswil*.

25. See Ernst Jünger, *In Stahlgewittern* (1920) [*The Storm of Steel*, London 1929]; and *Der Kampf als inneres Erlebnis*, Berlin 1922. On his early work in general, see Karl Heinz Bohrer, *Die Ästhetik des Schreckens. Die pessimistische Romantik und Ernst Jüngers Frühwerk*, Munich 1978.

26. An inner dialogue is involved here with Hans-Peter Schwarz: *Der Konservative Anarchist*, Freiburg 1962. In identifying himself as an anarch, Jünger returns to the fantasy of grandeur which treats the masters' resistance as an 'as if' existence. Although his early works and anti-Weimar journalism had helped to pave the way for the Third Reich, he soon found the reality repulsive and largely abstained from organizational incorporation in the party or propaganda machinery of National Socialism. Cf. his diary from the Second World War: *Strahlungen*, Tübingen 1949.

27. 'Right-Hegelianism' specifies only one of Jünger's intellectual sources – in addition to the nihilist heroicization of his war experiences, his aestheticism, his link to Nietzsche and Spengler, and his attraction to nature, mythology and an undefined metaphysics. It did, however, provide the main conceptual scaffolding for his principal diagnosis of the times: *Der Arbeiter. Herrschaft und Gestalt* (1932), Stuttgart 1982. Thus, the concept *Arbeiter* (or worker) is not understood empirically in terms of manual labour dependent on a wage, but refers to the rule of the Hegelian slave (as deliverance from a world of masters and slaves). The Hegelian gestures are even plainer in a programmatic abridgement printed in Karl O. Paetel, *Ernst Jünger in Selbstzeugnissen und Bilddokumenten*, Reinbek 1962, pp. 49ff.

28. See Rainer Gruenter, 'Formen des Dandytums. Eine problemgeschichtliche Studie über Ernst Jünger', *Euphorion* 46, (1952); Gerhard Loose, *Ernst Jünger. Gestalt und Werk*, Frankfurt/Main 1957, pp. 9ff. [cf. Loose's separate study in English, *Ernst Jünger*, New York 1974]. Schwarz (pp. 229ff.) sees him as an eccentric who has deserted, and thus also represents, his epoch.

29. 'In our epigone-world of flagging great empires and debased city-states, human striving is confined to coarse necessities. History is dead: that lightens the historical retrospect and keeps it free of prejudice, at least for those who have suffered and got over the pain.' *Eumeswil*, p. 382. The last image is an allusion to the treatise *Über den Schmerz* [Of Pain], 1934.

30. Part of the background experience lies in Jünger's second officership as a captain in the German administration in France, where he served in the mail censorship department among others.

31. *Eumeswil*, p. 355.

32. Ernst Jünger, *Der Waldgang* (1951), 6th edn, Stuttgart 1986, p. 40.

33. Ibid., pp. 40f.

34. In Paris on 30 July 1944, when the Americans were already in Normandy, Jünger documented his boundless self-pity by using the same image in his diary: 'By a remarkable mechanism of history the stains became visible on the German to the extent that the wheel of fate was swinging down for him. He is now learning the experience of the Jews: to be an object of scandal.' *Strahlungen*, II, Munich 1988, p. 291.

35. With the exception of de Jouvenel (b. 1903), all these writers were, like Jünger, from the generation born around 1890 and moulded by the First World War. On the backgrounds of the first three, see Christian Graf von Krockow, *Die Entscheidung. Eine Untersuchung über Ernst Jünger, Carl Schmitt, Martin Heidegger*, Stuttgart 1958, and Jean-Pierre Faye, *Langages totalitaires*, Paris 1972; and on individuals, Pierre Bourdieu, *The Political Ontology of Martin Heidegger*, Cambridge 1991, and Joseph W. Bendersky, *Carl Schmitt. Theorist for the Reich*, Princeton 1983. The type discussed here is presented in thirteen portraits (which also include Gottfried Benn, Hans Freyer, Arnold Gehlen among the key figures of the 'posthistory' syndrome) in Karl Corino, *Intellektuelle im Bann des Nationalsozialismus*, Hamburg 1980.

36. De Jouvenel, *L'Or au temps de Charles V et de Philippe II*, Paris 1943; de Man, *Jacques Coeur*, Berne 1950; Schmitt, *Der Nomos der Erde*, Cologne 1950.

37. Schmitt, *Ex captivitate salus*, Cologne 1950; de Man, *Cahiers de ma Montagne*, Brussels 1944; Heidegger, 'Der Feldweg', written in 1947, first published in 1953.

38. It was also used as a symbol for the wreck of progress in Hans Magnus Enzensberger's 'lyrical comedy' *Der Untergang der Titanic*, Frankfurt/Main 1978, and has become the title of a satirical magazine.

39. *Waldgang*, pp. 30f.

40. See the description by his assistant Armin Mohler in *Die Schleife. Dokumente zum Weg von Ernst Jünger*, Zurich 1955.

41. Hans Blumenberg, *Schiffbruch mit Zuschauer. Paradigma einer Daseinsmetapher*, Frankfurt/Main 1979. Of the wealth of references in this essay, we can give here only two which bear upon Jünger's own usage. First, in the late nineteenth century the distance from the shipwreck – which, since Lucretius, had allowed onlookers 'to enjoy their own untroubled vantage-point' – was narrowed and lost (p. 28). Thus, when Jakob Burckhardt saw himself being tossed in a frail ship by the waves set in motion by the storm of the French Revolution, he added: 'We ourselves are that wave' (p. 66). Second, Nietzsche among others evoked the revolution in the secure areas of thought and even – pushing on a beam – felt pleasure and freedom in the collapse. Blumenberg, thinking of the intellectuals of the conservative revolution, comments: 'The shipwreck that was sought for and called upon to test the solidity of well-being. . .will one day be called "heroic nihilism" ' (p. 22).

42. *Waldgang*, p. 37.

43. *Land und Meer* (Leipzig 1942, and Cologne 1981) is the title Schmitt gave to his 'reflection on world history'.

44. 'Der Führer schützt das Recht', *Deutsche Juristen-Zeitung* 39 (1934), pp. 945ff. An exemplary discussion of his activity in the Third Reich and his later ousting can be found in Bernd Rüthers, *Entartetes Recht. Rechtslehren und Kronjuristen im Dritten Reich*, 2nd edn, Munich 1989, pp. 101ff. Schmitt, who had become known as a Catholic intellectual and adviser to Papen and Schleicher in the anti-Weimar opposition, was won over by Heidegger in the spring of 1933 to involvement in the NSDAP. Over the next four years, before he was pushed into the background by rivals in the SS, he was particularly active in journalism, legal work and academic politics in support of the new regime. In 1936 he opened the anti-semitic campaign in jurisprudence with a congress at which he appealed to Hitler's motto: 'In fending off the Jews,. . . I fight for the works of the Lord' (quoted in ibid., p. 136). Jean-Pierre Faye has reported what Schmitt told him in the postwar years: 'he had only been a councillor of state – under President Göring! – and, well, had a car with a little banner that avoided any traffic problems. He was of the view that a Prussian councillor of state had absolutely no power. Such modes of expression revealed something of the person who, after all, was positioned within the state apparatus at a responsible and dangerous level.' 'Geschichte im Toben des phonischen Spiels. Ein Gespräch', *Schreibheft* 27 (1989), pp. 46ff.

45. See the attempt at a structural analysis of Schmitt's political biography and work: Manfred Lauermann, 'Versuch über Carl Schmitt im Nationalsozialismus', in Klaus Hansen and Hans Lietzmann, eds, *Carl Schmitt und die Liberalismuskritik*, Opladen 1988.

46. Carl Schmitt, *Völkerrechtliche Großraumordnung mit Interventionsverbot für raumfremde Mächte. Ein Beitrag zum Reichsbegriff im Völkerrecht*, Berlin 1939.
47. Carl Schmitt, 'Die Einheit der Welt', *Merkur* 6 (1952).
48. In his war diary from 1942 (*Strahlungen* I, p. 199), after the Allies had landed in North Africa, Jünger was already using this concept of a 'world civil war'. And it was to have a promising future: Ernst Nolte drew on this same world of ideas when he stirred up the historians' dispute in the mid eighties. According to Hanno Kesting, this central concept of his philosophy of history first became topical in 1947–49 with the foundation of Cominform and the proclamation of the Truman Doctrine. *Geschichtsphilosophie und Weltbürgerkrieg*, Heidelberg 1959, pp. 268ff.
49. See Ernst Jünger, *Der gordische Knoten*, Frankfurt/Main 1953.
50. Carl Schmitt, 'Die geschichtliche Struktur des heutigen Welt-Gegensatzes von Ost und West', in Mohler, ed.
51. *Ex captivitate salus* [Salvation Comes from Captivity], pp. 21 and 75. The background to Melville's short story in the slave trade and the American agitation for emancipation is documented in Marianne Kesting, ed., *Melville. Benito Cereno*, Frankfurt/Main 1972. The editor belonged to Schmitt's circle and was probably prompted by him. On Schmitt's interpretation of the story as a metaphor for the decline of Europe, see the contributions by Enrique T. Galvan and Sava Klickovic in the *Festschrift Carl Schmitt: 'Epirrhosis'*, West Berlin 1968. Jünger had already referred to *Benito Cereno* in his war diaries.
52. See the leading article, which was often reprinted in other journals as part of the campaign of Nazi officials for a general amnesty: 'Zeus an die Bundesregierung. Amnestie – Urform des Rechts', *Christ und Welt*, 10 November 1949. Faye (p. 50) answers as follows the question of whether Carl Schmitt ever felt any sense of guilt: 'I think he felt innocent and joyful; he was "gay science" in person. I naturally don't know what he really felt and thought. He made a very jovial impression on me.' According to Faye, he had nothing but scorn for other people, especially Jünger and Heidegger, whom he described as 'milkers of being'.
53. In *Anteile*, Frankfurt/Main 1950.
54. [The title is a play on the ambiguity of the German word *über*, which may mean either 'across' or 'concerning'. Trs. note.] In Mohler, ed., pp. 9ff, later republished as 'Zur Seinsfrage' in Heidegger, *Wegmarken*, Frankfurt/Main 1957. [For an English translation, see *The Question of Being*, New York 1959.]
55. 'Vom Ende des geschichtlichen Zeitalters', in Günther Neske, ed., *Festschrift Martin Heidegger zum 70. Geburtstag*, Pfullingen 1959. This then formed the central piece in Jünger's *An der Zeitmauer*.
56. The allusion is to Heidegger's 'Feldweg' and Jünger's *Waldgang*. [An English translation of 'Feldweg' appeared as 'The Pathway' in *Listening. Journal of Religion and Culture*, vol. 2 (1967), pp. 88–91.] This study, which would appear to have reinvigorated Heidegger's literary following, was written in 1947, published anonymously as a newspaper article in 1949, then reissued as a seven-page brochure in 1953: in all, 45,000 copies were sold. This enigmatic text whispers in the *Heimatstil* about Being. At the end the talk is of peace and seclusion: 'It reaches to those who were prematurely sacrificed in two world wars. The Simple has become still simpler. The Ever-the-Same disquietens and detaches. The words of the fieldway are now quite plain. Does the soul speak? Does the world speak? Does God speak? Everything speaks of renunciation in the Same. Renunciation does not take. Renunciation gives. It gives the inexhaustible strength of the Simple. The words make one feel at home in a long ancestry.' In 1947, after a two-year denazification process, Heidegger was compulsorily pensioned off. Two years later the new style was ready to be carved in granite: 'Stillness stills. What does it still? It stills Being into the coming to presence of world.' (*Die Technik und die Kehre*, 1949. English translation: 'The Turning', in *The Question Concerning Technology and Other Essays*, New York 1977, p. 49.) For a critique see Theodor Adorno, *The Jargon of Authenticity*, Evanston 1973, which also discusses the postwar use of the *Heimatstil* – esp. pp. 52ff.

57. Martin Heidegger, 'Foreword' to *Holzwege* (1950), Frankfurt/Main 1980. The use of the term *Holzwege* also involves an ironic play on words, since its only idiomatic use in German is in the expression 'auf dem Holzweg sein' – 'to be on the wrong track'.

58. At the same time, it refers to Jünger's wartime experience in Paris, where the expression *passage de la ligne* denoted withdrawal from the entanglements of collaboration by crossing from the occupied to the unoccupied zone of France. See, for example, the memoirs of Bertrand de Jouvenel, *Un voyageur dans le siècle*, Paris 1979.

59. Cf. Schwarz, p. 223, who plausibly analyses the chiliastic and individualist tensions in the salvationism underlying Jünger's picture of history.

60. See Max Bense, *Ptolemäer und Mauretanier. Oder die theologische Emigration der deutschen Literatur*, Cologne 1950, for a critique of Jünger's and Benn's use of imagery (pp. 28f.), as well as a terse location of Jünger in the spiritual world of the nineteenth century.

61. Martin Heidegger, *Sein und Zeit* (1927), translated as *Being and Time*, New York 1962.

62. See the affectionate recollections of Hannah Arendt, which are used apologetically for Biemel's discussion of the master's anti-semitic inclinations, in a work of paraphrase that otherwise skates over biographical aspects: Walter Biemel, *Martin Heidegger*, Reinbek 1973, pp. 10ff.

63. See Habermas, *The Philosophical Discourse of Modernity*, pp. 157ff. 'The basic concepts (left unchanged) of fundamental ontology were given a new content by Heidegger in 1933. If he had hitherto used "Dasein" in an unmistakable way for the existentially isolated individual on his course toward death, now he substitutes for this "in-each-case-mine" Dasein the collective Dasein of a fatefully existing and "in-each-case-our" people [*Volk*]. All the existential categories stay the same and yet with one stroke they change their very meaning – and not just the horizon of their expressive significance. The connotations they owe to their Christian origins, especially Kierkegaard, are transformed in the light of a New Paganism prevalent at that time.' And with the example of Heidegger's call for popular acclamation of Hitler as 'some final existential decision', Habermas draws our attention to the 'obscene intonation of its semantics'.

64. The debate was sparked off by Victor Farias's *Heidegger and Nazism*, Philadelphia 1989 (first published in French in 1987 and translated into German, with an introduction by Habermas, in 1989). In Germany it came as a kind of echo to the 'Historians' Dispute', while in France its indirect effect of politically compromising the deconstructivists brought forth some nervous reactions. For an overview, see collections such as Jürg Altwegg, ed., *Die Heidegger Kontroverse*, Frankfurt/Main 1988; and *Le Débat* 48 (1988), pp. 113ff. The status quo before the storm broke in France is displayed in Michel Haar, ed., *Cahier de l'Herne: Heidegger*, Paris 1983. Heidegger's defence against Farias has been conducted by François Fédier, *Heidegger: anatomie d'un scandale*, Paris 1988, and Ernst Nolte, 'Ein Höhepunkt der Heidegger-Kritik?', *Historische Zeitschrift* 247 (1988); see also the collection from a circle of students: Annemarie Gethmann-Siefert and Otto Pöggeler, eds, *Heidegger und die praktische Philosophie*, Frankfurt/Main 1988. An earlier collection of material on Farias's theme is contained in Guido Schneeberger, *Nachlese zu Heidegger*, Berne 1962. The results of painstaking historical research are now presented in Hugo Ott, *Martin Heidegger. Unterwegs zu seiner Biographie*, Frankfurt/New York 1988. Similar questioning dominated the discussion about the hushed-up early collaboration of the Belgian Paul de Man (a nephew of Hendrik) under the German Occupation and the two anti-semitic articles he wrote at that time; he later took on a second identity in the USA and became the leading deconstructivist in literary criticism. See Hans-Thies Lehmann, 'Paul de Man: Dekonstruktionen', *Merkur* 42 (1988); and, for a contrary position, Tsvetan Todorov in the *Times Literary Supplement*, 1988, pp. 676ff. The annoyance at these revelations shown by Jacques Derrida – who, precisely as de Man's friend, worked out the meaning of the concept of memory for the deconstructivists –

emerges from a comparison between his *Memoires for Paul de Man*, 2nd edn, New York 1989, written in 1984, and the piece 'Like the Sound of the Sea Deep within a Shell: Paul de Man's War', which is reprinted in the same volume.

65. In essence, this was already being argued in 1953 in Karl Löwith, 'Heidegger – Denker in dürftiger Zeit', now in *Sämtliche Schriften*, vol. 8, Stuttgart 1984, pp. 124–34.

66. Habermas, *The Philosophical Discourse of Modernity*, p. 131.

67. Of course, it is not as obsolete as Baudrillard makes out in 'Der Streit um Heidegger: Zu spät!', *Die Zeit*, 5 February 1988 (also in Altwegg, pp. 166ff.). For Baudrillard, the debate involves a 'necro-perspective' and is the sign of a loss of reality which covers up the incomprehensibility of history in the media-estranged contemporary world – a classical example of posthistorical repression by intellectual artefacts, which for this purposeful ex-Communist ought to make even the reality of Auschwitz a matter of debate. For a masterly exercise in simulative biographical repression, see Baudrillard's retelling of his own later work in *L'Autre par lui-même*, Paris 1987 – translated as *The Ecstasy of Communication*, New York 1988.

Quite different is George Steiner's desperate – and for a nationalist dilemma, inconclusive – mental wrestling over Heidegger's silence on the Third Reich and the Holocaust. (See the preface to the German edition of George Steiner, *Martin Heidegger. Eine Einführung*, Munich 1989 – first published as *Heidegger*, Glasgow 1978.) Steiner considers Heidegger's philosophy and interpretation of language to be the most important of the twentieth century. But he most sharply condemns the French deconstructivists, Derrida, Lacoue-Labarthes and Lyotard, for their recent attempts through deep interpretation to present Heidegger's National Socialist addresses as obsolete ('puffed-up brutality'), or even to raise them to models of political rhetoric. For Steiner himself, there remains only the schizophrenic split between 'great' thought and 'small' life in the 'mundane sense': namely, 'that Heidegger *in propria persona* was an ordinary character, an ageing man full of cunning and ambition, imbued with deep-seated "agrarian" traditions of concealment and exploitation. His field may have yielded the devil's harvest, but it belonged to him.' Ibid. [English], p. 93.

68. Martin Heidegger, 'The Self-Assertion of the German University: Address, Delivered on the Solemn Assumption of the Rectorate of the University of Freiburg', *Review of Metaphysics* 38, March 1985, pp. 470, 476–7. This address of 1933 is accompanied here by an essay, 'The Rectorate 1933/34: Facts and Thoughts', that Heidegger wrote in his own defence in 1945. On the context, see Farias, pp. 96ff., and Hans Ebeling, 'Das Ereignis des Führers. Heideggers Antwort', in Siegfried Blasche et al., eds, *Martin Heidegger: Innen- und Außenansichten*, Frankfurt/Main 1989.

69. See the bibliography in Otto Pöggeler, 'Den Führer führen? Heidegger und kein Ende', *Philosophische Rundschau* 32 (1985).

70. 'The Rectorate 1933/34', p. 483.

71. Winfried Franzen maintains that this 'wish to surpass and overshadow', which underlay all Heidegger's writings as well as his politics, can be understood as a personality trait. ('Die Sehnsucht nach Härte und Schwere. Über ein zum NS-Engagement disponierendes Motiv in Heideggers Vorlesung "Die Grundbegriffe der Metaphysik von 1929/30"', in Gethmann-Siefert/Pöggeler, pp. 78ff.) Nevertheless, intellectual delusions of grandeur are a structural mechanism for ideological production.

72. See Farias, p. 280.

73. Farias, p. 281. [Translation modified.]

74. See Franzen.

75. Löwith, p. 144.

76. In *The Philosophical Discourse of Modernity* (p. 155), Habermas rightly remarks that Heidegger's political 'error' is much less irritating than his later 'unwillingness . . . to admit his error with so much as one sentence'. The fact that, in the face of

questioning by the denazification committee, he took refuge in a psychiatric hospital, and that he forbade publication during his lifetime of his self-apologetic statements on National Socialism (see the posthumously published interview in *Der Spiegel*, 31 May 1976, translated as 'Only a God Can Save Us', in *Heidegger: The Man and the Thinker*, ed. Thomas Sheehan, Chicago 1981), also suggest attempts to prevent damage to his fantasy of grandeur. Cf. Habermas's introduction to the German edition of Farias's book, in which he refers to his own early Heideggerian errors.

77. This 'reversal', replete with denials of itself, was set out in a letter to a colleague in 1946. It was then sent on to France, where Heidegger's philosophy had a number of followers and the authorities of the French occupation zone might alter his fate. ('Letter on Humanism', in Heidegger, *Basic Writings*, ed. D.F. Krell, New York 1977.) Heidegger's own interpretation of his turn is discussed in the foreword to William J. Richardson, *Heidegger: From Phenomenology to Thought*, The Hague 1963. For a textual criticism of 'Heidegger II', see Bourdieu, *Die politische Ontologie Martin Heideggers*, Frankfurt/Main 1975, pp. 104ff. [cf. Bourdieu, *The Political Ontology of Martin Heidegger*, pp. 88ff., which is translated from the variant French edition of 1988.] It should be noted that by attaching so much contextual weight to the 'conservative revolution' and the academic establishment, Bourdieu misunderstands the character of the postwar situation. In the pompous banality of Heidegger's 1949 lecture on technology – which was not delivered until four years after his discharge – he actually sees the empty verbalism of a university mandarin!

78. In this new ambiguous style of writing, the philosopher who is apparently incapable of taking any distance from himself catches the central concept of *Sein und Zeit* in his new existence as a 'representative of the Sacred' and an ill-defined herald of the history of Being. Bourdieu reads the image-world of Heidegger's later work as the medium of an arbitrary censorship, whose aim is to overcome his earlier positivist political theology in a negative equivalent, as the 'system of everything that it excludes' (*Die politische Ontologie. . .*, p. 110; cf. *The Political Ontology. . .*, pp. 70ff.). It could also be read as the medium of the non-arbitrary.

79. This option explains Heidegger's popularity among some of those who are seeking alternative perspectives, so that he increasingly appears as the foster-father of postmodernity. See, for example, Richard Palmer, 'The Postmodernity of Heidegger', *Boundary 2* (1976). Wolfgang Welsch, however, in a comparison with Lyotard, has shown that Heidegger continues on an anti-modern basis the older tradition of unity-centred thought, whereas the basic postmodernist vision grounds its attitude to modernity and its diagnosis of the age on a new polymorphism. (*Unsere postmoderne Moderne*, Weinheim 1987, pp. 207ff.) Habermas also sees Heidegger's orientation as imprisoned in the past: 'But if, on the contrary, the disappointment with National Socialism could be elevated beyond the foreground sphere of responsible judgement and action and stylized into an objective error, to an error gradually revealing itself in history [i.e. in the history of Being, L.N.], the continuity with the point of departure of *Being and Time* need not be endangered. . . . From that time, he was able to view fascism itself as a symptom and to classify it, alongside Americanism and communism, as an expression of the metaphysical domination of technology.' *The Philosophical Discourse of Modernity*, pp. 159–60.

80. In the mid 1950s, Jaspers drew this sketch of Heidegger: 'A profound despair: No faith in communication, – awareness of total aloneness, – without actually suffering from it, – but in passive defiance – An awareness of the decline, – the end of human history – and the artificial, non-credible invoking of primitive possibilities – a contempt for man, – desire for the recognition he does not want to do without, – and yet a growing contempt against all who follow him – A modern phenomenon – many recognize themselves in it: Romantic sentimentalities at the periphery – Lack of obligation as a whole – Content with vague, non-binding

symbols lacking consequence, by means of which the self-illumination of the consciousness of one's own value within the negative is possible. "Place-Holder of Nothingness", "Guardian of Being".' Karl Jaspers, 'Note 129 (1954/55) on Heidegger' in *Basic Philosophical Writings*, Athens, Ohio 1986, pp. 503–504.

81. Heidegger, *An Introduction to Metaphysics*, New York 1961, pp. 37, 31–2. The leitmotif of this world-historical ethnocentrism linked him to Jünger and Schmitt and was later developed by Ernst Nolte in several works, such as *Deutschland und der Kalte Krieg*, Munich 1974.

82. Heidegger, *The Question of Being*, p. 49.

83. Ibid., p. 108.

84. Ernst Jünger, 'An der Zeitmauer', nos 42ff., in *Sämtliche Werke*, vol. 8, Stuttgart 1981, pp. 462ff.

85. Hans-Peter Schwarz (pp. 222ff.) concludes from a survey of Jünger's observations on history since the fundamental *Vom Geiste* of 1927 that 'a remarkably chiliastic moment' is the common element 'within an approach that is in principle unhistorical'.

86. Cf. the references to Bertaux and Teilhard de Chardin in chapter 3, section II above.

87. As defeat approached, Jünger came to view the Second World War as a 'world civil war'. This did not imply that he took the side of the partisans, however, but that he placed all the participants on an equal footing without regard to justice and history, thereby freeing the Germans of blame. (Cf. the remarks above on Carl Schmitt.) A similar meaning attaches to his memorandum *The Peace* (Hinsdale, Ill. 1948), conceived as an appeal to the youth of Europe, which he made available to the *frondeurs* in Paris on 20 July 1944, although he himself was against the use of assassination. Jünger was discharged from the Wehrmacht in the autumn of that year. See Loose, pp. 215ff.

88. Hendrik de Man, *Gegen den Strom. Memoiren eines europäischen Sozialisten*, Stuttgart 1953. See Peter Dodge, *Beyond Marxism: The Faith and Works of Hendrik de Man*, The Hague 1966; the introduction to Dodge, ed., *A Documentary Study of Hendrik de Man*, Princeton 1979; and Mieke Claeys-Van Haegendoren, *Hendrik de Man. Een Biografie*, Antwerp 1972. Both these authors confine themselves to external details for the period after 1940. An attempted reassessment of his theory and political biography took place at a conference organized in 1973, the contributions from which have appeared in Ivo Rens, ed., *Sur l'oeuvre d'Henri de Man*, special issue of *Revue Européenne des Sciences Sociales* and *Cahiers Vilfredo Pareto 12*, Geneva 1974, No. 31.

89. *Vermassung und Kulturverfall* (1951), 3rd edn, Munich 1953, p. 125. On Gehlen's covert use of it, see the editor's remarks in Arnold Gehlen, *Gesammelte Werke*, vol. 7, Frankfurt/Main 1978, pp. 468ff.

90. *The Psychology of Socialism*, London 1928; *Joy in Work*, London 1929. His major work analysed the motives of those who embraced socialism, including its bourgeois supporters, in terms of the split between inherited value-traditions and the actual life-situation of the proletariat. This made him few friends in the SPD, but in retrospect it earned him the reputation of a thirties precursor of the Bad Godesberg turn. His programmatic text for an idealist socialism of reform (*Die sozialistische Idee*, Jena 1933) was confiscated immediately after publication; and as we have seen, Kojève translated it into French together with Henri Corbin as *L'Idée socialiste*, Paris 1935.

91. De Man, *Jacques Coeur*, p. 8.

92. *Gegen den Strom*, p. 272.

93. Ibid., pp. 287f.

94. *Vermassung*, p. 124. Referring to the war machine he writes: 'Nothing can outdo the impression of human helplessness made by contact with this machine; and the impression is all the stronger, the closer one draws to its central driving mechanism. For one is then astonished to discover that the machine, as it were, continues under

its own power independently of the will of individuals, in a direction conditioned purely by its original impetus and mass.'

95. *Gegen den Strom*, p. 288. He also mentions here briefly the problems that are dealt with more thoroughly in *Vermassung*: 'Massification, bureaucratization, depersonalization, autonomization and unmanageability of giant apparatuses, hypertrophy of national states and empires, mass war psychoses born out of mass fears – the outcome being a permanent war that endangers all social and moral achievements of our culture's phase of ascent, and perhaps even calls into question the continued existence of humanity.'

96. There is no reference to a particular text by Jouvenel, but the two had renewed their prewar aquaintance in Switzerland and were writing to each other. According to information supplied by Michel Brélaz in Geneva, their letters did not specifically mention the concept of 'posthistory'. My own examination of Jouvenel's numerous writings before 1945, which mostly deal with current affairs, also indicates that he did not formulate there the idea of a dawning of posthistory. In his later writings on political theory, we find references to Cournot's morphogenetic views, but not to his prognosis of a posthistorical society. I shall therefore assume that de Man was referring to *On Power*, a work first published in 1945 in which Jouvenel surveyed the regimes of the twentieth century and developed the idea of a 'social protectorate'. Personal conversations in exile may then have added further substance.

97. *Vermassung*, p. 125. Michel Brélaz also advises me that the first draft of *Vermassung und Kulturverfall* was an unpublished text in English, *The Age of Doom* (1949), which appealed to Cournot in developing above all the ideas of a morphological stabilization and mutation, and a speeding-up of history. For L. Arénilla ('La fin de l'histoire. Le point de vue de Cournot', *Diogène* 79 1972), the fact that Cournot did not pose the alternative of death or mutation, but looked forward to a more rational development of society, identifies him as a precursor of technocratic visions, somewhere between Saint-Simon and Rathenau, whom de Man had also picked up on in the interwar period.

98. *Vermassung*, p. 125. On de Man's view of history, see Sven Stelling-Michaud and Janine Buenzod, 'L'Itinéraire d'Henri de Man: de l'histoire à la philosophie de l'histoire', in Ivo Rens, ed.

99. Hendrik de Man, *Cavalier Seul*, Geneva 1948.

100. Bertrand de Jouvenel, *On Power: Its Nature and the History of Its Growth* (1945), New York 1949.

101. There is still no full-scale biography. Jouvenel's memoirs, *Un voyageur dans le siècle*, are of substance only in relation to the prewar period. See Ganslandt's afterword in the German edition of *On Power*: *Über die Staatsgewalt*, Freiburg 1969; Pierre Hassner, 'Bertrand de Jouvenel', in *International Encyclopedia of the Social Sciences*, vol. 18 (1979); and Roy Pierce, *Contemporary French Political Thought*, London 1966, pp. 24ff., 185ff.

102. For extracts from this unusually intimate interview, as well as a comparison with the rather selective memoirs, see Zeev Sternhell, *Neither Right nor Left*, Berkeley 1986. Cf. de Jouvenel, *Un voyageur*, pp. 250ff. Jouvenel's role in the reception of de Man and in the Doriot movement makes him a key figure in Sternhell's investigation of fascist ideology in France, which shows how it extended out of some of the ideas of 'reform socialism'. The suggestion that Jouvenel was an agent of the German ambassador, Otto Abetz (see *Un voyageur* for his own account of their friendship since 1931), gave rise to legal disputes.

103. See Dieter Wolf, *Die Doriot-Bewegung*, Stuttgart 1967, pp. 139ff., 205ff; *Un voyageur dans le siècle*, pp. 287ff; and Sternhell, passim. Hassner (p. 359) skates round Jouvenel's involvement in the PPF and emphasizes his activity in the Resistance, without going into the reasons why he remained in exile in Switzerland for several years after the end of the war. Nor is this clear from the memoirs – except that he complained in his diary for 1944 how little his patriotism was appreciated at home.

104. See Gerard Loiseaux, *La littérature de la défaite et de la collaboration d'après 'Phönix oder Asche' de Bernhard Payr*, Paris 1984, pp. 70, 92, 97f., 156f., 313f., shows that Jouvenel was one of the political writers most favoured and courted by the Occupation authorities. He was translated into German and became a committee member of the German–French Association, which probably brought him into contact with Ernst Jünger and even Carl Schmitt (who gave a talk at the German Institute in Paris in October 1941). Being a 'half-Jew', Jouvenel did however moderate the anti-semitism of other collaborators who were calling for a 'biopolitician' to keep the 'French nation' pure.

105. During an early trip to the USA he met Leo Strauss in Chicago, who wrote to Kojève that Jouvenel valued his interpretation of Hegel as well as his activity as a political official, but had been surprised to learn that one and the same person was involved.

106. Arnold Gehlen published a piece on his posthistorical views in the institute bulletin, *Futuribles* (50/1963) – presumably after a talk there on the same subject.

107. *On Sovereignty: An Inquiry into the Political Good*, Cambridge 1957; *The Pure Theory of Politics*, Cambridge 1963; *The Art of Conjecture*, London 1967; *Arcadie*, Paris 1968; *La civilisation de puissance*, Paris 1976.

108. *On Power*: 'The State as Permanent Revolution' (pp. 157ff.); 'Liberty's Aristocratic Roots' (pp. 317ff.)

109. Ibid., pp. 215ff.

110. Ibid., pp. 2, 254ff. ('Totalitarian Democracy'), 336ff. ('Liberty or Security') and 356ff. ('Order or Social Protectorate').

111. Ibid., p. 362.

112. In March 1944, at roughly the same time that Jouvenel was writing this in his Swiss exile, Jünger noted in his diary: 'If Kniebolo [a cover-name for Hitler] falls, the hydra will form a new head.' *Strahlungen* I, p. 497.

113. *On Power*, p. 353.

114. One can hardly avoid quoting here the Romanian–French essayist E.M. Cioran: 'The tired intellectual sums up the deformities and the vices of a world adrift. . . . Only the strength that grinds him into the dust seduces him. . . . Thus he will fling himself, eyes closed, into any mythology which will assure him the protection and the peace of the yoke. Declining the honour of assuming his own anxieties, he will engage in enterprises from which he anticipates sensations he could not derive from himself, so that the excesses of his lassitude will confirm the tyrannies. Churches, ideologies, police – seek out their origin in the horror he feels for his own lucidity, rather than in the stupidity of the masses.' *The Temptation to Exist*, London 1987, pp. 57–8. Cioran too has an analysis of the end of history, although in his case it goes together with an aestheticized, Schopenhaurian disgust with life. See his 'Après l'histoire', in *Écartèlement*, Paris 1979; and Fernando Savater, *Versuch über Cioran*, Munich 1985, pp. 101ff.

115. *Lutte des Jeunes*, 27 May 1934, p. 3, translated from Slama, p. 188.

116. *On Power*, p. 364.

117. Ibid., pp. 354–5.

6

The Blown-Away Angel:
On the Posthistory of a Historical
Epistemology of Danger

At the Moment of Danger

In late September 1940 a small group of Jewish refugees – five women, a boy and a 48-year-old man – are climbing a mountain path from France across the Pyrenees, which at that point jut out into the Mediterranean. They want to reach the Spanish frontier post at Port Bou without going through the police controls of the Vichy regime. They have their visas to pass through Spain and to enter the United States, but not to leave France. The man is carrying only a black briefcase whose contents, he says, are more important than his life. To avoid any risk he has, unlike the others, spent the night in the open; but his heart condition has been worse since his internment at the beginning of the war, and he has suffered an attack during the night. When the group rejoin him in the morning things are still not going well; now and again he has to be relieved of his case, and he must take a rest every ten minutes. When they catch sight of Port Bou from the cliff and feel themselves to be on Spanish territory, he is unable to go any further and kneels down to drink at a pool. The woman guide, who has it in mind to turn back, tries to stop him by pointing out that it will now be downhill all the way and that he might catch typhus here. He replies: 'Yes, maybe. But you see, the worst that can happen now is that I'll die of typhus *after* crossing the border. The Gestapo won't be able to get its hands on me. And my manuscript will be safe. Please forgive me.' And he starts drinking.

He did not die of typhus. But when the Spanish border guards refused to let him in without a French exit stamp, he poisoned himself the following night in his hotel by taking an overdose of morphine. He entrusted his briefcase to a fellow-émigré and her son, who were to be allowed in the next day, and begged them to get its contents ('*mes pensées*') through to Theodor Adorno in New York. Apparently, however, the police forced the woman to destroy the farewell letter, and the briefcase itself was impounded. The authorities listed the dead man's baggage of exile as consisting of 'a leather briefcase, such as businessmen use, a man's watch, a pipe, six photographs, an X-ray, a pair of spectacles, various letters, magazines and a few other papers of unfamiliar content, as well as some money amounting to 273 pesetas after deductions for costs incurred'.[1]

The impounded testament was afterwards presumed lost,[2] together with those few papers of unfamiliar content which the émigré, unwilling to emigrate any further, absolutely needed to remove from the Third Reich's sphere of influence before his death and to carry into the light of the world. It would seem to follow then, that this testament was different in character from the rest of his work known to émigré friends.[3] In this respect it should be viewed historically, by reference to the moment of danger in which it was first capable of being formulated, rather than used for over-hasty conjectures based on the rest of his work.[4]

It would seem that copies of the letter and the manuscript finally reached their destination three-quarters of a year later.[5] Adorno, after his failure in New York, had just moved to Los Angeles to work with Max Horkheimer on philosophical studies and a series of essays that would work through his American culture shock. Towards the end of the Weimar Republic, the man with the briefcase, the literary critic and cultural historian Walter Benjamin, had been the intellectual mentor of the philosopher and music critic ten years his junior: Teddie Wiesengrund. When Hitler came to power Teddie at first remained in Germany, considering like Papen that the Third Reich was a transitory petty-bourgeois regime. But in 1934 he went to live in England and took the surname Adorno after his mother (whose family had long ago originated in Corsica), presumably so that the Jewish name of his Protestant-convert father, with whom he anyway had few ties, would not cause difficulties on his frequent trips to Germany. Before this, in 1933, Benjamin had emigrated to France to collect material for his life's project, a paradigmatic cultural history of Paris in the nineteenth century, and had soon found himself in an extremely precarious financial situation. Later, when Horkheimer took Adorno under his wing and found him a post as an assistant of the Frankfurt School in exile, Benjamin's meagre income was stabilized through payments from the New York Institute. But this also gave him a feeling of dependence, and the tension had sharpened in the last years before the war. Most seriously, the young music theorist Adorno, framing his cultural pessimism in Marxist terms, had criticized as vulgar Marxist the work that his highly sensitive friend was doing on literary history. At the same time Benjamin, who was trying to develop a new approach to history, had seen the collapse of his bourgeois existence and felt instinctively close to the Communists without ever becoming a Party member.[6]

In the spring of 1940, before the German army completely conquered France, Benjamin set down eighteen reflections 'on the concept of history'[7] – some of them on old newspaper wrappers – so that his major project would have more purchase both for himself and for friends. But he did not yet want to publish what the Frankfurt School later rather misleadingly called his 'Theses'. He explained his real motive in writing them, as well as his hesitation, in a letter to Adorno's wife, with whom he was more open than with his colleagues. (At the time, however, he did not keep his promise to send her a copy of the text.)

> The war and its resulting constellation have led me to put down some thoughts of which I can say that I have kept them in safekeeping – yes, safekeeping – from myself for some twenty years. . . . Even today I am handing them over to you more as a bunch of whispering grass gathered on pensive walks, than as a collection of theses. . . . Moreover, the reflections have such an experimental character that they will not serve alone as the methodical preparation for a sequel to the Baudelaire piece.[8] They make me suspect that the problem of memory (and of forgetting) will occupy me for a long time yet.[9]

The last sentence now seems quite cryptic, appearing as it does in one of the last letters from a writer who would take his life a few months later – at a time when he must have considered his major work to have been lost to him.[10] We can also see in this short quotation, however, the vulnerable sensitivity with which he faced his own attempt to gain some general bearings in the crisis.[11] This clearly differentiates it both from the tone of interpretative certainty typical of posthistorical intellectuals and from the genre of 'epistemological considerations' (which was Adorno's mistaken understanding of the 'theses'). The true occasion for the text – namely, the 'historyless time' following the Hitler–Stalin Pact and the expansion of fascism – is naturally only spoken in code, but spoken none the less. There is a threefold threat: to his existence as a Jew; to his work as a historian bound up with Paris; and to his political perspectives as a man of the Left.[12] He certainly has to flee, but not at all to the forest.[13] Instead, he achieves identity with a final work in his own area, in which he mobilizes the Jewish religious tradition for a reinvigoration of his intellectual practice as left-winger and historian.

The reflections 'on the concept of history' are a terse document rich in imagery, consisting of individual parts which obtained their sequential order only in a later version. The accumulation of images shows the groping character of the text as it rushes ahead towards the concept. This also makes it difficult to read – for although the parts hang together, they demand to be read as signposts rather than as a coherent system.[14] The metaphorical wealth, allegorical terseness and allusive complexity meant that when it awoke from its long slumber and found numerous interpreters at the time of the student revolt, it became a canvas screen on which the discussion of base and superstructure, theory and practice and the quality of progress was projected.[15] Since projections often slightly mistake their object, the discrepancies may allow us to read more accurately both the text itself and the excess of interpretation in discussions since that time. We shall attempt to do this in relation to two dominant images that come at the beginning and in the middle, in Reflections I and IX.

The Chess Automaton

After the Benjamin revival in the mid sixties, the first disputes centred on the question of whether his Reflections followed from his Communist tendencies of the 1930s, or whether they harked back to his early theological interests. The posing of such an alternative is rather surprising, given that the first Reflection already combines both dimensions in a single image. Referring to Edgar Allan Poe's story of a chess automaton, Benjamin here counsels historical materialism to enlist the services of theology for its match to decide the fate of history, theology here being represented by a dwarf chess expert who, from his concealed position beneath the table, guides and animates the puppet. Since the puppet 'historical materialism', as the agent of the automaton who challenges people to play, would not be able to move at all without the brilliant string-pulling dwarf 'theology', it might seem fairly evident that the dwarf here recruits the puppet to conceal his own ugliness: that is, to make up for the fact that he is not a subject in the class struggle. In fact, this is the central point in Habermas's reading of the image, in a justly famous essay which dissects Benjamin's concept of experience by examining the whole of his *oeuvre*. Habermas concludes that even as a 'conservative-revolutionary' he remained a theologian who sought in the proletariat, via historical materialism, a subject for his rich but aporetic theory of experience. But the dwarf cannot take the puppet into his service:

> Historical materialism, which reckons in progressive steps. . ., cannot be covered over with an anti-evolutionary conception of history as with a monk's cowl. My thesis is that Benjamin did not succeed in his intention of uniting enlightenment and mysticism because the theologian in him could not bring himself to make the messianic theory of experience serviceable for historical materialism.[16]

For Habermas, this error must be corrected by a reversal of the relationship between Marxism and theology. The final three pages of his essay, however, are decisive only for his own work, because there he sketches out, 'on the verge of Posthistoire',[17] his turn from the Marxist theory of emancipation to the theory of communicative action. We shall have to return to these points. But for the moment we must remain with the text.

Who, then, takes whom into their service? For Benjamin, the puppet historical materialism 'can easily be a match for anyone if it enlists the services of theology'. That seems clear enough linguistically, whilst sounding implausible in its content. But Habermas's plausible alternative reading of the German syntax, reinforced by Adorno's habit of unorthodox displacement of the object of the verb, results in an interpretation in which theology is the master of events![18] Such a conclusion is wrong, however, for Benjamin literally meant what he wrote. His fine German never causes any difficulty, even if his thoughts set many a puzzle. In his own French translation the puppet unambiguously takes the dwarf into its service, and another draft spells it out in German, too.

> I could easily imagine a counterpart to this apparatus in philosophy, especially since the dispute over the true concept of history can well be thought of as a game between two partners. The winner, if it is up to me, will be the Turkish puppet, for whom the philosophers' name is materialism. It can easily be a match for anyone if assured of the services of theology, which today, however, is small and ugly and nowhere to be seen.[19]

We are dealing therefore not with a historical subject but with the revival of a historical construction (the puppet materialism) — and in the interests not of that construction itself but of the one who seeks its victory in the struggle with any other conception of history that needs to be challenged. These other conceptions should be imagined not as constructions but as animate or historically sentient beings, and thus as one variant or another of the historicism actually existing in the operation of the society. The subject is the author.

The Germanist Gerhard Kaiser was also unable to tolerate the unwieldiness of the image. He accepted that the puppet was to take the dwarf into its service, and not vice versa; but common sense and an observer's blindness prevented him from entering more deeply into the question. Instead he dissolved the inherent tension with the help of dialectical wordplay ('Insofar as [the dwarf] serves the puppet, he serves himself'[20]). The puppet could thus be identified with the dwarf, but theology was again the mistress – at least insofar as it 'was' the theologically enriched historical materialism of the following theses. Such an abstract solution did not solve the problem but merely eliminated it.

Heinz-Dieter Kittsteiner, who as a Berlin student in the circle around Jacob Taubes launched the discussion of Benjamin's 'Theses' in the student movement in 1967,[21] has been rubbing away at this image for more than two decades. It is not that he has failed to understand it: on the contrary, his paraphrase is one of the most precise. But it does not suit him. He feels disturbed by the dwarf. In the rediscovery of a tabooed Marxist tradition and the orientation of youth towards a supposedly revolutionary situation, the fascinating aspect of Walter Benjamin was his combination of 'Marxism' with an idea of historical discontinuity that would make possible a new beginning and a new history.[22] New life therefore had to be breathed into the puppet itself, and the dwarf relegated to the collection of curios of a particular situation (wrongly dated in 1938). The solution lay in the framework of a philosophy of history which 'incorporated itself into Marxism and insisted on class struggle', but which abstained from 'a linear calculation of progress'. In this way, 'under the pressure of a particular situation, an appropriately secularized theological vocabulary will be added to Marxism as its manifest rational kernel'. Finally, Kittsteiner transformed Benjamin's association of materialism and theology into a division of labour between historical theory and political practice: 'The chess-playing puppet with the theological dwarf inside, who together are capable of combating fascism, have each their own function: the historical materialist faces the present as a Marxist and the past as a theologian of remembrance.'[23]

Kittsteiner, who had not yet become the historian of conscience we know today, felt that this reversal was justified by another reflection of Benjamin's. New readings of the tradition, establishing new traditions of meaning through a powerful contemporary definition of the problematic, would be constructed with the image of a heliotrope turning towards the dawn. From this primeval metaphor, however, the politically committed student drew a cultural-revolutionary slogan: the past was not only to be reinterpreted (or 'redeemed') but itself transformed. After the removal of their theological waste-product, the theses would sparkle forever in the rising sun of Marxist activism; they 'have changed on the printed paper'.

In 1975, when this sun was evidently setting, Kittsteiner distanced himself from its key idea of not only turning Benjamin into a heliotrope but also transforming his text. This made it easier to use the text as a bridge from the bourgeois world to Marxism: 'It could certainly tell us a lot about how a bourgeois individual experiences capitalism, but not very much about capitalism itself. Instead of searching for a Marxist Benjamin, we now began to read Marx.'[24] There is no longer any talk of practice. And Kittsteiner's Afterword of 1975 gives only a moment's attention to the transition from role-model commitment to Marxology as the staple of the Left in 'posthistory'. A decade further on, Kittsteiner again returned to Benjamin in connection with his recently published preparatory material, now using philosophical–historical erudition to range him among those whom he saw as the adversary – that is, historicists.[25] To this he counterposed a reflective reading of Marx which freed him from his practical intentions and results ('no longer a valid therapy today') and celebrated him as an analyst of encroaching progress as end in itself. It will be remembered that in 1967 the author had already wanted to pull Benjamin over to the side of progress.[26]

> The true myth of modernity is the myth of a complete heteronomy, one in which no gods, heroes or men appear – only things. Karl Marx told the story: the one about the birth of money from the mutual reflection of twenty yards of linen and one skirt.[27]

Marxism, having gone out of fashion, is now assigned the role of dwarf in the chess automaton, which no longer has either a player or an author. Kittsteiner quotes Marx's view that revolutions are the loco-motives of world history, and Benjamin's retort that they are rather the alarm handle for which the human race reaches on the train. And he concludes: 'Fine. Here is the train. But where is the emergency brake? And who has the long arm to reach it and the strength to pull it?'[28] Or perhaps we are already in posthistory and even this worry has been cleared away: 'It is worth considering whether Marx wrote to exorcise the fear that this society [capitalism] might not prove itself to be "an organism constantly in the process of transformation" [*Das Kapital*, MEW 23, p. 16], but rather a "solid crystal".'[29]

The quotation from Marx actually seems to say the opposite, that capitalism is not a solid crystal (an image which recalls Gehlen's central concept of 'crystallization'). Not long afterwards, however, in a contribution to the posthistory debate, what was 'worth considering' has become what 'may be assumed'. Kittsteiner now has Marx turning like a heliotrope towards the rising sun of posthistory, in an act of disengagement within an eternally posited capitalism. All rebellion has proved to be ineffective, and in retrospect merely had the significance of a fashion, an aesthetically simulated expression of life. If it is now a thing of the past, a piece of life that used to protect itself with 'as if' armour is also dying away. An opponent who has bared himself so completely must be almighty. Diagnosis now becomes autobiography.

> The decline into crystal is irreversible, like all the phenomena typical of the age. The only thing of interest is to observe how life reacts to reified, abstract-universal social labour. Life, being Darwinist, reacts by adaptation. . . . Life is not a category which effectively confronts the historical process. What it grasps is not history but only commodities, and it is rescued in their design. . . . Fashions, including intellectual ones, are that 'mysterious atmosphere' which life needs in order to persist. They give the signal for the appropriate armour in which life thinks that it can take up the struggle with things. In fashion, body skin becomes like the skin of commodities; the protection is destroyed and life understandably reacts with fear. . . . But this adaptation, which makes people capable of survival, exacts its price. For each adaptation . . . is a partial death, the surrender of a part of individuality.[30]

The Angel

In the middle of his reflections on history, Benjamin again takes up a thought-provoking image that has been widely interpreted in recent years.[31] Reflection IX reads:

> A Klee painting named 'Angelus Novus' shows an angel looking as though he is about to move away from something he is fixedly contemplating. His eyes are staring, his mouth is open, his wings are spread. This is how one pictures the angel of history. His face is turned toward the past. Where *we* perceive a chain of events, *he* sees one single catastrophe which keeps piling wreckage upon wreckage and hurls it in front of his feet. The angel would like to stay, awaken the dead, and make whole what has been smashed. But a storm is blowing from Paradise; it has got caught in his wings with such violence that the angel can no longer close them. This storm irresistibly propels him into the future to which his back is turned, while the pile of debris before him grows skyward. *This* storm is what we call progress.[32]

In attempting to decipher this passage, various interpreters have brought to bear a wide range of materials and angles of vision from Benjamin's own biography, from Klee's subjects and views on art, from the spread of angelic allegory in nineteenth-century cultural history, from Marxism, from the angelology of the Kabbala, from the Torah and the mythology of Antiquity, and from the science of thermodynamics. Although there is generally little agreement among them, most share the conviction that Benjamin himself identified with the angel in the text.[33] The only direct evidence for this is that Benjamin, who bought this picture by Klee in 1921 and kept it with him in Berlin and Paris, hanging it either above his desk or over his sofa, referred to it in several of his writings as an allegory of varying content; and that when he was once in a state of frenzy or delirium, during a life-crisis following his emigration from Germany, he saw it as a 'satanic angel', a 'monster' with clawed hands and a 'man-eating' face, and in this fantastic shape of a fallen, retreating angel – or, others would say, of Jacob's struggle with the angel – was reminded of his own unfulfilled erotic attachments.[34] But this prehistory is not enough to answer the question whether it was carried over seven years later into a quite different context, or, if so, whether he should then be seen as a *flâneur* swimming against the stream of the city masses (Arendt), as a 'critical but paralysed observer' (Christoph Hering), as an isolated and defeated historian (Otto Karl Werckmeister), as a 'true historian' (Heinrich Kaulen), or – according to the account in which he reconverted from Marxism to Jewish religiosity – as 'man qua universal being' (Gershom Scholem). Simply to identify Benjamin with the angel seems to involve spontaneous projections which are not worked through in the text, and sometimes also an ignorance of theology among his left-wing Germanist or philosophical interpreters, who, without further ado, associate it with mysticism and 'the monk's cowl' or endow it with a surfeit of unquestioned deep meaning. In contrast, the sober contribution of a theologian, using the tools of historical–critical exegesis of the Hebrew Bible, provides a refreshing dose of rationality.[35]

Rudolf Bahro, for his part, in a critique of 'identifications, fixations and prejudices' as the core of the 'disorder of our whole psychodynamic', describes Benjamin's Reflection IX as a 'bad dream' and moves quickly on to anthropologize its theological associations.

> Now, in dream all the visualized elements are aspects of the dreaming subject, who is here the bearer of history. Man is not only this angel driven from paradise. He also piles up the wreckage, and produces the storm. And the Good Lord, who blows him from paradise, [also] exists in man himself. *History is psychodynamics*. The logic of self-destruction is an affliction of the human soul. Our suicidal devices, our technical and social structures are not our first nature. Concrete is not 'material' in the sense that rock is. It is

all *culture* that we have made *second* nature, and on which we are foundering. It is the unconquered side of our human, our psychic existence.[36]

Benjamin's allegory of history, drawing on Klee's picture on which he had already projected many various thoughts, is thus first explained by Bahro as a dream, an unconscious psychic phenomenon. It is true that Benjamin himself often sought to interpret dream-images as memories of the unconscious. But in these reflections there is not the slightest reference to a dream; rather, he constructs an angel as the symbol of the exhausted strength of a theological tradition. In the second stage of Bahro's argument, all the elements of the picture – the angel, time, energies, wreckage, dead and crushed people – as well as the telescoping of contrary interpretations, are transcended in one central instance: 'man' as the 'bearer of history'. And from the backdrop of the human soul steps the 'Good Lord', who was certainly concealed from Benjamin. In a further move, we learn that this all-powerful being, man, is a sick soul who constructs for himself a second nature (which Bahro describes as a 'megamachine') and that man is now foundering on this. For Bahro, of course, as he later makes clear, the point is not to settle into posthistory but to end the 'deadly spiral' through historical action – which requires that man should overcome the egocentricity of his dislocation from nature.[37] But this idea does not seem to be derived from consideration of Benjamin's complex imagery; indeed, it is supposed to prevent the general anthropological implosion of this imagery through the grasping of its historical tension.

Reflection IX was evidently written neither in dream nor in delirium, but with great deliberation. Its author stressed in correspondence that he wished to concentrate the fruit of two decades of reflection, which was to have entered into the introduction to the *Passagenwerk*, by then in preparation for twelve years. As this *magnum opus* had been in extreme danger since the German attack on France and was unlikely ever to be finished, Benjamin wanted at least to set out its underlying conceptions. After a number of preliminary drafts,[38] the few pages that emerged in the course of several months did not yet seem suitable for publication; but in the end their handing down was more important to him than his own life. It is thus not excessive to study even tiny signals in the text.

In Reflection IX three words are emphasized: *this* storm which drives the angel off course from his work of redemption, and which we call progress; and before that, the opposition between what *we* perceive in history (a chain of events) and what *he* sees (one single catastrophe, wreckage reaching up to the sky). Now, one could certainly object that in the other theses the author always conceals his ego beneath an abstraction ('historical materialism', 'the materialist historian'), or at least makes it appear in the third person. However, this programmatic encapsulation of 'I' in 'He' is never counterposed to 'We' but always to named adversaries. If the significance of the 'Angelus Novus' picture involves an opposition between the angel's view (catastrophe) and ours (events, progress), the author conceives himself as part of 'We', of the most general assumptions of our culture, and does not set himself against it as a higher being.

A second remark concerns the angel and his flight. Why is he flying against the storm?[39] First, let us confess our surprise at the peculiar image of an *angel* of history. Usually historians have chosen a muse as their higher being; the various angels who appear in the Bible and the Jewish tradition act as divine messengers, protectors, awakeners or avengers, or as ephemeral beings who exist only to sing their hymn in praise of God and then fade away. Each time the angel relates to God or humanity or both, but not to history. Besides, history in the singular – as in the modern philosophy of history which joins together past and future as a social process – is foreign to the Hebrew Bible. What the Bible knows is the past: in Hebrew this is typically denoted by the same word that refers to what the face is turned towards in attention; while the word for the future also signifies what is hidden behind one's back. The position and line of vision of the new (or still young) angel in the storm thus evoke the religious tradition, as does the storm itself. Furthermore, given that the Hebrew word *ruach* means both 'wind' and 'spirit', the storm here refers to the dynamic of human exploitation and domination of nature, which develops out of the termination of the Edenic order.[40] This dynamic of progress and reason, which since the Enlightenment has grown into a uniform historical process and promises to fulfil religious hopes through secular evolution, makes it impossible for the angel to carry through his message of redemption.

The herald of religious tradition, who knows of paradise, has another measure: namely, the hopes stored from the beginning in the religious tradition and in the dreams of childhood. He is startled at what he sees, because he cannot console himself with the philosophical promises that future history will indemnify the victims of the past according to a cost-benefit model of calculation. What is swept away by the history of progress piles up at his feet like massed debris of disappointments, defeats and sacrifices. But the victims no longer have access to the power of religious redemption; for in the raging wind of disenchantment the angel is driven up and away.

After all the erudition that has been brought to bear on Benjamin's angel, these few remarks on the text will probably seem all too slender. Nevertheless, important conclusions follow from the insight that it was not Benjamin and others like him, but the divine messenger, who was incapable of action. Thus, it is not the case that Benjamin was fleeing from the catastrophe into religion. Rather, he was recalling the hopes of redemption stored in the religious tradition,[41] so as to introduce them as a meaning and yardstick into human contact with history – both in reference to the past and for political action in the present.

Excursus on Recent Consideration of the Gender of Angels

One of the differences between Benjamin and representatives of the conservative revolution – whose work originated and took effect within similarly masculine milieux – is that women have recently been prominent in the reception of his thought. In particular, Susan Buck-Morss, Jeanne-Marie Gagnebin, Krista Greffrath, Karin-Maria Neuss, Marleen Stoessel, Sigrid Weigel and Liselotte Wiesenthal have been able to identify the dialectical tension in Benjamin's images of the angel and chess automaton and to appreciate their significance and historical context, whereas many male interpreters, from various political backgrounds, have almost compulsively eradicated this tension.[42] On the other hand, gender is evidently not sufficient as an intellectual category; for we also find Hannah Arendt in the radius of predominantly male projections, and not all men have remained under their sway when considering these texts.

A study of the 'angel' by the Parisian philosopher Christine Buci-Glucksmann – which, unlike other interpretations, states its angle of vision in the very title of the book, *Walter Benjamin and the Utopia of the Feminine*[43] – may help us to understand this difference better. The essay in question first appeared in the early 1980s, within a deconstructivist framework influenced by Nietzsche, Derrida and Lacan – evidently a new departure in the intellectual life of the author, who had previously been in the circle around Nicos Poulantzas and written orthodox Marxist works 'for Gramsci' and against social democracy.[44] In fact, after the turn to deconstructivism and feminism we no longer find any reference to this earlier layer of work.

The central idea of Buci-Glucksmann's interpretation is that Benjamin's early writings already displayed a fascination with constructions of femininity in Saint-Simonism and Baudelaire, particularly with the androgynous as a heroic ideal,[45] and that this was then combined with

Gershom Scholem's observations on the double gender (or 'bisexuality', as she calls it) of the godhead in parts of the Kabbala and Jewish mysticism since the Middle Ages.[46] It can be assumed that Benjamin was familiar with Scholem's early work of the 1920s, if not also with his deepening research from the years after the war to which Buci-Glucksmann refers. As to Benjamin's reception of Scholem, and Buci-Glucksmann's own work on nineteenth-century perceptions of femininity and the dual-gender potential of the sexes, she uncovers a great deal of evidence and embeds it within a presentation of the *oeuvre* as a succession of theatrical scenes. Finally, she offers a thought-provoking psychoanalytic interpretation of a dream about 'reading' that Benjamin had in the French internment camp. This dream, rich in sexual symbolism, gave him a rare sense of happiness which he reported in a letter to Gretel Adorno.[47] Buci-Glucksmann interprets this dream in Derridean language as 'arche-traces' of an incestuous primal scene, 'in which material and text are exchanged'. The details of her analysis are clear but not compelling – at least there is a (personal) motif of sudden, retrospective awareness: 'Something primeval is being repeated, something extreme, a catastrophe that has always happened before.'

From here on, the language becomes more obscure and emphatic, drawing on previously constructed associations from Benjamin's work, or from Derrida and Lacan, which have a weaker grasp on the text.[48] This leads up to a generalization from which the question of the angel is then developed: 'Performing in this well-known "border region" are the traces of blood, traces of writing [*écritures*], traces of social architecture deposited in the cities. Is the key perhaps that angel's stage, that Jewish Ariadne's thread?'[49] The imagery is quite bewildering. Performing traces? Can Ariadne's thread be transposed to the Jewish tradition and there be equated with a stage, 'the' angel's stage, even though there are so many different angels in that tradition? Can the key to a border region (of recall powers) be a stage? And to what is it the key: to the region, or to the play of blood, text and society? It all remains open. Then we are referred back to the feverish text of 1933 about the fallen angel with the anagram Agesilaus Santander, in which the angel's possible sexual duality is mentioned. The author associates this with the pseudonym Benedix Schönfliess , derived from the name of his maternal grandmother, which he had intended to use but never actually did. At the same time, the Kabbalistic hope in redemption is revived as the reunification of the sexually divided. Mysticism and scholasticism now mingle together:

> The bisexual angel, the secret name of the mother in the midst of the textual
> signifier, the trace of all traces: are these not the sign of a deviant and
> heretical name facing the dominant/paternal extraction? The stage of the
> text is anchored here – the stage from which Benjamin sets out towards the
> repressed, the outcast and the working class, to those who are 'nameless'.
> Here the angel of the 'family novel' tallies with those of the text and of
> history. And, of course, here is played out the fate of the writer Benjamin,
> whose cipher was 'catastrophe'.[50]

The trace of all traces to the mother has suddenly brought us, on the
second-to-last page, to the angel of history and thus to the theme of the
essay. The author provides us with new insights into the relationship
between family novel and writing; but history appears as apocryphal
and is simply appended to the problematic of the intellectual. If we look
at Benjamin's text in Reflection IX, however, we see that his image of
an angel of history does not display – or, if one prefers, betray – the
slightest trace of bisexuality. Maybe it is simply not the same angel. He
does use the ordinary German masculine form throughout, but
obviously not to rescue him for a male divinity. It is as if the angel's
gender, and therefore the conventional pronoun, were a matter of the
utmost indifference to him.

After a 45-page prolegomenon about angelic sexuality, writing and
dream memory, we are left with just one page for the tension in the
dialectical image to explode.[51] The author sees its dialectic not in the
contradiction between progress and the striving for redemption of the
angel who is incapable of action, but rather, as a good post-Marxist, in
progress as such, understood as a confrontation of victors and vanquished 'in the mute namelessness of a history still to be rewritten.'

> The other, complementary world of Kafka and Klee, the world/language of
> the 'theological dwarf' and the angel is undialectical. It refers to the
> interruption of history, to the catastrophe, the inhuman, and the flourishing
> and decline of the subject. It shows us the archaic, and barbaric side of our
> civilized society, the 'thing-like substance' of big cities, mass politics, the
> anthill state and modern bureaucracies.[52]

And that is all: keywords of deconstruction and posthistory, for which
a reading of Benjamin was hardly necessary. We have reached again the
safety of the ivory tower where Benjamin, in view of 'these two
languages and worlds', is certified as having a 'split style of writing'.
The Other of instrumental reason is here severed off and made incapable of acting upon it, even in a female manner; it thus becomes
ephemeral, a realm of shadows as the side on view. This was already
contained in the starting-point of the argument, which quotes Lacan's

wordplay on the feminine and the theological: '*Étrange* [alien] is a word that can be broken down into *Être-ange* [Angel-Being].'[53]

This excursus started from the observation that women hardly participated in the posthistory debate, but have played an important role in the interpretation of Benjamin, because they have mostly been better able than male colleagues to face and interpret the inner tension of his multilayered images. In the notes to this chapter, they have been a kind of constant countermelody to the dominant male styles of reading, with their tendency to activist projection and posthistorical retreat. Christine Buci-Glucksmann's interpretation of Benjamin is in this respect truly androgynous, but that has turned out to be not wholly advantageous. She shares with other women an inclination towards psychoanalytically informed analysis of references within Benjamin's imagery and life-history; but like many male interpreters, she largely dissociates this perceptual field from the social dimension, albeit with opposite effect. It is not the Other of reason that she masks over, but reason itself.

In Buci-Glucksmann's recent work the pre-feminist Marxist layer, which I assume to have been part of her life-history and theoretical formation, is sealed up with unexplained *topoi* of deconstruction and posthistory. The contents of this layer do not therefore develop but occasionally intrude as foreign bodies. Thus, whereas Benjamin sought to breathe new life into dialectics by means of active perceptions, her own apparatus concept of dialectics is dragged along unaltered. Free from any hindrance, it pushes forward the concept of the social, only now without a subject or subjectivity. This masking of the old layer, however, reacts upon the new and makes it appear ephemeral and often imprecise – especially when the object of enquiry oversteps the self-imposed limits of intellectual understanding. Anything beyond those limits lies in a kind of cloud, in which feelings and appreciations wander fancy-free or join up with spurious judgements. Let us take a single example. Just after the paragraph quoted above, where the author uses posthistorical platitudes to distance herself from now-time [*Jetzteit*], she signs off on a remarkably optimistic yet resigned note: 'This world is the prehistory of a history – one prophesied by Marx, but investigated by Benjamin's "weakened messianism".'[54] Mixed feelings here join together modules in a judgement in which literally nothing stands up to scrutiny. 'Posthistory' is not a prehistory: it was not as such either prophesied by Marx or investigated by Benjamin. Nor was Benjamin a political Messiah on study leave: he wanted to win back for the oppressed the hopes invested in almighty deities of this world and the next. And, in his view, each and every one of them had a 'weak messianic power'.

Thinking History in Danger

Benjamin's thinking on history, which he rather unconventionally describes as historical materialism, is situated within the tradition of Blanqui, Fourier and Marx. He would like to reunite this tradition, on a thoroughly human basis, with the meanings handed down in religious hopes (particularly in their Jewish expression). But his thinking also owes a great deal to Carl Schmitt, who is actually alluded to in the text of the Reflections. Benjamin knew and admired Schmitt's writings on 'political theology', 'political romanticism' and 'dictatorship', and he shared their problematic insofar as he also believed that a secularized society could not simply evade such basic questions as sovereignty or state of emergency which used to be stored in religion, but had to take them over and deal with them itself. Far from agreeing with Schmitt's answer to this problem, however, the left-wing Jewish émigré felt himself to be the enemy of the Catholic crown jurist and anti-semite.[55] Whereas Schmitt legitimated domination by the juridical equivalent of the religious, and increasingly sought to build the legal order on ontological or situational foundations and the decisionism of the rulers of the day, Benjamin adopted a completely different approach. In his central concepts of 'remembrance', 'now-time' and 'weak messianic power' is contained an appeal for the activation of alternative traditions. By making history contemporary, he seeks to redeem the hopes of those who have been passed over by history: that is, to release them for the freedom of further effectivity, so that their existential tradition-affirming power may be brought to bear in the struggle that must halt the catastrophic storm of history. That storm is already blowing from paradise, and is thus a force moving all history. For Benjamin, however, its basic momentum towards catastrophe had become fully evident with the devastating impact of fascism – and especially with the undermining of alternative orientations centred on Soviet Communism as a moral and state-political support after the Hitler–Stalin pact.

The weak messianic power 'given to each generation', which is conceived as a fundamental human capacity in every age, might learn from the Jewish tradition of expectation of the future, where 'every second of time was the strait gate through which the Messiah might enter'. The heavenly messenger evokes a capacity which today – when the dynamic of instrumental reason (or catastrophic progress) prevents him from awakening the dead and assembling the debris – must be taken over by humanity itself. And for this to be achieved, Benjamin says elsewhere, our contact with history must shake off the glorification of progress and its victors in the dubious continuum of empty time. Instead, it must open itself to the primal hopes of humanity which used to be stored in theology, but which more and more have to be redeemed, through historical awareness, from the hopes of the vanquished that are not bound to any current of tradition. In striving to put a revolutionary end to the domination of progress, the subject of historical emancipation ('the struggling, oppressed class') must as always return to the hopes of those who paved the way and were defeated – through a 'tiger's leap into the past' in appropriate historical forms.

Such a conception must have been hard to arrive at for a Jewish materialist who was in the most desperate personal straits, and who after the Hitler–Stalin Pact had lost his points of reference in the class struggle and been placed in precautionary internment during the *drôle de guerre*. At that time Benjamin was in agreement with Brecht about the depressing prospect of a 'time without history' – that is, without class struggles. (This symptom alone establishes a certain affinity with the later adepts of 'posthistory', despite his maintenance of a social and historical approach.) Characteristically, however, as a supporter of the Communist movement, Benjamin did not openly condemn Stalinism. In the Reflections he waged a surrogate battle against social democracy, accusing it of that blind faith in progress and exploitation of nature which marked the Communists of his time still more strongly.[56] Given the blocking of any practical political orientation, which he mentions only briefly with reference to the defeat and betrayal by unspecified leaders of the Left, the 'political worldling' creates room for himself to return to theoretical labour and draws a parallel between his considerations and the cloister meditations of medieval monks.

> At a moment when the politicians in whom the opponents of Fascism had placed their hopes are prostrate and confirm their defeat by betraying their own cause, these observations are intended to disentangle the political worldlings from the snares in which the traitors have entrapped them. Our consideration proceeds from the insight that the politicians' stubborn faith in progress, their confidence in their 'mass basis', and, finally, their servile integration in an uncontrollable apparatus have been three aspects of the same thing.[57]

It should be stressed that this global critique, which avoids any examination of his own errors of orientation, does not involve a more general withdrawal of the political worldling into the cloister, nor any

posthistorical levelling of the external world to dehumanized mono-
tony. Benjamin never acted the role of a political prophet. He belonged
among the victims, not the perpetrators. The political bearings for his
hope of survival were lost, but not the context of social meaning that
underlay his intellectual practice. Indeed, he 'regards it as his task to
brush history against the grain'. He seeks to attain a conception of
history for which the state of emergency is the rule, with the aim of
grasping the necessity of a 'real (that is, revolutionary) state of emergency' and 'improv[ing] our position in the struggle against Fascism'.

At the moment of danger, when he compressed the fruits of decades
of theoretical reflection, Benjamin used the space remaining to him to
outline the conception of a new historical practice that required a break
with historicism and the emptying of time.

> Historicism rightly culminates in universal history. Materialistic historio-
> graphy differs from it as to method more clearly than from any other kind.
> Universal history has no theoretical armature. Its method is additive; it
> musters a mass of data to fill the homogeneous, empty time. Materialistic
> historiography, on the other hand, is based on a constructive principle.
> Thinking involves not only the flow of thoughts, but their arrest as well.
> Where thinking suddenly stops in a configuration pregnant with tensions, it
> gives that configuration a shock, by which it crystallizes into a monad. A
> historical materialist approaches a historical subject only where he
> encounters it as a monad. In this structure he recognizes the sign of a
> Messianic cessation of happening, or, put differently, a revolutionary
> chance in the fight for the oppressed past. He takes cognizance of it in order
> to blast a specific era out of the homogeneous course of history – blasting a
> specific life out of the era or a specific work out of the lifework. As a result of
> this method the lifework is preserved in this work and at the same time
> cancelled [*aufgehoben*]; in the lifework, the era; and in the era, the entire
> course of history. The nourishing fruit of the historically understood
> contains time as a precious but tasteless seed.[58]

It has been said of this conception that it reflects the limited work
opportunities for an intellectual outsider.[59] That may be so. But it is not
thereby reduced to the level of an ineffectual tragedy, as the interpreter
in question would have it. Rather, it thinks the tragedy through in its
long-range perspectives.[60] The impetus given by Benjamin for the
building of a tradition of the oppressed – which can always be
conceived only individually – secures for itself theoretical constructs
such as the puppet which remain in the error-friendly state of the
hypothetical. That is sensible enough, because the whole cannot be
investigated – or, as Adorno might have put it, the whole is the untrue.
Without the fitting of such theoretical constructs, the tiger's leap into

the past would lead to random literary monads, whose relations with one another and to the Now would only be open to intuitive guesses, but could never be articulated and therefore criticized and revised. Or else, we would find ourselves with that synthetic historiography which is neither true in the particular nor discussible in the general; because it does not whole-heartedly orient towards the individual, it inevitably adds up the available traditions of the rulers and sticks together, in a pseudo-empirical or relativist manner, the principles on which the connections are constructed. Benjamin's struggle with what he calls historicism is actually directed against a filibustering meta-narrative about how wonderfully far we have got.[61]

Benjamin polemicized with equal clarity against the conversion of theoretical constructs into uncorroborated statements about the present or the future – a practice which legitimized either passivity or terror or both. The first he laid at the door of Kautskyite Social Democracy and the Popular Front; the second he considered only in letters. The seemingly peaceful variant, which aimed economistically at emancipation through overall social growth, was exposed as a short-sighted perspective liable to end in disaster; for the social alliance in question, by deadening the human energy of the oppressed with the promise of future goods, was grounded on the repressed exploitation of natural resources mistakenly held to be free. In the final Reflection, where he stressed the immensity of the nature thus abused by the catastrophe of progress, Benjamin took organic life on earth as one day and described the history of civilized man as one-fifth of the last second of the last hour, while messianic now-time compressed the whole history of humanity in the universe.

Benjamin opposes to this a historical experience of revolution, whose energy is destructive of existing relations. It feeds off the longing for a life without domination and exploitation, which is experienced in childhood and formulated in the religious tradition. In the Reflections, this thesis is not so much argued as presented in metaphors of time at a standstill. But later research into revolutions, from Günther Franz to Edward Thompson, has provided ample evidence in its support. It has been shown, for example, that in the Peasants' War or the revolts that took place during the Industrial Revolution, 'revolutionary masses at the moment of action' looked much more to the restoration of remembered conditions of justice than to the unfettering of the productive forces. Benjamin's hope is that, before this impetus falls victim to the erection of a new apparatus of rule and the onward march of production, it will be possible for him and the masses to bring time to a halt, to let this momentum develop, and to reach beyond the most insupportable

conditions to assist the species-recollection of the good life – or, as he
puts it, happiness – as the guide to human action. Through his tiger
leaps, the historian must stand at their side and blast the repressed
hopes out of the progress-levelled past. The further he reaches back, the
more clearly will he unearth the most general expectation of redemption preserved in the religious tradition. Now that secularization has
broken the link to the Beyond, which certainly displaced the realization
of justice yet made it present to everyone, the oppression remains
unresolved. No one will rouse the fallen; no one will reach paradise.[62]
But a weak power of redemption and reorientation persists within our
memory of the buried and repressed, as a constant challenge to
empirical experience. That is neither mysticism nor millenarianism,[63]
but an attempt to release, where historically possible, the desires that
have been sacrificed to the progress compulsion. A less far-reaching
quest for traditions would give the oppressed neither an orientation to
truth (that is, to the treasury of human experience buried in parts of the
tradition) nor the courage to take action. Benjamin saw the danger that
the Left would be crippled by fascism in power, and he sensed that
history was continuing its advance to catastrophes of unprecedented
scope. In the months when he was compressing his reflections on
history for the Left, the German authorities in Poland were renaming a
small village as Auschwitz and secretly building a camp there.[64]

Reason Unfit to Fly

Benjamin's friends in exile were all dismayed to learn of his death,[65] but
they reacted differently to his text of his reflections on history. Hannah
Arendt – who had seen the first draft in Paris and later described
Benjamin's dangerous frailness to a hardier sister, writing with
empathy but in a lightly disparaging tone – had a superficial and
misguided understanding of the core of the reflections.[66] Anders found
the text 'obscure and confused', while Brecht appreciated the clarification of a different way of thinking.[67] Adorno may have best grasped the
rejection of progress; but he found alien Benjamin's historical concre-
tism,[68] as well as his early closeness to the messianic tradition[69] and his
political hopes. Though deeply moved, he kept his distance: 'Benjamin's death makes publication a duty. The text has become his bequest.
Its fragmentary form implies the task of remaining faithful to the truth
of these reflections through ongoing thought.'[70]

Horkheimer wrote two essays which display some parallels to
Benjamin's movement of thought, but they distinguish themselves from
it by not finding any political perspective at the level of the philosophy

of history. In the first, whose English version is headed 'End of Reason',[71] Horkheimer looks back at the process whereby reason, now 'allegory without function' or a 'meaningless sign', has been reduced to an instrument of self-preservation – what he will later term 'instrumental reason' – and accentuated and neutralized in fascism. At the centre stands sorrow at the decline of the bourgeois individual, in whom the full ambivalence of reason was still embodied. The category of individuality has 'not stood up to large-scale industry', but has 'contracted' into an adaptive cell of the social struggle for survival, 'without dreams and without history'.[72] In the end the prospects are bleak. But in the self-produced hell, at least the dual nature of reason – to serve goals, and to escape them and call things by their right name – means that it still has the possibility of becoming aware, 'in the space of a moment', that 'when progress comes to an end' it will be left with nothing other than 'relapse into barbarism or the beginning of history'.[73] The ending is bleak, first, because the abrupt appearance of a 'beginning of history' leaves it open whether we are being referred once more to Marx's hope of an emancipated history after the revolution, or whether reason will be left just with the history of itself. But secondly, and more important, the hope that the preceding analysis might allow a sudden flash of insight ('Ideology lies within the nature of men themselves, of their mental atrophy and their dependence on banding together') has proved in practice to be implausible, even if it is theoretically granted to all. For although the fully rationalized world could also free everyone from the primacy of self-preservation, the social subject of such reason is dispersed in common humanity, so that any hope in it assumes a messianic quality: to all intents and purposes there is very little chance but then a possibility is suddenly introduced throught the insight of independent late-bourgeois intellectuals capable of shaking off the restraints.

In the second essay, which, like Benjamin's reflections on history, was written in spring 1940 under the impact of the Hitler–Stalin Pact, Horkheimer turned his attention to the 'authoritarian state'.[74] Essentially bidding farewell to his own Marxist analysis of fascism, which just a year before had still strongly marked his essay on the Jews,[75] he lays the basis for his theory of totalitarianism and its extension to Western industrialized societies. In his view, the three model orders of his time (New Deal, fascism, Stalinism) share a common element of politically mediated economics, and thus appear to be moving together towards variants of the same 'state capitalism'. Hence the focus shifts to the authoritarian state, of which Soviet-style 'integral statism' is only the 'most consistent' form, and nurtures the 'terrifying prospect of a universal period of authoritarianism'.

In Los Angeles, then, the course was being set for the Frankfurt variant of nascent posthistory, the 'administered world'[76] in which there would be no possibility of dialectical practice.[77] Although Adorno's negative dialectics of aesthetic–theological opening would later reclaim meaning for the 'Other',[78] the new course was made irreversible during the war as a result of the extermination of European Jewry. It found its form in a figure of thought relating to the philosophy of history: 'Myth is already enlightenment', and 'enlightenment with every step becomes more deeply engulfed in mythology'.[79] In common with other posthistorical constructs, such as Seidenberg's opposition between instinct and intellect,[80] this involved a conception of history as the middle phase in a dichotomous analysis of the domination of instrumental reason. The third phase was so total that it resembled the first in its annihilation of social subjectivity and freedom – which was now achieved through universalization of the blindness of an instrumentally shrunken reason. Now, however, the perspective was one of complete resignation. The sense of what it is like to be alive 'after Doomsday' – or, as he would later say, 'after Auschwitz'[81] – is expressed in a reflection written in autumn 1944 and published in Adorno's book of essays *Minima Moralia*.[82] Analysing the media war 'out of the firing-line', he engages in a kind of inner dialogue with Benjamin, whose hope in stilled time becomes a kind of catastrophic bullet hole in a formerly epic sense of life. 'Life has changed into a timeless succession of shocks, interspaced with empty, paralysed intervals.' The idea of a normal life and a rebuilding of culture, after the war and the murder of millions of Jews, appears to him 'idiotic'. More likely is the perpetuation of catastrophe, as he contemplates in helpless ambivalence the prospect of a revival of vendetta, with 'whole nations as the subjectless subjects' in an estranged homeland. The logic of history appears to him as destructive as the people who bring it about: 'Normality is death.'[83]

Adorno's feeling of meaninglessness crystallizes in the image of something flying. Of course, it is not an angel incapable of action, nor a dialectical image of any kind, but the negation of Kojève's position, as it were, which amounts to much the same thing for all that is to come.

> Had Hegel's philosophy of history embraced this age, Hitler's robot-bombs would have found their place. . .as one of the selected empirical facts by which the state of the world-spirit manifests itself directly in symbols. Like Fascism itself, the robots career without a subject. Like it they combine utmost technical perfection with total blindness. And like it they arouse mortal terror and are wholly futile. 'I have seen the world spirit', not on

horseback, but on wings and without a head, and that refutes, at the same stroke, Hegel's philosophy of history.[84]

Half a year before the Allied victory such associations moved out of context to America. Was there still a public for the evaluations made by the principal figures of the Frankfurt School, now that they had parted from the historical optimism of even a bourgeois Marxism? In 1944 and again in 1947 – after a further cleansing of Marxist concepts – they published their 'philosophical fragments' almost secretly. This was in keeping with one of their last reflections, whose depressive content was criticized by younger members of the School with the coded expression 'message in a bottle'. 'If words can be directed to anyone today, it is not to the so-called masses nor to the individual, who is without power, but rather to an imaginary witness to whom we leave them so that they will not completely perish with ourselves.'[85]

Horkheimer and Adorno returned to Frankfurt at a time when most West Germans, under the aegis of the new protecting powers, were seeking to practise precisely what Adorno described as 'idiotic': that is, a return to normality and a rebuilding of culture, in both cases secretly harking back to the prewar period. The terrain was thus rather unfavourable for the reception of their thought. Moreover, they had sealed up their memories of their earlier Marxist ideas, which might have undermined their authority by displaying changes in their thinking. Habermas, who was an assistant at the Institute for Social Research in the 1950s, reports the most grotesque symbolic action, when Horkheimer nailed into a box in the Institute cellar the only set of the *Zeitschrift für Sozialforschung* from the thirties, which had been the forum of erstwhile Critical Theory.[86] In the end, of course, the Undead resisted such incarceration and, once released, sucked all the more vigorously the blood of the following generation. In the newly receptive boom of the 1960s, the resigned diagnoses of the wartime years intersected with the critical theory of the thirties. The coffin opened, the bottle-message came ashore and – to the irritation of its authors – sharpened the contradictions of a detached activism which for a while celebrated the loss of reality as a seizure of power by the imagination.

Those with more experience at least pressed for a clarification of perspectives. As we have already seen, Habermas singled out Benjamin's 'theses' in order to free the puppet of historical materialism from the mystical wire-puller hidden beneath the table. Shortly before, Ulrich Sonnemann had urged the angel – who was still expected to issue directives on the philosophy of history – to improve his navigation by using a rear-view mirror. In his plea against the West Germans' fixation on the ruins of history, and for a strengthening of their powers of judgement, he sneered at Benjamin's ninth Reflection in the most confusing terms:

> But according to the theme of Marx's historical prophecy, which Benjamin made his own and which, thus undefeated, survives its own errors, the storm first becomes progress that can be called by no other name when the angel no longer allows himself to be driven by it, and the forward movement becomes his own. He must therefore turn round and face away from the pile of wreckage: the simplest aerodynamic consideration makes it clear that only in this way can he close his wings and perhaps even use them for the benefit of his journey, in which a start against the wind, perhaps made necessary by another turning back, must on no account be denied to him, so that he can determine his own flight path by using cross currents. He is thrown back on himself more fearfully than the most heretical Hegelian might have thought: if he turns around he sees that there is no trace of a road ahead, and if he wants to secure his course he must keep in rear view the path of the storm, which in a whirlwind is somewhat circular. If he does not escape, he will be driven back into paradise – something that even Benjamin did not imagine, because his storm was not a tornado. Paradise is life if you are coming away from it, but death if you must go back. What the angel of history needs, therefore, is a rear-view mirror. The idea of a critique of history fixes one's mind on such an installation.[87]

Readers will forgive me if I do not spoil their enjoyment with a critique of these lines. It may suffice to point out that the author has since offered the thesis of Germany's 'special way' [*Sonderweg*] for the angel's creative, dynamic take-off into the future – that is, the anti-Prussian critical variant of modernization theory.[88]

That the angel of history should turn to the future was also the view of the neo-Marxist opposition, before its horizon blurred into posthistory. And in the 1970s, as the more sensitive section of Marxist intellectuals in the GDR touched the limits of a realizable future, they began to feel that rational social action was impossible and to engrave the shadows of the past in their life-history.[89] The dramatist Heiner Müller perhaps most clearly traced back to national history the ossification of future perspectives in 'actually existing socialism', and froze the contradictions between tradition and action in posthistorical images. In the process meaningful action turned out to be deadly, 'survival to be a betrayal of the dead'.[90] Benjamin's hope that historical action might thrive on expectations buried in the past no longer had any support in history and appeared to have been almost systematically stifled. Some time earlier, in the context of a reissue of Brecht's fragment 'Travels of the God of Luck',[91] Müller had used the image of a 'luckless angel' for a contemporary reading of Benjamin, which he republished separately in 1982.

> The past is washed up behind him and debris rains down on his wings and shoulders, with the sound of funeral drums. Meanwhile the future piles up before him, presses his eyes in their sockets, bursts his eyeballs like a stone, turns his words round into a mouth gag, chokes him with his own breath. For a while longer the beating of his wings can still be seen, the rocks can be heard crashing down behind him, his futile movements become louder and more violent, from time to time, if also slower. Then the moment closes in on him. At the fast-buried stopping place the luckless angel finds rest, waiting for history in the petrification of flight vision breathing – until the renewed sound of powerfully beating wings spreads in waves through the stone and indicates that he is flying.[92]

Müller's angel is incomparably more weighed down than Benjamin's, to which it alludes. For the debris of history does not pile up at his feet but has actually buried him; and instead of seeking to redeem those who have been crushed, he himself represents the historical dialectic of progress at a standstill. And yet, beneath the ruins he starts to beat his wings again. In the context of a late Stalinism unwilling to accept its end, that must have been the expression of a desperate optimism which could not give up identification with secularized transcendence. But by the late 1980s it sounded to Müller's interpreters like a diagnosis of posthistory, and they advised the angel that his salvation lay in the standstill which lifted him out of history.[93]

Habermas has many times stressed the social progress involved in 'institutionalized freedoms' and a 'relatively conflict-free mode of collective life' in the Federal Republic.[94] Here he sees the main difference separating him from the basic assumptions of *The Dialectic of Enlightenment*, according to which 'instrumental reason has gained such dominance that there is really no way out of a total system of delusion [*Verblendungszusammenhang*], in which insight is achieved only in flashes by isolated individuals'. On the other hand, many symptoms of West German society 'frighten' him, and 'on an intuitive level [he is] quite convinced that something in this system is deeply amiss'. This contradiction irritates him and causes 'a certain oscillation' in his theoretical labour.[95] As if this oscillation were itself tied up, he used the image of an unserviceable flying-machine in 1980 to express the kernel of his cognitive interests, at the end of a road that began 'on the verge of posthistory'[96] and led him through historical materialism to the 'theory of communicative action'. It is a fine but sad image.

> The problem which made itself more clearly felt in the 1970s, and which an eloquent neo-conservatism would like to suppress all the more quickly, is the following. How is it possible to open up the compartmentalized expert fields of science, morals and art, and to connect them to the impoverished traditions of the lifeworld without losing their fragile distinctive meaning, in such a way that the separated moments of reason fit together again in the communicative practice of everyday life? As I see it today, the interpretive role of philosophy focused on the lifeworld is to help restart the interaction of the cognitive–instrumental with the moral–practical and the aesthetic–expressive, which is standing still like a moving body caught on a hook.
>
> Of course, the hook is rather well fixed. The life-forms of capitalist-modernized societies – of which bureaucratic socialism offers only a less attractive variant – are doubly disfigured: by the unstoppable invalidation of the substance of tradition, and by subjugation under the imperatives of a one-sided rationality confined to the cognitive–instrumental.[97]

There is no more talk of the storm; apparently it has blown itself out or the window has been shut. But the interaction has become confused, and the author has trouble in restoring equilibrium between its elements. Certainly it is hard to understand why this aesthetic machine, which keeps the appearance of flight before one's mind, has become caught up – and why that on which it is caught is called a hook. Presumably, as he was writing, another consequence of this perfect image of stationary mobility intruded itself: namely, that the moving body was hanging on a hook, and that what it was hanging from had not been built into the picture.

Notes

1. Lisa Fitko, ' "Der alte Benjamin". Flucht über die Pyrenäen', *Merkur* 36 (1982), pp. 35ff.
2. See the editor's report of his investigations, in Walter Benjamin, *Gesammelte Schriften* [henceforward *GS*], vol. V.2, ed. Rolf Tiedemann, pp. 1183–1205. At least since this extensive fragment became available, it has been clear that although Benjamin's friends continued to see him in exile as a literary critic, he actually had in mind a major project for what we would today call a history of everyday life in bourgeois society. His reflections, which so far have been the object of study only within the fields of literature and philosophy, were conceived with the aim of a history.
3. The historical character of this text is best defined in Heinrich Kaulen, *Rettung und Destruktion. Untersuchungen zur Hermeneutik Walter Benjamins*, Tübingen 1987, pp. 198ff. See also Susan Buck-Morss, *The Origin of Negative Dialectics. Theodor W. Adorno, Walter Benjamin and the Frankfurt Institute*, Hassocks 1977, pp. 43ff., 168ff.; and Chryssoula Kambas, *Walter Benjamin im Exil. Zum Verhältnis von Literaturpolitik und Ästhetik*, Tübingen 1983, pp. 201ff.

4. This, in my view, is the objection to the numerous, and often fertile, interpretations of these few pages – perhaps the most numerous in the recent history of ideas. Apart from Benjamin's existential straining to smuggle his secret message into the after-world, there are also signs in the text and in its unusually well-documented prehistory that he had the thought of death before him. To be more precise, there is the idea of the 'presence of mind' at the moment of danger, developed from the 'deathbed film', whereby the most important scenes in a person's life suddenly 'flash by' without any epic connection during the conscious stages of dying. The Day of Judgement thus appears as a 'summary court-martial' of the soul (Kafka), on a day like any other. It seems to me that Benjamin wanted to transpose this last capacity of human memory to a culture threatened by death.

5. This would have happened through Hannah Arendt and/or the American Consulate in Barcelona. See *GS* V.2, p. 1196, and the letter on p. 1203. Cf. *GS* I.3, p. 1223, which suggests that the manuscript was delivered to the Institute for Social Research in June 1941.

6. The biographical background is clarified in Hartmut Scheible, *Theodor W. Adorno*, Reinbek 1989, esp. pp. 68ff.; and Werner Fuld, *Walter Benjamin. Zwischen den Stühlen*, Munich/Vienna 1979. Hannah Arendt's characterization of Benjamin is at once empathetic and somewhat condescending: 'Introduction' to Walter Benjamin, *Illuminations*, London 1970, pp. 1ff.

7. The text of this first draft is in *GS* I.2, pp. 691ff. Important preparatory materials and Benjamin's own French translation are contained in *GS* I.3, pp. 1223ff. In earlier editions the text was accompanied by an early theological fragment which obscured its special character.

8. This was intended as the first stage of Benjamin's *Passagenwerk* project. See Walter Benjamin, *Charles Baudelaire*, London 1973.

9. Letter to Gretel Adorno, April 1940, in *GS* I.3, pp. 1226f.

10. He entrusted the advance work for the *Passagenwerk* to his friend Georges Bataille, who deposited it with the Bibliothèque Nationale. It survived the war and occupation, and was finally published forty-two years later.

11. In the last two years of his life, moreover, Benjamin aged in phases as a result of a heart-muscle disorder. The last pictures show a face that has noticeably spread out – wounded, defensive, furrowed and depressed. See Fuld's analysis of a picture from 1938 (pp. 271f.), and a photo from 1939 in Bernd Witte, *Walter Benjamin*, Reinbek 1985, p. 125.

12. On the background to the production of the 'theses', see *inter alia* Fuld, pp. 283ff., which refers to Franz von Baader's *Elementarbegriffe über die Zeit*. For a contrary view, see Gershom Scholem, *Walter Benjamin und sein Engel*, ed. Rolf Tiedemann, Frankfurt/Main 1983, pp. 201ff., which calls to our attention Leo Löwenthal's 1923 doctoral thesis on 'Franz von Baader's Philosophy of Society'. (*Schriften*, vol. 5, Frankfurt/Main, pp. 99ff.; cf. his recollection of Benjamin's interest in Baader – in ibid., vol. 4, pp. 123f.) Kambas refers to the fact that the conversations between Brecht and Benjamin in 1938 did not assume a victory over fascism in the foreseeable future, but rather the imminence of a 'historyless epoch'. 'Wider den "Geist der Zeit". Die antifaschistische Politik Fritz Liebs und Walter Benjamins', in Jacob Taubes, ed., *Der Fürst dieser Welt. Carl Schmitt und die Folgen*, Munich 1985, p. 287.

13. See chapter 5, section II above on Jünger's forest way.

14. For this reason the images do not allow of reciprocal interpretation – for example, when productive interest in history is described as 'a tiger's leap into the past', and its selective perception is compared to the sun's effect upon a heliotrope.

15. See Siegfried Unseld, ed., *Zur Aktualität Walter Benjamins*, Frankfurt/Main 1972; Peter Bulthaupt, ed, *Materialien zu Benjamins Thesen 'Über den Begriff der Geschichte'*, Frankfurt 1975; Christoph Hering, *Die Rekonstruktion der Revolution. Walter Benjamins messianischer Materialismus in den Thesen 'Über den Begriff der Geschichte'*, Frankfurt 1983. Earlier approaches are briefly surveyed in Gerhard

Kaiser, *Benjamin. Adorno. Zwei Studien*, Frankfurt/Main 1974, pp. 1–13. Since the publication of the *Passagen* fragments, discussion of Benjamin's later view of history has proceeded from a broader foundation; it can best be followed in the three volumes edited by Bolz and others: Norbert Bolz and Richard Faber, eds, *Walter Benjamin. Profane Erleuchtung und rettende Kritik*, 2nd edn, Würzburg 1985; Bolz, ed., *Antike und Moderne. Zu Walter Benjamins Passagen*, Würzburg 1986; and Bolz and Bernd Witte, eds, *Passagen. Walter Benjamins Urgeschichte des XIX. Jahrhunderts*, Munich 1984. On the international discussion see the report in Klaus Garber, 'Walter Benjamin in Paris und Berlin', in Bolz/Faber, pp. 9ff.

16. Jürgen Habermas, 'Consciousness-Raising or Rescuing Critique', in Gary Smith, ed., *On Walter Benjamin: Critical Essays and Recollections*, Cambridge, Mass. 1988, pp. 113–14. The generational and gender difference of approach is expressed in the sharp criticism of Habermas by, for example, Karin-Maria Neuss (*Auf der Suche nach Walter Benjamin*, diss., Zurich/Constance 1987, pp. 94ff.), who investigates Benjamin's intermediate position between Marxism and Judaism in terms of his life-history. A caustic critique of science is contained in Liselotte Wiesenthal, *Zur Wissenschaftstheorie Walter Benjamins*, Frankfurt/Main 1973. See also Seyla Benhabib's critique of the reformist atrophy of the utopian concept of emancipation: *Critique, Norm and Utopia: A Study of the Foundations of Critical Theory*, New York 1986, pp. 327ff.

17. Habermas, 'Consciousness-Raising or Rescuing Critique', p. 121.

18. The German text reads: *Sie kann es ohne weiteres mit jedem aufnehmen, wenn sie die Theologie in ihren Dienst nimmt*, so that the question is whether the second *sie* (a pronoun referring to the puppet) is subject or object of the verb *nimmt. Trs. note.*

19. *GS* I.3, p. 1247. Several authors have referred to this same passage. See, for example, Hering (p. 22), who mostly varies in the closest possible way on Benjamin's own words in his otherwise extremely dogmatic study that tends towards idealization. Similarly close to the text but without such dogmatism is the excellent work of Jeanne-Marie Gagnebin, *Zur Geschichtsphilosophie Walter Benjamins. Die Unabgeschlossenheit des Sinns*, Erlangen 1978, esp. pp. 149f.

20. Kaiser, p. 16. The same essential point is repeated in his ' "Der profane Text eines profanen Autors" oder "Rückübersetzung des Materialismus in Theologie" ', in idem, *Neue Antithesen eines Germanisten 1974–1975*, Kronberg 1976, pp. 99ff. Kambas offers a similar view in *Benjamin im Exil*, p. 216. The misreading of Benjamin's purpose by Habermas and Kaiser was corrected in Krista Greffrath's painstaking study of his ambiguities: *Metaphorischer Materialismus. Untersuchungen zum Geschichtsbegriff Walter Benjamins*, Munich 1981, pp. 11ff. and p. 146, note 15; cf. Alo Allkemper, *Rettung und Utopie. Studien zu Adorno*, Paderborn 1981, p. 34. The whole controversy, though ignoring Habermas, has now been carefully reappraised in Kaulen, pp. 239ff.

21. Heinz-Dieter Kittsteiner, 'Die "Geschichtsphilosophischen Thesen" ', *alternative* 10 (1967). The directness of Benjamin's requisitioning for anti-imperialist agitation is illustrated by Helmut Salzinger, 'Walter Benjamin – Theologe der Revolution', *Kürsbiskern* (1968), pp. 629ff. At that time the Frankfurt students wanted to name their institute after Benjamin. See Momme Brodersen, ed., *Benjamin auf Italienisch. Aspekte einer Rezeption*, Frankfurt/Main 1982, p 110.

22. Eight years later Kittsteiner wrote in the preface to a reissue of his article: 'The bursting contradictions of what was then called "late capitalism". . .appeared to many as the possibility of breaking open the bad continuum of history and producing a "profane order" geared to "happiness". In the process a tradition suppressed by the "rulers" gradually revealed itself; as we learnt of its tabooed theories, we felt tied to all previously vanquished fighters against repression and exploitation. Our pictures, banners and red flags were to shine back into history and recharge the poor excluded ones with revolutionary "now-time". We were expected on earth.' In Bulthaupt, p. 39.

23. Kittsteiner, 'Die "Geschichtsphilosophischen Thesen", pp. 243ff. Cf. the contrary views of Helmut Pfotenhauer in 'Eine Puppe in türkischer Tracht', in Bulthaupt, esp.

pp. 279ff. and 289; and *Ästhetische Erfahrung und gesellschaftliches System. Untersuchungen zu Methodenproblemen einer materialistischen Literaturanalyse am Spätwerk Walter Benjamins*, Stuttgart 1975, p. 26.

24. In Bulthaupt, p. 40.

25. H.D. Kittsteiner, 'Walter Benjamin's Historicism', *New German Critique* 39, (1986). By referring principally to Karl Heussi, Hermann Lotze and Leopold von Ranke, Kittsteiner was able to locate Benjamin as a materialist version of the historicist tradition in the philosophy of history, including its critique of progress and its partly monadological sense of the concrete. That is certainly a step forward in relation to the current philosophical over-elevation of Benjamin, for it moves the so-called theses closer to their problematic of a dialectical contribution to an epistemology of history. On the other hand, it increases the danger of conceptual confusion, because Benjamin, like many of his contemporaries, understood something different by 'historicism': namely, the tendency of academic historiography to descriptive evolutionism and a vision focused on the successful.

26. See his concluding formulation from 1967, apparently directed against Adorno, Scholem and their followers: 'Today the method of interpreting Benjamin theologically has its correlate in the negation of possible progress as social transformation.'

27. 'Walter Benjamin's Historicism', p. 214.

28. Ibid., p. 215.

29. Ibid., p. 212.

30. Kittsteiner, 'Über das Verhältnis von Lebenszeit und Geschichtszeit', in D. Kamper and Ch. Wulf, eds, *Die sterbende Zeit*, Darmstadt 1987, pp. 72ff., 76f. (originally a contribution to the series on aesthetics in posthistory edited by Taubes and Kamper).

31. In addition to other sources already mentioned, see especially Renato Solmi, 'Einleitung in den Angelus Novus' (1962), in Brodersen, pp. 38ff; Ulrich Sonnemann, *Negative Anthropologie. Vorstudien zur Sabotage des Schicksals*, Reinbek 1969, p. 277; Hannah Arendt, 'Introduction', pp. 12–13; Gershom Scholem, 'Walter Benjamin and His Angel' (1972), in Smith, pp. 51ff.; Peter von Haselberg, 'Benjamins Engel' in Bulthaupt, pp. 337ff.; Rolf Tiedemann, 'Historical Materialism or Political Messianism? An Interpretation of the Theses "On the Concept of History"', *The Philosophical Forum* 15, 1–2, pp. 76ff.; Gianni Vattimo, 'Ursprung und Bedeutung des utopischen Marxismus (Marxismus und Geist der Avantgarde)', in Brodersen, pp. 64ff.; Gagnebin, pp. 84ff.; Otto Karl Werckmeister, 'Walter Benjamin, Paul Klee, and the Angel of History', *Oppositions* 25 (Fall 1982), pp. 103ff.; Karol Sauerland, 'Benjamins Revision der bisherigen materialistischen Geschichtsbetrachtung', *Neue Rundschau* 93 (1982), pp. 60ff.; Marleen Stoessel, *Aura. Das vergessene Menschliche. Zu Sprache und Erfahrung bei Walter Benjamin*, Munich 1983, pp. 166ff.; Christine Buci-Glucksmann, *Walter Benjamin und die Utopie des Weiblichen*, Hamburg 1984; Jürgen Ebach, 'Der Blick des Engels', in Bolz/Faber, eds, *Walter Benjamin*, pp. 67ff.; Sigrid Weigel, *Die Stimme der Medusa. Schreibweisen in der Gegenwartsliteratur von Frauen*, Reinbek 1989, pp. 270ff.; Kaulen, pp. 212ff.

32. 'Theses on the Philosophy of History', in *Illuminations*, pp. 259–60. Emphases restored from German original.

33. This is true of Solmi, Arendt, Scholem, Haselberg, Tiedemann, Fuld, Werckmeister, Sauerland, Witte, Kaulen and others. Weigel's reading is the most accurate (p. 273), resting on Freud's distinction between the non-simultaneity of consciousness and memory traces. (On this problematic see Christine Bange, *Die zurückgewiesene Faszination. Zeit, Tod und Gedächtnis als Erfahrungskategorien bei Baudelaire, Benjamin und Marguerite Duras*, Weinheim/Basle 1987, p. 175.) Cf. Gagnebin, pp. 88f. and Stoessel, pp. 187f.

34. Scholem ('Walter Benjamin and His Angel', pp. 57ff.) reproduces the notes which Benjamin wrote in August 1933 under the name Agesilaus Santander (supposedly an anagram of *Der Angelus Satanas*). The minor controversy over their significance is discussed in Jürgen Ebach, 'Agesilaus Santander und Benedix Schönflies', in Bolz/

Faber, eds, *Antike und Moderne*, pp. 148ff., where biblical references further corroborate Benjamin's identification with the picture at that time. See also the excursus on pp. 112ff. above.

35. See Ebach, 'Der Blick des Engels' and 'Agesilaus Santander'.

36. Rudolf Bahro, *Logik der Rettung. Wer kann die Apokalypse aufhalten?* Stuttgart 1987, pp. 101f. The chapter heading is 'The Drive of the Rationalist Demon', and the sub-heading 'History is Psychodynamics'.

37. The defect consists in overdevelopment of the intellect ('the brain') as the separate organ of self-preservation. 'The ego turns out to be. . .not only a spiritual prison but a material armour which drags the hero into the depths.' Ibid., p. 197.

38. Interpreters tend to draw on these drafts as if they had not been discarded. The distorting effect of such montages, which are alien to the multilayered drafting of an author's thought, can be most clearly seen in Kaulen's otherwise scrupulous interpretation: *Rettung und Destruktion*, p. 217. In fact, Reflection IX seems to be the only one which Benjamin composed in one burst without a series of drafts; there is only a note indicating that he originally intended to place it at the beginning. Kaulen puts this note together with fragments from earlier drafts of other theses, in which the historian appears to support himself on Friedrich Schlegel as a 'backward looking prophet', and uses various signs of omission to assemble a sequence whose only justification is the fact that both figures looked towards the past. Soon the historian (and the interpreter) are rising into thin air.

39. It is incomprehensible why Scholem, arguing against Arendt (and his own text), considers that the storm drives the angel 'forwards not backwards into the future, before which he rushes ahead as its herald', so that in the end he is forced to ascribe a cyclical view of history to Benjamin, rather than one of the contradictoriness of progress and historical endeavour. See Scholem, 'Walter Benjamin und sein Engel', in Unseld, p. 138, n. 25.

40. See Ebach, 'Der Blick des Engels', pp. 72f., 85.

41. Rainer St Zons completely evacuates this dimension in talking of Benjamin's 'coded longing to undo' the past. ('Walter Benjamins "Thesen über den Begriff der Geschichte" ', *Zeitschrift für philosophische Forschung* 34 (1980), p. 375.) Here again a great deal of confusion is caused by montages speculatively assembled from preliminary materials. Several interpreters deduce Benjamin's concept of theology from a seemingly fine image in the *Passagenwerk* apocrypha, which appears to them to make Marxism a kind of mirror-writing or erasing of Revelation. (See, for example, Kaiser, 'Der profane Text', pp. 115f.) Benjamin, however, seems to have understood the weakness of the image and, although he noted it down, he did not use it in the text of the Reflections: 'My thinking is related to theology as blotting-paper is to ink. It becomes saturated with it. But if it was just up to the blotting-paper, nothing would remain of what was written.' (*GS* I.3, p. 1235; I.5, p. 588.) Blotting-paper does indeed soak up surplus ink, but it also serves to fix the script. In reality nothing is left up to the blotting-paper: it must let the words stand as they are. Perhaps, in view of the author's profane pattern of meditation, this consideration first led him to think himself out of, rather than into, the angel. But that is not something we can know.

42. Gagnebin (p. 1) writes that her 'sometimes stolid reading' is 'a reaction to a tendency in the reception of Benjamin's work to take his writings as a dark treasury of beautiful quotations for use in profound disquisitions. Benjamin comes out of this rather badly.. . . Here we shall venture to suppose that Benjamin's text has a certain coherence which can be rendered explicit.'

43. Buci-Glucksmann, *Walter Benjamin und die Utopie des Weiblichen*, which includes an essay published in French in 1982 as 'Walter Benjamin et l'ange de l'histoire'.

44. *Gramsci and the State*, London 1980; *L'État social-democrate*, Paris 1981; *La gauche, le pouvoir, le socialisme. Hommage à Nicos Poulantzas*, Paris 1983. Since then Buci-Glucksmann has mainly published work on the baroque prompted by readings of Foucault and Benjamin.

45. *Walter Benjamin und die Utopie des Weiblichen*, pp. 11ff.

46. She may be referring here to the incorporation of gnostic and archaic notions of a dual-gender divinity into the Kabbala, and to the early heretical ideas of women's emancipation in the 'messiah' of the Sabbatian movement within seventeenth-century Jewish thought. See Gershom Scholem, *Ursprünge und Anfänge der Kabbala*, Frankfurt/Main 1962, pp. 143ff. (of which the studies on the book *Bahir* date back to the 1920s); *On the Kabbalah and Its Symbolism*, New York 1965; *Main Trends in Jewish Mysticism*, New York 1961, esp. pp. 287ff.; and *Sabbatai Sevi. The Mystical Messiah*, London 1973, pp. 403ff.

47. Benjamin, *Briefe*, vol. 2, Frankfurt 1978, pp. 828ff.; Buci-Glucksmann, *Walter Benjamin und die Utopie des Weiblichen*, pp. 78ff.

48. The leitmotif of the associations is provided by Karl Kraus's motto: 'Origin is the goal', which Benjamin placed at the head of Reflection XIV on the 'tiger's leap into the past' (for example, from the French Revolution back to Ancient Rome). Reflection IX on the angel, however, is preceded by a verse from a private poem of Scholem's about the Klee picture:

> My wing is ready for flight,
> I would like to turn back.
> If I stayed timeless time,
> I would have little luck.

49. Buci-Glucksmann, *Walter Benjamin und die Utopie des Weiblichen*, p. 82.

50. Ibid., p. 85.

51. Cf. ibid., p. 53, where the puppet–hunchback relation in the image of the chess automaton is described as a 'duel that cannot be decided'.

52. Ibid., p. 86.

53. Ibid., p. 43.

54. Ibid., p. 86.

55. This is why the positive references from the Weimar Republic are dropped once Benjamin goes into exile. See Michael Rumpf, 'Radikale Theologie. Benjamins Beziehung zu Carl Schmitt', in Peter Gebhardt et al., eds, *Walter Benjamin – Zeitgenosse der Moderne*, Kronberg 1976; Ellen Kennedy, 'Carl Schmitt and the Frankfurt School', *Telos* 73 (1987); and the discussion sparked off by it in Germany, in *Geschichte und Gesellschaft*: Alfons Söllner, 'Jenseits von Carl Schmitt. Wissenschaftliche Richtigstellungen zur politischen Theorie im Umkreis der "Frankfurter Schule" ', No. 12 (1988) pp. 502ff., and Ulrich K. Preuß, 'Carl Schmitt und die Frankfurter Schule', No. 13 (1987), pp. 400ff. Liselotte Wiesenthal (pp. 9ff.) shows the conceptual significance of the Extreme in Benjamin's debt to Cassirer and Schmitt. The reference to Schmitt's *Political Theology* and to the Jewish theological revival led by Franz Rosenberg goes back to Benjamin himself. It should be sharply distinguished from the posthistorical attempt to capture him by the followers of Jacob Taubes (described by the rearguard of the avant-garde as a 'messiah clique'), who place him in the same context as authors like Oswald Spengler, Martin Heidegger and Ernst Jünger – whom Benjamin already regarded as enemies in the Weimar Republic and openly attacked. See, for example, Norbert Bolz, 'Vorschule der profanen Erleuchtung', in Bolz/Faber, eds, *Profane Erleuchtung*, pp. 190ff.; and 'Prostituiertes Sein' in Bolz/Faber, eds, *Antike und Moderne*, pp. 191ff. In his varied interpretations of Benjamin from a posthistorical viewpoint, Bolz is almost compulsively led to draw parallels with the conservative revolution. Such provocative recourse to the latency level of mere contemporaneity reduces the difference between their answers – and hence the specificity of the authors themselves – to the status of an escape clause. For his part, Julian Roberts completely fails to appreciate the historical problematic of the 'Theses', in his reading of them as a left-utopian variation on Klages and Heidegger. *Walter Benjamin*, London 1982, pp. 196ff.

56. Kambas demonstrates Benjamin's internal critique of Stalinism, but also shows that it directly related, on the one hand, to the Popular Front Socialists, and on the other

hand to the context of his work on the nineteenth century. *Walter Benjamin im Exil*, pp. 203ff.

57. Reflection X, *Illuminations*, p. 260.
58. Reflection XVII, ibid., p. 141.
59. Werckmeister, pp. 118ff.
60. Since historians appear to have slept right through the Benjamin debate – which was of no use either to them or to the discussion – their contributions left something to be desired in the unfortunate and falsely polarized debate over empirical versus structural history, as well as in the efforts to reinvigorate the discipline in general. The significance of Benjamin's theory of experience for historical practice, which already emerged in Habermas's 'rescuing critique', has now been demonstrated in Kaulen, *Rettung und Destruktion*, and in various contributions to the volumes edited by Norbert Bolz et al. See especially Michael Löwy, 'Kritik des Fortschritts', in Bolz/Faber, eds, *Antike und Moderne;* 'Revolution against "Progress": Walter Benjamin's Romantic Anarchism', *New Left Review* 152, July–August 1985.
61. Josef Fürnkäs refers, in connection with Benjamin's prose, to the surrealist and messianic elements in his idea of universal history: a 'world of all-round, integral actuality' in which 'the past has become quotable in each of its moments'; 'integral prose which has burst the chains of the script and is understood by all men'. *Surrealismus als Erkenntnis. Walter Benjamin – Weimarer Einbahnstraße und Pariser Passagen*, Stuttgart 1988, p. 7.
62. See Benjamin's correspondence with Horkheimer from spring 1937, which is reported in Tiedemann, 'Historischer Materialismus', pp. 87f.
63. Roland Kany sees Benjamin as merely an irrational 'posthistorical' prophet of the Apocalypse, sacrificing historical truth and continuity to a political instruction about access to the past – something for which the Nazis also strove, and which in the end serves the mobilization of the instincts. Kany's furious judgements, however, should be seen against a background of epistemological fictions alien to history. *Mnemosyne als Program. Geschichte, Erinnerung und die Andacht zum Unbedeutenden im Werk von Usener, Warburg und Benjamin*, Tübingen 1987, pp. 237ff.
64. Wolfgang Kraushaar refers to this coincidence in 'Auschwitz ante', in Dan Diner, ed., *Zivilisationsbruch. Denken nach Auschwitz*, Frankfurt/Main 1988, pp. 201ff., 240f. Remarkably he thinks it possible to reconstruct Benjamin's thinking about empirical history without taking into account his specific observations at the moment of danger.
65. The distance of such news in the emigration, as well as the closeness of a weak power that could be delivered from despair, can be sensed in a poem that Brecht wrote in Los Angeles.

> I'm told you raised your hand against yourself
> Anticipating the butcher.
> After eight years in exile, observing the rise of the enemy
> Then at last, brought up against an impassable frontier,
> You passed, they say, a passable one.

> Empires collapse. Gang leaders
> Are strutting about like statesmen. The peoples
> Can no longer be seen under all these armaments.

> So the future lies in darkness and the forces of right
> Are weak. All this was plain to you
> When you destroyed a torturable body.

'On the Suicide of the Refugee W.B.', trs John Willett, in *Bertolt Brecht Poems*, ed. John Willett and Ralph Manheim, London 1976, p. 363; *Gesammelte Werke*, p. 828.
66. See Arendt, 'Introduction', pp. 19–38.

67. See the editorial documentation in *GS* I.3, pp. 1227f.

68. Adorno saw Benjamin as a philosopher, not a historian seeking to provide a foundation for his practice. In retrospect he formulated the perfect expression of his male-bourgeois expectations: 'From the very beginning I had the highest and the greatest hopes of Benjamin.' The draft of the *Passagenwerk* appeared to him to involve the idea of a 'philosophy at once concrete and transcendent'. 'When I received the news of his death in autumn 1940 in New York, I really and quite literally had the feeling that by this death. . .philosophy had been robbed of the best it could have hoped for.' (*Über Walter Benjamin*, Frankfurt/Main 1968, pp. 14f.) Cf. Wiesenthal (pp. 179ff.), who speaks for Adorno against Tiedemann in showing that Benjamin was no Hegelian. Horkheimer, on the other hand, in an early essay on Bergson which also bore heavily on Benjamin's concept of experience, noted the redemptive task of the historian that followed from his atheism of the time. *Zeitschrift für Sozialforschung* 3 (1934), pp. 321ff.

69. See Anson Rabinbach, 'Between Enlightenment and Apocalypse: Benjamin, Bloch and Modern German Jewish Messianism', *New German Critique* 34 (1985); and on Adorno's negative theology, Micha Brumlik, 'Theologie und Messianismus im Denken Adornos', in H. Schröter and S. Gürtler, eds, *Ende der Geschichte*, Münster 1986.

70. In Benjamin, *GS* I.3, p. 1224 – the unpublished draft of a preface to the small-run hectograph edition of the text in Institut für Sozialforschung, ed., *Walter Benjamin zum Gedächtnis*, Los Angeles 1942. On Horkheimer's and Adorno's selective and rather crude appreciation of the theses, see Rolf Wiggershaus, *Die Frankfurter Schule. Geschichte, Theoretische Entwicklung, Politische Bedeutung*, Munich 1988, pp. 348f. On Benjamin's significance for Adorno and the latter's replacement of redemptive history with the utopian content of art, see Buck-Morss.

71. In *Studies in Philosophy and Social Science* 9 (1942), pp. 366ff.

72. 'Vernunft und Selbsterhaltung', in Max Horkheimer, *Gesammelte Schriften*, vol. 5, Frankfurt/Main 1987, pp. 320ff. and esp. 334ff.

73. Ibid., p. 350.

74. Ibid., pp. 293ff.

75. See Diner, pp. 30ff.

76. See the retrospective interview with Horkheimer: *Verwaltete Welt?*, Zurich 1970.

77. Brumlik (p. 47) dates the despair, the 'gateway of knowledge', to the beginning of the Second World War.

78. See Theodor Adorno, *Negative Dialectics*, New York 1973.

79. Theodor Adorno and Max Horkheimer, *Dialectic of Enlightenment* (1944), London 1986, pp. 11–12.

80. See chapter 3 above.

81. See Detlev Claussen, 'Nach Auschwitz', in Diner, pp. 54ff. On the later conception of history, see Hartmut Scheible, 'Geschichte im Stillstand. Zür Ästhetischen Theorie Theodor W. Adornos', in Heinz Ludwig Arnold, ed., *Theodor W. Adorno*, Munich 1977, pp. 92ff.

82. Theodor Adorno, *Minima Moralia: Reflections from Damaged Life*, London 1978, p. 54.

83. Ibid., pp. 55–6.

84. Ibid., p. 55.

85. Horkheimer, *Gesammelte Schriften*, 5, p. 288.

86. Jürgen Habermas, *Philosophisch-politische Profile*, Frankfurt/Main 1987, p. 415.

87. Sonnemann, p. 277.

88. Most recently, in the context of the historians' dispute, he polemicized against Habermas's view that the unreserved opening of the Federal Republic to the political culture of the West had been a 'great intellectual achievement of our postwar period'. See Sonnemann, 'Geschichte als Flucht vor ihr', in Christoph Türke, ed., *Perspektiven: Kritischer Theorie*, Lüneburg 1988, pp. 31ff., where he refers –

presumably with a faded rear-view mirror – to Hans-Ulrich Wehler as a psychohistorian shrouded by public silence who had at least 'begun' with a reappraisal of the past.

89. Even in the thaw of the 1950s, the idea of progress consolidated in catastrophe was the greatest obstacle to the reception of Benjamin in the GDR. Hans Heinz Holz, in a major essay on Benjamin which was otherwise at pains to be thorough and accurate, got himself out of it by simply ignoring Reflection IX and covering up the angel of history with half a sentence: 'Benjamin also polemicized against the smug faith in progress.' 'Prismatisches Denken. Über Walter Benjamin aus Anlaß der Veröffentlichung seiner ausgewählten Schriften', *Sinn und Form* 8 (1956), p. 544.

90. Rolf Günter Renner, *Die postmoderne Konstellation*, p. 327.

91. 'Reisen des Glücksgotts'. Only a few songs have been published from this work that Brecht began in 1941 and continued during the war. It cannot be established, therefore, whether there is a Brechtian source for Müller's 'luckless angel'. But it would be interesting to know, because Brecht had learnt of Benjamin's 'On the Concept of History' shortly before starting work on this desperately optimistic project in Los Angeles. It may be, of course, that Müller contributed this himself, following the publication of Benjamin's selected works in 1955.

92. Heiner Müller, 'Glücksgott', in idem, *Theater-Arbeit*, West Berlin 1986, p. 18. The text was written in 1958, and included in Müller, *Rotwelsch*, West Berlin 1982, p. 87.

93. See Renner, p. 327. More circumspect is Georg Wieghaus, *Heiner Müller*, Munich 1981, pp. 83ff.

94. 'Political Experience and the Renewal of Marxist Theory', an interview from 1979 with Detlef Horster and William van Reijen, reprinted in Peter Dews, ed., *Habermas: Autonomy and Solidarity*, London 1986, p. 79. For the context see Helmut Dubiel, *Kritische Theorie der Gesellschaft. Eine einführende Rekonstruktion von den Anfängen im Horkheimer–Kreis bis Habermas*, Weinheim/Munich 1988, pp. 87ff.

95. Ibid., pp. 78–9. Cf. Habermas, 'The Entwinement of Myth and Enlightenment: Re-Reading *Dialectic of Enlightenment*', *New German Critique* 35 (1985).

96. In 'Consciousness-Raising or Rescuing Critique', p. 121, Habermas could not help suspecting 'that an emancipation without happiness and lacking in fulfilment might not be just as possible as relative prosperity without the elimination of repression. This question is not without risks; however, on the verge of *posthistoire*, where symbolic structures are exhausted, worn thin and stripped of their imperative functions, neither is it entirely idle.'

97. Jürgen Habermas, *Philosophisch-politische Profile*, enlarged edition, Frankfurt/Main 1987, pp. 12f.

7

The Dissolution of History

And here we still are, acting with slogans from the last century, splitting hairs and struggling with our greater fatigue. We know that is not what we live and could die for. Our blood will be spilt, and no one will tell us why.

Christa Wolf (1979) No Place on Earth

I THE LEGACY OF SALVATIONIST HISTORY

In Jewish–Christian culture three aspects of history are combined in a unique manner. The origin myth (history of creation) extends into a temporal structure of the world in which the believer's expectation of redemption is embedded (history of salvation), so that the imminence of salvation or judgement is secured or announced through a humanization of the Divine. The Western religious tradition thus passes down an understanding of the world as history, which is interwoven with hopes of individual redemption and with the identity of God and man as the decisive turning-point. Within this framework, however, an empirical science of the course of the world developed out of precursors in Antiquity. Its aim was to safeguard tradition in the particular (including exceptional events and deeds) and to provide a normative evaluation of ever recurring situations.

This preservation of chronological and analogical thinking within the framework of salvationist history inevitably ended in crisis. For it eventually became apparent that there were worldly reasons to change the basic conditions of existence and to detach them from the cyclicity of nature. Once new discoveries burst the limits of the world, and trade, technology and institutionalized relations of power freed part of society from direct ties with the sequences of nature, elements of a total explanation of the world could be transferred from the jurisdiction of salvationist history to the scientific processing of experience. At the same time, the latter increasingly had to measure itself against the comprehensiveness and meaning-content of the former. In other words,

out of the various histories through which men and women reached
agreement over the origins and institutions of their group and passed
on experience that fitted it for continued existence, a new *universal*
history had to come into being, with a perspective that would provide
an understanding of the cosmos to replace the religious world-view.

The critical point in this process was reached when it became
possible to demand that the historical aspect of salvationism should be
made an area of human responsibility, and that religion should be
limited to a relationship between God and the individual soul. In this
respect the Reformation laid the groundwork, while the Enlightenment
carried it to the level of thought (in what might be called the 'axial age')
and began to restructure social space through the political and technical–
industrial revolutions.[1]

The advance of scientific pretensions into the domain of religion
produced truly magnificent intellectual endeavours, since they had to
outmatch the power of myth. It was the heroic age of the intelligentsia,
whose dimensions have never ceased to inspire a sense of nostalgia
among the educated middle classes and cultural producers. The mind
breathed power. In the period when the cultured bourgeoisie was
making one conquest after another, its claims were staked out in the
spaces wrested from salvationist history, through systems of thought
that apprehended the world as a whole, sought to structure it genetically, and filled it with a meaning which linked individual strivings with
the development of the world. In fact, the most successful of these
projects had an influence which cannot be separated from the evolution
of bourgeois society in the nineteenth and twentieth centuries. All
subsequent theoreticians stood on the shoulders of giants such as Kant,
Hegel or Marx, whose Promethean achievements corresponded to the
gigantic challenge of substituting reason for myth. And yet, the world-
historical replacement remained closely bound up with the casting
form of myth. This was most clearly expressed in the fact that the early
philosophy of history took to thinking about an end of history. In the
tradition of earlier hopes in the Beyond, history would give rise to
perpetual peace, spirit would be at home with itself, or society would
live without exploitation or estrangement.

The overview of world history, and especially the disclosing of its
principles of motion, could be completed only by means of a sweeping
reductionism and a number of hefty assumptions. In particular, the
supposition of meaning could be satisfied only insofar as its essential
features could be introduced into history. Nevertheless, the early
philosophy of history acquired a concrete legitimacy which strengthened the claims of science to political leadership and the hope of

replacing the Beyond here on earth. This farewell to modesty contradicted the experiential wealth of all older cultures. But it was kindled by the same unchaining of the productive forces which had allowed the rolling back of religion, and it strengthened the expansion of the new civilization. In other words, the teleologically defined and historically authenticated meaning of progress became the motor oil of the social dynamic – for it gave the winners a good conscience and the losers a modicum of hope.

But only for a certain time. The philosophy of history wore itself out in the real world. The empirical concern with history, which it had itself stimulated, showed that this was much too contingent and differentiated for grand conclusions or overall perspectives to be derived from it. Above all, the course of progress in society itself did not yield the predicted goals of fraternity, perpetual peace, self-sustaining liberty, spirit at home with itself and an empire of beauty, nor that social revolution which was supposed to satisfy the needs of one and all. It was precisely the more sensitive minds who, towards the end of the nineteenth century, diagnosed a society of hardening structures and apparatuses – one driven with the force of compulsion to bind the vitality and intellect of the bourgeoisie in economic and bureaucratic fetters, and to spread throughout the world the condition of a proletariat whose misery had been alleviated only in small pockets. The masters had not remained masters, but the slaves were still slaves.

The answer seemed to lie in renouncing the idea of a necessary course of history which one could clarify and thereby accelerate by reflecting and falling in with it. If God was dead, the humility owing to him did not need to be transferred to history; one could break free and impose on it the goals of the will to power, for whose sake men had appropriated salvationist history. For bourgeois individualism this might involve – as it did for Nietzsche – destroying history in an eternal return of the same, so as to replace its invested meaning with the leadership claims or the ill-socialized aesthetic of the great personality. In the intermediate layers, a renewal of vitality could be sought through Sorelian violence, politically mediated in the name of the nation, which offered to carve out a third way between 'capital' and 'labour'. And in the proletariat, following Lenin, historical regularities which did not suffice in themselves could be made to prevail through the collective organization of power in centralized party apparatuses. In each case, the programmes corresponding to these voluntarist approaches remained a minority phenomenon before the First World War, but through the experience of war they acquired a mass base and later developed into dynamic forces which sought fulfilment in pursuing

goals legitimated by the philosophy of history (leadership by intellectual elites, the achievement of national greatness, or a classless society,
if possible on a world scale). All the authors who have formulated
visions of posthistory since the Second World War were marked by
such regroupments.

We can set out this initial finding in more general terms. The history
which is supposed to end with posthistory is a conceptual construction
about the course of the world as a whole. Its core consists in the
generalization of empirical knowledge about reality (earlier events,
human nature, the dynamic of structural processes) in such a way that
it does not conflict with, but rather gives support to, the setting of a
comprehensive goal. Since this empirical knowledge exceeds individual
powers of understanding, it is essentially a question of selective interpretation, according to criteria ultimately obtained from speculative or
normative statements about the future. Insofar as freedom is awarded
to humanity, the interpretation can therefore appeal to its will to
change through action the perceived trends of history. If such action is
unsuccessful, or if it proves to be catastrophic or downright criminal,
then either the interpretation (or appeal) or the freedom comes into
question. The second possibility is closer to the type of the active
interpreter.

II THE WILL TO POWERLESSNESS

Posthistory is not a developed theory; it is more a symptomatic
sensibility. The word itself is an allusive code which refers to a mood
but also presupposes a great deal of theory. Thus, it measures itself
against the grand directionality of the classical philosophy of history,
and seeks to effect a voluntarist turn which, by drawing on the
resources of power, will attain the meaning and purpose that is no
longer to be found in historical reality. Such a marriage of spirit and
power does not, however, correspond to that common *mésalliance*
whereby science and art submit to being a tool and adornment of the
existing rulers. On the contrary, spirit seeks to recruit and instrumenta-
lize power among revolutionary members of the educated middle
classes, in order to use it for its own designs against the power
structures within society. This revolt before the chasm of meaninglessness derives from the contradictory consciousness involved in claims to
spiritual greatness that fail to take effect on the 'unconscious' masses.[2]
However, insofar as this spirit of bourgeois decadence seeks to revolt
against the social structures of power, rather than take flight from them

in an aesthetic form of existence, it is forced into alliance with its Other, the masses. Which brings us back to the third presupposition of posthistory: namely, that this enterprise has collapsed.

The attempt and the failure have both a subjective and an objective side, a type and a condition. It is easy enough to define the temporal context: the postwar years, and a second wave since the 1970s. The condition is biographically determined, on the Right, by prior experience of fascism and its downfall, and, on the Left, by withdrawal from various forms of Communist organization, first Stalinism and then the smaller groups. But that is only one element, for one is struck by the unusual combinations in our group of authors. In later years Jouvenel became a member of the Club of Rome, Carl Schmitt wrote on Che Guevara, Jünger experimented with drug culture, Kojève went to visit Schmitt, and de Man presented his extract from the life of a European socialist to the German Institute of Industry. I shall therefore try to identify more closely the distinguishing characteristics of ten posthistory theorists.[3]

The term I used above – 'revolutionary members of the educated middle classes' – is intended as a descriptive contrast to those revolutionary intellectuals who dedicated themselves for a long period to a political organization. In our group de Man was the only one in this latter category: he held posts in the Belgian Socialist Party for a full decade, though he also held a professorship. At least five others were members of radical mass parties (NSDAP, PPF, KPD, PCF), without being functionaries in the sense of an existential form. Their organizational involvement was either too short-lived (as with Jouvenel's two-year editorship of Doriot's Party paper) or too peripheral (as with Baudrillard's participation alongside Althusser in a PCF think-tank, or Gehlen's attempt to organize Leipzig university teachers for the NSDAP). All our authors had at least a middle-bourgeois existence – only Heidegger and Schmitt had climbed into it from below[4] – and displayed great intellectual abilities. They were neither disposed nor fated to enter professional politics – the fastest but also the riskiest social ladder in the twentieth century. Seven of the ten were professors, two well-known writers, and one eventually a top official. But such positions only describe them externally; all were or still are, by their temperament and interests, political intellectuals, public men, *hommes de lettres*, insiders of the Zeitgeist, and by any criteria (especially their own) an elite.

Roughly half of our group belonged at important periods of their life to either the far Left or the far Right, in the sense that their programmatic or propagandist activity related to political forces that sought to train the masses for action to transform the system. However, such alliances between intellectual circles and large organizations providing a political direction did not typically last for long, and were marked by a social–cultural tension. In eight of the ten authors, one can observe a more or less spontaneous shift in their basic political positions. That would not be particularly remarkable given the vicissitudes of twentieth-century European history, except that they subsequently spoke and acted as if they had remained the same or had always been in the right. With two exceptions, they were born before or just after the turn of the century and lived beyond the age of seventy, some considerably longer. Most of them lived through two world wars and at least three cultural and two political breaks in continuity – times that were changing at a faster pace than ever before. They therefore had to change with them, painfully withdrawing from their era, if sometimes with gestures of seeming indifference. At least two were marked intellectually by the First World War. One had to leave his Russian homeland because of an unsuitable social profile, even though he sympathized with the October Revolution. One grew up abroad because his father had to emigrate as a rabbi. Five moved to and fro between countries, for professional and political reasons that cannot always be clearly distinguished from each other. One had to emigrate from Germany, as a left-wing Jew, and returned to Austria in 1950. Two so-called half-Jews – one from a Communist parental home, the other after a phase of involvement with fascism – looked for 'safety off the beaten track'.[5] Five lost their employment for a period of time during or after the Second World War; and four had to change their country of residence. A minority – all on the Right: Jouvenel, Freyer, Gehlen, Jünger – were successful under every regime, allowing for a brief waiting period. Whereas most obtained a more or less respected elite position after the early fifties, others had a rather more difficult time of it. The last left-wing figure was scapegoated into the wilderness after the 'German autumn' – unlawfully, as the courts ruled – and was only rehabilitated shortly before his death in 1980.

If one were to look more closely at the curricula vitae and the shifting affiliations, the picture would be altogether more confused. Thus Peter Brückner, who as a young man had belonged to a National Socialist organization, considered himself a Communist, played an active role in East Germany after 1945, moved to the West and became one of the leaders of the New Left, fell under suspicion as a foster-father of the Red Army Faction, and studied Gehlen to work out a diagnosis of the contemporary world. To take another example, the radical left-liberal Jouvenel started out as an advocate of economic planning, became a fascist, then perhaps a member of the Resistance, then a right-liberal, and finally an ecologist. Jünger, for his part, discovered a form of right-elitist opposition to every regime. Freyer, a member of the right-populist Youth Movement in the 1920s, became the 'Führer of German sociology' in 1933, dissolved its organization a year later without breaking from the regime, withdrew to Hungary during the war, kept his chair in Leipzig in the Soviet Occupation Zone, then received emeritus status in the West and became an honorary member of the faculty in Münster. Hendrik de Man, an established socialist theoretician, found himself in approving correspondence with Mussolini in 1930. Men of the Left such as Anders, Kojève or Taubes came under the influence of Heidegger or deferred 'with a struggle' to Carl Schmitt. Jean Baudrillard, a bourgeois Communist with a 'political economy of the sign' to his name, was shortly afterwards sneering at the 'divine Left' and bowing enthusiastically to Nietzsche, about whom his former teacher Henri Lefebvre – a Catholic-educated, highly active Marxist expelled from the PCF in 1956 – had written an appreciative book during the Popular Front period. And then there is a half-hearted reactionary like Gehlen who, after an early *völkisch* period and a house appointment in the Third Reich, commended the firmness of every authoritarian institution and organized a constant flow of articles to make his presence felt in the front-line against the Left, the impulsive masses and the Zeitgeist. Despite having been a Nazi functionary, by 1947 he was already a professor instructing top officials in the French occupation zone: he changed his discipline three times and was continually moved to comment on the modern art that he condemned so bitterly. His was almost what one could call a straight life-line!

Now, these breaks and tensions in the biographies of our authors are not random examples of twentieth-century confusion. Nor, in most cases, can their often evident change of position be explained simply by the surplus energy of the 'renegade'. They were not mere playthings of history, and they did not seek to protect the world from the error of their ways. Indeed, they kept up their intellectual production, as if it were a question of proving that their intellect was not dependent on any system.[6] Either the work was kept free of any biographical self-analysis (Gehlen and Heidegger), or it was removed from history through self-referring interpretation and consolidation in terms of basic principles (Kojève and again Heidegger). Or else, as in the case of Jünger or de Man, the autobiography was constantly reworked until it reached a level of personal consistency that was tantamount to a declaration of independence from society.

Indeed they were not mere playthings, as were most of the untold victims of dictatorship and war. They threw in their lot with radical currents in the name of the meaningfulness of 'history', lending their pens, their names and their counsel. Not even their elitist conception of themselves was mere illusion, for they did have a portion of intellectual power at their disposal. The illusory aspect of their fantasies of grandeur referred to their practice – to the notion that the masses and the apparatuses could both be led and kept at a distance. This became evident at the latest when their political commitment, radicalized through the quest for meaning, was transferred from the candour of opposition to an invidious association with an established regime. For the need to compromise themselves in particulars had not been anticipated in the grandeur of their original project. Encounters with the power of the apparatus then wounded the self-respect of these bearers of meaning so deeply that all meaning seemed to be lost. Instead of leading the alliance between bourgeois intellect and the masses, they felt themselves to be the ornamentation on an alliance between power and the masses.

In proportion to their self-esteem and the chances of survival, this awareness led to a withdrawal from the space of history. Practical defeat was compensated for in intellectual production, which took up the resources from 'before' and tried to rescue them from the suspicion that they had been responsible for the defeat and for the historical effects of the misconceived alliance. Defensive measures against this suspicion, which deeply threatened the self-understanding of intellectual leadership, prevented any concrete discussion of his own involvement and experience of history. In their place came a self-exonerating diagnosis of the external world. The alliance between the masses and power, on the historical basis of the technological domination of nature, was now supposed to have developed into a self-steering system which, with marginal differences of political expression, spanned virtually the whole world and constantly reproduced itself despite all wars and revolutionary changes. This 'second system', which neither needed nor permitted new thinking, was detaching itself from nature, from the possibility of learning about reality, from time as a meaningful sequence of development, and from the intervention of any individual. Freedom of the individual could no longer be meaningfully related to the aggregate course of events, but asserted itself at most in niches, in recollective fantasy, in myth, in the 'as if'.

III HISTORY AND POSTHISTOIRE

My interpretation of the genesis of the posthistory concept, as a specific form of projective self-exoneration, is based on a reading of these authors that cuts across the grain. It fits together pieces of the mosaic which refer to the loss of meaning of historical thought. It turns inward where the authors point to the external world. But if we strip the concept of its defensive surplus and its voluntarist inflection of the Hegelian concept of history, the diagnosis is not thereby left without an object. Rather, it is opened up for more discriminating evaluation in the work of historians.

In all the posthistory theorists there is an assessment of world civilization, often seen in terms of crystallization. This metaphor, drawn from the biological theory of evolution, implies that random genetic mutation, together with survival of the fittest, fashions species which then harden in their genetic make-up and go on reproducing so long as their environment allows it. Transposed to history, this gives us a socio-cultural development process which, by virtue of the considerable autonomy from nature of technical-industrial civilization and its uniform extension on a world scale, eventually comes to the end of its qualitative changes and petrifies into a self-reproducing structure. This might be seen as a theory of modernization with a broader, evolutionary content; but it is set, as it were, in a minor key. For crystallization also entails the end of freedom and meaning, and therefore a reanimalization of man.

De Man and Anders see a further consequence: namely, a tendency towards death. The writings of both these authors respond to the destructive energy unshackled in the Second World War, and to the rise of machines of war and extermination which cannot be controlled because of a failure of human intelligence. Curiously enough, it was the inventor of the posthistory concept who also – like Teilhard de Chardin, Bertaux or Serres – hoped for a 'mutation' involving the radical transformation of social structures and attitudes, and therefore an epochal historical change. The main keywords on the agenda have thus been: the abandonment of 'exterminism', limits to growth, decentralization, saving of resources, peaceful relations between the environment and society, non-material satisfactions.

Although this list may with a little effort be understood as an adaptation of the Enlightenment programme – that is, as an inward recovery of externalized progress by the powers of reason – the whole framework is broken up by more general theories which bring keywords such as 'entropy' or 'death instinct' to bear upon society. In the expansive hope in progress characteristic of the 'axial age', the global conceptions of diminishing life-energy and room for manoeuvre, as well as the vision of life itself as a detour on the road to death, were not conceived as the last historical 'mutation'. Since the historicity of nature, one of the great discoveries of the past hundred years, has relativized the opposition between human and natural sciences, one might have expected alternatives to the growth and modernization paradigm to have emerged at the level of historical and social theory from the correlation between the finitude of human existence and that of the world. But the posthistorical use of socio-biological metaphors (crystallization, termite states, etc.), which has accompanied such discourse ever since the Enlightenment, does not offer anything of the kind. Instead of conceptualizing culture in both a natural framework and a social dimension, it represents a sort of frozen social Darwinism that arbitrarily mixes together the dimensions of nature and culture and remains, in a number of ways, tied to traditions that it rejects. Thus, in keeping with the Enlightenment tradition, it disregards the mortality of nature, transposes the death of the individual subject to the history of the species, flattens out social conflicts of interest and irregularities, and thus evacuates all movement from history for the purposes of enquiry.

The perspective of posthistory, understood as an elitist, culturally pessimistic inversion of the optimism of progress, therefore seems to me to blinker rather than illuminate the diagnosis of the age. Most of its adepts place the weight on their own special concerns rather than on the new problems of the twentieth century: they do not draw attention to the modern capacity for self-annihilation, but remain fascinated by exaggerated symptoms of the petrification of civilization. The question of meaning thus obscures the question of existence. From Kojève through Gehlen to Baudrillard, the end of history (or the crossing of traditional horizons of meaning) is proclaimed as the fantasy of a meaningless but ever continuing course of events.

Beyond that, posthistory presupposes constructions of meaning in the form of meta-narratives about world history – and so remains marked by the legacy of salvationist history. Within this traditional mould the polarity is simply reversed, so that instead of the euphoria of progress we have the fear of apocalypse as the basis for a concept of the historical that reflects the finitude of man and the world. On the other hand, the pseudo-empirical narrative structure of world history is retained, as if we knew something substantive about the beginning and the end. Since we do not know this, a macro-theoretical framework of the historical always remains at the level of hypothetical thinking. The

production of theory has a different origin and a different epistemological status from the historical–critical processing of what has been
handed down. As a rule, meaningful history is created through
advances in the interpretation of traces of real events from the past.
However, for the relationship between history and any practical endeavour, what is decisive is that the status of macro-historical interpretative models and deductions – without which it is impossible to
demonstrate a significant relation between details – should not become
so blurred that the interpretation appears immanent within the events
themselves. A number of posthistory theorists have taken an interest in
seemingly empirical attempts to flesh out the tentative character of
world history – as in the theories of cultural cycles advanced by
Spengler or (more cautiously) Toynbee. But instead of setting up a
tension between various modes of orientation to the historical world,
this has led to delusions of grandeur and prognostic certainty.

Most of the posthistorians stand in one of the traditions descending
from Hegel's philosophy of history, which sought to uncover meaning
genetically in the course of the world. This has given rise to at least two
difficulties. On the one hand, the construction of meaning has always
preceded the analysis of historical reality, so that the latter can be
considered only in parts or through a sweeping reduction of its
complexity (the so-called straining of the concept). But even in the best
of cases, selective reduction limits the capacity of the concept for
prognosis, which in retrospect always proves to have been overtaken
by history. On the other hand, because of its narrative structure, a
history finds its meaning only at its completion. The conceptual plan
therefore assumes that aggregate history comes to an end in the epoch
when its meaning is established as having been fulfilled. This allows us
to see the proximity of material philosophy of history to various
chiliastic currents – whether those which, like Romanticism, believe the
Apocalypse to be nigh; or those which, like Marxism, consider annul-
ment of the movement-compulsion to be both indicated by history and
realizable in practice within the desired form of society. Or perhaps the
interpreter, like Hegel, sees himself as part of Absolute Knowledge – so
that, at this level, the end of history can only be followed by an eternal
return of the Same. In each of these cases involving a short-circuit
between the starting-point and the goal of real historical meaning, the
end of history turns out to be an artefact of thought.

Despite all these considerations, however, the posthistory diagnosis
cannot be simply discarded. For at another level, there is still a debate
to be had about its actual characterization of the contemporary social
formation and the latter's relationship to the individual. Here we can

see the common ground between postwar diagnoses of the 'mega-machine' (Mumford) or 'post-industrial society' (Bell) and those of a 'social protectorate' (Jouvenel), 'secondary systems' (Freyer) or 'the new normality' (Brückner): namely, an attempt to downplay the significance in technically developed societies of constitutionality, property relations and other basic references of traditional social theory, and to emphasize accordingly the existence of a common, self-reproducing techno-social structure which slips out of control and thus makes the preconditions of control a factor of secondary importance. This structure is conceptualized in its historically generated but no longer historical condition. It is as if developed societies no longer displayed a fundamental contradiction pressing for structural changes – or rather, as if contradictions were now only partial or marginal and not subject to the force of inertia of the basic social structures, as if they tended not towards revolution or social transformation, but to their own discharge through rebelliousness or a retreat into inwardness.

There are thus several levels at which the dynamic of social standard-ization can be understood and related to technological advances. In economic terms, rises in productivity have made prosperity possible on a fairly broad scale, without class struggle, and the contradictions between capitalists and proletarians have been converted into a tense relationship of cooperation between capital and labour, one which is held together by corporatist organizations and at once supported and relativized by the secular growth of public and private services. In the socialist countries, where state control has displaced the means and organization of violence between capital and labour, this standardiza-tion has made more headway but is less efficiently organized. At the political level, spaces free of the state – and hence any pure form of social autonomy – have given way before bureaucratization, the grow-ing power and presence of state apparatuses of violence, the saturation of society by state regulation, and the dependence of every individual and every 'private' function (especially those involving social protec-tion) upon state funds and services. The growth of this compact yet immobile power shrinks the space in which a fundamental opposition might develop, and hinders even minor political corrections of course. On the other hand, the internal regulation of conflict is extensively based upon distribution of the results of economic growth, and this fixes the systems in their dynamic of expansion. Finally, at the cultural level, the relative autonomy of regional and class cultures is blurred by mobility, by the state education and training systems, and by the ubiquitous presence of the mass media. What replaces them is a market-organized culture of atomized masses in which temporal and spatial horizons become blurred, appearance and reality can no longer be distinguished, and simulations are often more fascinating and even more realistic than the primary experience. The primary reference of this culture is a contradiction shifted to the individual, whose practical conduct is determined by market and bureaucratic forces that define the basic daily routine, but whose perceptions and expressions are released in all manner of imaginary fantasies.

There would seem much to be said for such a rough sketch of contemporary societies, which can accommodate a wide range of individual observations from everyday life and scientific enquiry. The problem is the perspective within which it is drawn. The man in the moon would give a good tip-off,[7] but can it come from one of those who have succumbed to the development of empirical knowledge and to the inevitability of the structures that are described as being inevitable within it?

Perhaps there really are beings like the man in the moon — alienated observers who, though contemporaries, are so little part of the epoch that they can, as it were, look at it from outside. If one wishes to expose oneself to the diagnostic power of those who have fallen or been driven out of history, one should listen attentively and not take any more from them than they can give — even though they have no awareness of their own limitations. The basic problem of the posthistory authors is that at a critical juncture they misunderstood the relationship between the intellectual and the masses. As educated bourgeois — elite or avant-garde — they could not bear thinking of themselves as part of the masses, and so dissolved the concept of the masses into that of individual subjects. In this sense, their error coincides with that very distance which for us makes them important as alienated observers. But that distance can be essentially qualified in terms of the authors' distinctive perspective: on the one hand, a grouping of contemporaries in the object-concept of 'the masses'; on the other hand, an attempt to cover over their own responsibility for the effects of their political commitment. We have to work back from these excess features. In the latter case, the necessary corrective is already to hand: namely, a refocusing of attention on the differences between the systems, so that they are measured by the life-qualities they permit, the victims they produce and the capacity they contain to grasp and reflect their problems. Such a mode of differentiation could profit, however, from insight into the latent common features of its epochal 'infrastructure'.

As to the relationship between subjectivity and the masses, the problem is more complex because it concerns the vantage-point itself. The posthistory authors do not see themselves as part of the masses, but regard the latter as something which, in reacting instinctively and mechanically to the demands of society, does not constitute a subjectivity in its own right or hold any capacity for historical knowledge and change. This conception of social structures, in which the masses are the mediation between economics, politics and culture, therefore carries these authors outside history. Their schema would be less objectivist and despairing if the individuals of which the masses are composed were endowed with subjectivity. That would mean conceiving the totality of structural constraints in such a way that it allowed some of that degree of freedom which the observer, after all, has no difficulty in claiming for himself. Were the observer to realize that he is part of the mass, it would immediately break down into individuals who are able to perceive, reflect upon and measure themselves against their integration into socially structured processes. One should certainly have no illusions that the individual alone can change these structures in any fundamental way. But in fact he or she is not alone; everyone else has the same possibility, however small it may initially seem in comparison with the scale of the problems. The basis for hope lies precisely in the mass character of reflecting and communicating subjectivity, not in a subjectification of the mass object or some other collective singular.

The posthistory diagnosis sees the social formation as marked to its core by an objective, power-structured process of standardization, which no longer promises any qualitative movement but is moving towards petrification. Whatever deviates from it is a hangover from prehistory (the non-European world[8]) or a posthistorical, aesthetic 'as if'. In this derealized dialectic of core and periphery is reflected the marginalization of the intellectual leader. But what if the conflict between intellectuals and the masses, which here appears so inescapable, were to be resolved within a perspective of mass subjectivity? Then the true differences within and between societies could again be grasped as the starting-point for historical action, without forfeiting everything of value in the posthistorical account of the existing formation. But the latter would have to undergo a change of status. If the risks of annihilation are brought into the argument, the paralysing diagnosis of structural autonomization becomes a horror-image which drives reflective subjectivity to seek for a basis of action. Posthistory becomes historical if it is read not as a universal diagnosis, but as a negative utopia peculiar to the loss of perspectives in the advanced industrialized societies.

But is it at all possible to imagine a historical perception and reflection of mass subjectivity in the contemporary culture? In Jünger's novel *Eumeswil*, a kind of cross between Nietzsche and Baudrillard, history was precisely the paradigmatic occupation of the posthistorical anarch; with the derealization of meta-narrative systems of meaning, history had degenerated into a video archive of past forms and events, whose fascination consoled him for the loss of meaning in his existence and in the world. Here we find, in visionary form, the elitist variant of the target reference of the culture industry and bureaucracy. The recipient really is posthistorical, in the sense that he is constantly faced with fragments of the past which alienate him from his own historical situation and subjectivity. They do not make him present to himself, but flood him with the past and thereby allow him to escape from his historical existence.

I have attempted to show that, at the most general level, the posthistory diagnosis is a disenchanted postscript to the nineteenth-century philosophy of history which misses the key problems in understanding world history today, and that its substantive interpretation of the contemporary world makes sense only with major corrections. On the other hand, the aesthetic or media-centred dimension of posthistorical theory is thoroughly practical and abreast of the times. The quest for a critical alternative would have to begin by asking what kind of service historians, or people with an education in history, can perform to support the subjectivity of individuals in their historical perception of themselves. Such a perspective may take up the legacy of bourgeois individualism, but must dispense with its ideal of greatness and power in order to arrive at a realistic assessment of the space for action within and against the existing social structures. It may also draw upon material instincts and collective traditions, but if it is to find and use such space, it must not hope that objective characteristics will suddenly be converted into actions. Such a perspective might also be described as 'history from below', because it places the traditional hierarchy of historical tasks 'the right side up'. It does not seek to guarantee meaning through a philosophy of history aesthetically translated into structural edifices or narrative representations, in which the truth of great systems, events and personalities is proven and ultimately adapted for didactic purposes.

The approach I have in mind starts by attempting to classify the life-history of individuals within a particular social and historical context — their experiences and failures, as well as their capacity to reflect on them, to tell others true stories about themselves, and to reach agreement with each other about the history that binds them together. Such a process inevitably extends to the historical context of the time and to the prehistories of the family, the group, the workplace, the locality, the movement, etc., because it needs them to throw light on the subject. Many already use exemplary models in trying to understand their own life-history – hence the present interest in oral history and chat shows, among other things. Everyone needs the help of professional historians in tracing the context and genesis of the present day, and the broader their temporal and thematic references, the more they rely upon the reconstructive and organizing functions of historical science. What does history have to offer if, instead of subjecting individuals to the fiction of an objectively meaningful process or fobbing them off with all manner of aestheticized fragments, it seeks to do the groundwork for their historical self-understanding and their capacity for historical action? The answer to this question would appear to involve at least three major components.

First, it can provide narratives of the contemporary context and historical premises of a particular group, stretching from its objective preconditions through its political choices to the socio-cultural effects on its everyday practice and the various collective and exemplary individual experiences. In other words, it offers elements of a social dimension for the individual's widening attempt to understand his or her life-history.

Second, the structuring of broad historical contexts (up to and including world history) always rests upon hypothetical constructions. Such a framework is essential for historical self-understanding; but it is just as important to avoid taking these constructs for the reality, to realize that they have the character of a rough outline. Thus, in the opening up of older and broader fields of history, readable theoretical synopses and discussions are more useful than grand pseudo-empirical syntheses.

Finally, an understanding of history that starts from the conditions and events of one's own existence must also include that area of social fantasy which concerns the experience of otherness, for this makes it possible to recognize one's own certainties as specific and therefore changeable. Such experience of otherness should not be rashly trans-ferred to the here and now: it makes us aware of this in the perception of distance. Nor need it involve the construction of a context, although it may excite curiosity about one. What it requires is rather a complex sense of the concrete, which also sheds light by example on the deep layers of another culture.

Historical groundwork linked to clarification of one's own exper-ience breaks open the apparent certainties of that experience. It allows us to orient ourselves by sketching out historical contexts, and over-comes that opposition between intellectual leaders and the masses in which interpreters take too much upon themselves while individuals are effectively discouraged from making history in accordance with their powers and abilities. An against the grain reading of posthistorical diagnoses shows that such an opposition freezes or explodes history – not just in the imagination, but also in reality. Explosions threaten when the groundwork for historical self-understanding does not get through to individual subjects, and when their quest for bearings is discharged in fundamentalist collective identities and a short-circuiting of the relationship between the masses and political power. The return of political theology is then a sign of the bankruptcy of the culture and the violent clash of irreconcilable identities. The other extreme might be described as a (crystalline or atomic) 'cold death', growing out of the spontaneous course of 'secondary systems', their cultural petrification and the risk they pose of a disaster for humanity. Intellectuals can certainly summon this systemic danger before the mind. But it can be averted only by the 'masses', who are actually composed of individuals with a modicum of freedom and responsibility, and to whom intellectuals also belong.

Notes

1. A seminal work for an understanding of this process is Karl Löwith, *Weltgeschichte und Heilsgeschehen. Die theologischen Voraussetzungen der Geschichtsphilosophie*, Stuttgart 1952. See also Reinhart Koselleck, *Futures Past: On the Semantics of Historical Time*, Cambridge, Mass. 1985, especially the section entitled 'Historia Magistra Vitae'. Jacob Taubes follows the impact of Jewish apocalyptic thought through to nineteenth-century philosophy in *Abendländlische Eschatologie*, Berne 1947. From the circle of influence of Carl Schmitt and Arnold Gehlen, see Kesting, *Geschichtsphilosophie und Weltbürgerkrieg*, and Koselleck, *Critique and Crisis: Enlightenment and the Pathogenesis of Modern Society*, Oxford 1988; and from the standpoint of positivism, Karl Popper's violently polemical *The Poverty of Historicism*, London 1957. The legacy of the Frankfurt School is expressed in Horkheimer and Adorno, *Dialectic of Enlightenment*, and the neo-Marxist basis of a history of everyday life in Henri Lefebvre, *La fin de l'histoire*, Paris 1970.
2. A typical symptom of the crisis of meaning for bourgeois intellectuals is the allocation to themselves of a specially authoritative role, defined as a rescheduling of the sequence constructed by the philosophy of history. The conservative section of the intelligentsia thus reveals its nobility of mind, which raises the bourgeois intellectual above the material debris of bourgeois society and supposedly provides him with the hearing due to the grandees of the ancien régime. This is the predominant form of conduct among posthistory theorists. But the party of movement conceives itself as an aristocracy of speed, an 'avant-garde' which experiments ahead of the march of history and marks out new directions.
3. I shall name the core group of this older generation in the order in which they came to a posthistorical perspective: Jouvenel, Kojève, Jünger, de Man, Gehlen, Freyer, Anders, Baudrillard, Brückner and Taubes. Other figures to be taken into account include, on the one side, Gottfried Benn, Heidegger, Schelsky and Carl Schmitt, and, on the other, Adorno, Seidenberg, Brown and Lefebvre – and, less directly, the French

poststructuralists and a number of younger German philosophers and anthropologists.

4. Perhaps the lack of an alternative social position (such as Jünger's profession as a writer) is one of the reasons why these two seem to have been most clearly marked by a determination to establish the continuity of their own thought, and by sudden fantasies of grandeur that might be described as a deep, stylized delusion.

5. An allusion to Peter Brückner's *Abseits als sicherer Ort*: see chapter 2 above. *Trs. note*.

6. These remarks are valid only for those authors who stood in a relationship with radical political groups that came to power, or for whom the problematic of collaboration or Communist internationalism indirectly involved them in the systems of fascist or Stalinist dictatorships. Moreover, those whose reference was oppositional movements that never came close to power (Anders, Taubes and the late Brückner) do not display that defensive hardening which we have seen in the work and biography of the others. But insofar as political failure was experienced as disappointment with the immobility of the masses and their association with power, it could equally lead to the adoption of a posthistorical perspective.

7. He already appeared by projection in 1932, in Jünger's radio presentation of his diagnosis of the age: *Der Arbeiter*. 'I have attempted', he said, 'to depict our present reality as if it had to be explained . . . to a man from the moon, and I leave it to you to decide how far I have been successful.' (Quoted in Paetel.)

8. The exclusion of nations that do not belong to the Club of Rome, and their reduction to the status of time-warped antecedents of industrialized societies, might prove to be a fateful blindness of European arrogance. Either it underestimates the historical impact of collective interests and hopes in those peoples who make up the underprivileged majority of the world's population, or it entails conscious reliance upon weapons with a capacity for mass destruction.

Index